WHERE IS THUMBKIN?

▼▼▼▼▼▼▼▼▼▼▼

Over 500 Activities To Use
With Songs You Already Know

Where is

Thumbkin?

By
Pam Schiller
and
Thomas Moore

Illustrations by Cheryl Kirk Noll

gryphon house
Beltsville, Maryland

Includes Special Toddler Section

@ 1993 Pam Schilller and Thomas Moore

Published by Gryphon House, Inc.
10726 Tucker street, Beltsville, MD 20705

Cover Design: Beverly Hightshoe
Cover Illustration: Cheryl Kirk Noll

Library of Congress Cataloging-in-Publication Data

Schiller, Pamela Byrne.
    Where is Thumbkin? : over 500 activities to use with songs you already know / by Pam Schiller and Thomas Moore : illustra-tions by Cheryl Kirk Noll.
      P. cm.
    Includes bibliographical references and index.
    ISBN 0-87659-164-0 : $14.95
    1. Movement education. 2. Games with music. 3. Creative activities and seat work. I. Moore, Thomas, 1950-
GV452.S375 1993   93-8227
372.86—dc20   CIP

TABLE OF CONTENTS

Children are born with a love of rhythm and rhyme, music and song. Music is, therefore, an integral part of the early childhood experience. Teachers have long recognized the magical appeal of music to children and have used it to teach concepts and skills, to develop language patterns, to elevate moods and to develop social skills. With this in mind, we have created a book that not only encourages the use of songs in the classroom, but also provides a multitude of ideas for extending the teaching potential of a song into all areas of the curriculum. It makes good sense to take what children already love and build on it.

Using this book

This book shows teachers how to take popular childhood songs and use them as a springboard for curriculum development. We have attempted to use songs that teachers use most frequently in their classrooms. The book is divided into a section for 3-, 4-, 5- and 6-year-olds and a section for toddlers. Each song is extended through the following sections: Things to Talk About, Thematic Connections, Curriculum Extensions, Related Bibliography and Related Records and Tapes.

Things to Talk About

Here you will find questions or thoughts to stimulate classroom discussion related to the song. Most questions or suggestions are open-ended to provide for a variety of responses.

Thematic Connections

Many early childhood classrooms use themes as an approach to curriculum development. We list possible thematic connections for all songs.

Curriculum Extensions

Each song is extended into five activities, including ones in Language, Math, Science, Art, Dramatic Play, Cooking and Fine and Gross Motor Development. All activities are easy to implement and require little or no preparation.

Each activity includes information for age appropriateness, a list of materials needed, directions for completing the activity and a developmental bonus which highlights the educational value of the activity. These guideposts make curriculum planning an easy process.

Related Bibliography

Children's literature is an important part of an early childhood curriculum. This section is a great resource for combining children's songs and literature. A short summary of each book is included.

Related Records and Tapes

Records and tapes with the highlighted song recorded on them or with a song that relates thematically are included in this section.

We hope this book will be a useful resource and will serve as a model for your own creative use of songs in the classroom. It was a joy to create. Music is like a smile—it's understood in any language, at any age. It is a common thread within humanity—across cultures and across time. We hope you will enjoy using it across the curriculum.

1

▼▼▼▼▼▼▼▼▼▼▼▼

SEPTEMBER

Head, Shoulders, Knees and Toes
Hokey Pokey
If You're Happy and You Know It
Open, Shut Them
Where Is the Table?
We're So Glad You're Here

Head, Shoulders, Knees and Toes

Head, shoulders, knees and toes, knees and toes,
Head, shoulders, knees and toes, knees and toes,
And eyes and ears and mouth and nose.
Head, shoulders, knees and toes, knees and toes.

Thematic Connections
Me, Myself and I
Body Awareness

Things to Talk About
1. Do animals have heads, shoulders, knees and toes?
2. What would happen if we didn't have toes? What about knees?

Curriculum Extension
For Art: Body Tracing

Ages
3,4,5,6

Materials
Bulletin board or butcher paper, crayons, markers

Procedure
1. Cut sheets of bulletin board paper into lengths long enough to accommodate a child's body height.
2. Divide the children into pairs. Each pair takes turns tracing each other's body out- line onto the butcher paper.
(Younger children may need adult assistance.)
3. Allow the children to create their own clever body positions.
4. After tracing, the children can then color in their outlines.
5. Label heads, shoulders, knees and toes.

Developmental Bonus
Concept development
Creative expression

Curriculum Extension
For Fine Motor: Another Set of Hands?

Ages
4,5,6

Materials
Scarves, bucket

Procedure
1. The children use their toes to pick up scarves and put them in a bucket.
2. Then they can try to pick up other items (straws, cray- ons, etc.) with their toes.

Developmental Bonus
Coordination
Small muscle development

Curriculum Extension
For Gross Motor: Beanbag Carry

Ages
4,5,6

Materials
Beanbag, masking tape

Procedure
1. Place masking tape on the floor to create a pathway.
2. The children attempt to follow the path while balancing a beanbag on their head, then on their shoulder.
3. They can use the same pathway for hopping with the beanbag on one knee or and the toes of one foot.

Developmental Bonus
Coordination
Balance
Large muscle development

Curriculum Extension
For Language: Body Language

Ages
4,5,6

Materials
Chart tablet paper, marker

Procedure
1. Brainstorm with the children about ways they use their heads to communicate, for example, shake yes or no, talk, facial expressions, listening, etc.
2. List their ideas on chart tablet paper.
3. Talk about ways to communicate that do not use the head, for example, shrug shoulders, hand movements, etc.

Developmental Bonus
Creative thinking

Curriculum Extension
For Science: Animal Parts

Ages
4,5,6

Materials
Collection of animal pictures or photographs

Procedure
1. Ask the children to examine the animal pictures looking for heads, shoulders, knees and toes.
2. Be sure to include insect photos.

3. Categorize the animals into those that have all four parts—heads, shoulders, knees and toes—and those that do not.

Developmental Bonus
Analytical skills

Related Bibliography

Ahlberg, Alan. Illustrated by Janet Ahlberg. *Funnybones*. Greenwillow, 1980. A big and little skeleton go looking for someone to frighten.

Burton, Marilee Robin. *Tails Toes Eyes Ears Nose*. HarperCollins, 1988. Children guess the identity of animals by looking at only part of the animal.

Hennessy, B. G. *A, B, C, D, Tummy, Toes, Hands, Knees*. Puffin, 1989. A rhyming, wonderfully delightful book.

Martin, Bill, Jr. and John Archambault. *Here Are My Hands*. Holt, 1987. A verse about body parts and how they are used.

Silverstein, Shel. "The Loser" from *Where the Sidewalk Ends*. HarperCollins, 1974. A funny poem about a man who loses his head.

Related Records and Tapes

Beall, Pamela Conn and Susan Hagen Nipp. "Head, Shoulders, Knees, and Toes" from *Wee Sing Children's Songs and Fingerplays*. Price Stern Sloan, 1979.

Palmer, Hap. "Put Your Hands in the Air" from *Learning Basic Skills Through Music*, Volume I. Activity Records, 1969.

Palmer, Hap. *Learning Basic Skills Through Music: Vocabulary*. Educational Activities, 1981.

"Head, Shoulders, Knees and Toes" from It's Toddler Time. Kimbo, 1982.

Hokey Pokey

You put your right hand in,
You put your right hand out,
You put your right hand in,
And you shake it all about.
You do the hokey pokey ,
And you turn yourself around,
That's what it's all about.

You put your left hand in....

You put your right foot in....

You put your left foot in....

You put your right elbow in....

You put your left elbow in....

You put your backside in....

You put your head in....

You put your whole self in....

Thematic Connections
Me, Myself and I
Body Awareness

Things to Talk About
1. What other parts of the body are not mentioned in the song?
2. What other ways could you turn around other than to walk?

Curriculum Extension
For Cooking: Milk Shakes

Ages
3,4,5,6

Materials
Blender, ice cream, milk, chocolate syrup, vanilla flavoring, measuring cup, cups

Procedure
1. Ask the children if they want a chocolate or vanilla shake.

2. Make shakes by blending one scoop of ice cream, one-half cup of milk and chocolate syrup or vanilla flavoring, depending on the child's choice, in the blender.
3. Serve and enjoy!

Developmental Bonus
Concept development

Curriculum Extension
For Creative Movement: Corn Shakers

Ages
3,4,5,6

Materials
Popcorn, heavy cardboard plates (two for each child), crayons, stapler

Procedure
1. Ask the children to decorate the bottoms of the paper plates.
2. Place the two plates together with a few grains of corn inside and staple.

3. Use the shakers to emphasize the words in the song "shake it all about."

Developmental Bonus
Listening
Coordination
Muscle development

Curriculum Extension
For Language: In and Out

Ages
3,4,5

Materials
None needed

Procedure
1. Play Jack-in-the-box, Jack-out-of-the-box.
2. One child is "it."
3. When the child who is it says "Jack-in-the-box," all the children squat down; when the child who is it says, "Jack-out-of-the-box," all the children pop up.
4. Mix the sequence, Jack-in-the-box, Jack-in-the-box, Jack-in-the-box, Jack-out-of-the box, Jack-out-of-the-box, Jack-in-the-box, etc.
5. After the game, ask the children to look around the room and find things "in" their place and "out" of their place.

Developmental Bonus
Spatial relations concepts

Curriculum Extension
For Math: Footprint Patterns

Ages
4,5,6

Materials
Two colors of construction paper, tape, markers, scissors

Procedure
1. Cut footprints from construction paper.
2. Cut right feet from one color and left feet from another.
3. Tape cut-out prints on the floor in a left, right pattern.
4. The children follow the prints saying, "left, right, left, right" as they go.
5. Create other patterns with the children.

Developmental Bonus
Patterning
Left/right concepts

Curriculum Extension
For Science: Sound Canisters

Ages
3,4,5,6

Materials
Eight potato chip cans with lids, dried rice, dried beans, dried corn, salt, colored tape or dot stickers

Procedure
1. Fill two cans one-half full with corn, two with beans, two with rice and two with salt.
2. Use colored tape or dot stickers on the bottom of the cans to indicate pairs, for example, blue dots on the two cans that contain beans, red dots on the two cans that contain corn, etc.
3. The children shake the cans, listen to the sounds and without looking on the bottom of the can attempt to match the sounds.

Developmental Bonus
Auditory discrimination

Related Bibliography

Aruego, José. *Look What I Can Do*. Macmillan, 1988. Two lively caribou romp through a game of copycat, frightening their neighbors and themselves.

Brown, Marc. *Hand Rhymes*. E. P. Dutton, 1985. Full-color illustrations to fourteen entertaining hand games.

Hughes, Shirley. *Alfie's Feet*. Lothrop, 1983. Alfie's new boots end up on the wrong feet.

Martin, Bill, Jr. and John Archambault. *Here Are My Hands*. Holt, 1987. A rhyme about the uses of various parts of the body.

Winthrop, Elizabeth. *Shoes*. HarperCollins, 1986. A funny rhyme about the uses of feet.

Related Records and Tapes

Lucky, Sharron. *Channel Three*. Melody House.

Lucky, Sharron. *Hokey Pokey*. Melody House.

Moore, Thomas. "Hokey Pokey Dokey" from *Singing, Moving and Learning*. Thomas Moore Records.

If You're Happy and You Know It

If you're happy and you know it,
Clap your hands. (clap, clap)
If you're happy and you know it,
Clap your hands. (clap, clap)
If you're happy and you know it,
Then your life will surely show it.
If you're happy and you know it,
Clap your hands. (clap, clap)

If you're happy and you know it,
Stomp your feet (stomp, stomp)...

If you're happy and you know it,
Shout "Hooray!" (shout "hooray")...

Thematic Connections
Me, Myself and I
Self-Concept

Things to Talk About
1. What things make you happy, sad, frightened, etc.?
2. How many ways can you think of to show you are happy? sad? afraid?

Curriculum Extension
For Art: Textured Hands and Feet

Ages
4,5,6

Materials
Textured paper (wallpaper samples), markers, scissors

Procedure
1. The children trace around their hands and feet on textured paper (wallpaper is great!).
2. Cut them out. Younger children may need help cutting out their hands and feet.
3. Use for bulletin boards or to create a mural or collage.

Developmental Bonus
Fine motor development

Curriculum Extension
For Language: Happy/Sad Feelings

Ages
4,5,6

Materials
Happy and sad paper plate faces

Procedure
1. Each child selects a happy face and a sad face. They take turns telling what makes them happy or sad.
2. This could also be a "tell-me-how-you-feel-today activity."

Developmental Bonus
Language development

For Math: Adding and Subtracting Beats

Ages
5,6

Materials
None needed

Procedure
1. Sing the song and add a beat, for example, "If you're happy and you know it, clap your hands (clap, clap, clap)."
2. Now try subtracting a beat (only one clap).

Developmental Bonus
Patterning

For Music: Shakers

Ages
3,4

Materials
Dried beans, plastic egg, masking tape

Procedure
1. Make shakers by putting dried beans inside a plastic egg and taping it closed. This makes a perfect shaker.
2. The children use the shakers for the places in the song where there are claps and stomps.

Developmental Bonus
Patterning

For Science: Through a Looking Glass

Ages
4,5,6

Materials
Finger paint, drawing paper, magnifying glass

Procedure
1. The children cover the palms of their hands in finger paint and make hand prints on drawing paper.
2. Provide a magnifying glass and encourage the children to compare lines in their hand printsto lines in the other children's hand prints.

Developmental Bonus
Observation

Related Bibliography

Baer, Edith. *The Wonder of Hands*. Macmillan, 1992. A look at all we do with our hands.

Baylor, Byrd. *I'm in Charge of Celebrations*. Scribners, 1986. A little girl celebrates the desert by special recognition of natural events.

Martin, Bill, Jr. and John Archambault. *Here Are My Hands*. Holt, 1987. A verse about body parts and how they are used.

Murphy, Joanne B. *Feelings*. Black Moss Press, 1985. A little boy goes through his daily activities and shares his feelings about each one.

Weiss, Nicki. *If You're Happy and You Know It*. Greenwillow, 1987. Eighteen story songs set to pictures.

Related Records and Tapes

Moore, Thomas. "I Am Special" from *I Am Special*. Thomas Moore Records.

"A Really Good Feeling" from *Bert and Ernie Sing-Along*. Sesame Street, 1975.

Moore, Thomas. "I Get Mad At My Family" from *The Family*. Thomas Moore Records.

Scelsa, Steve and Greg Millang. "Sing a Happy Song" from *We All Live Together, Vol. 3*. Youngheart Records, 1979.

Weissman, Jackie. "I'm So Mad I Could Scream" from *Miss Jackie and Her Friends Sing About Peanut Butter, Tarzan and Roosters*. Miss Jackie, 1981.

Open, Shut Them

Open, shut them, open, shut them,
Give a little clap.
Open, shut them, open, shut them
Put them in your lap.

Creep them, creep them, creep them,
creep them,
Right up to your chin.
Open wide your smiling mouth,
But do not let them in.

Creep them, creep them, creep them,
creep them,
Past your cheeks and chin.
Open wide your smiling eyes,
Peeking in—BOO.

Creep them, creep them, creep them,
creep them,
Right down to your toes.
Let them fly up in the air and,
Bop you on the nose.

Open, shut them, open, shut them,
Give a little clap.
Open, shut them, open, shut them,
Put them in your lap.

Thematic Connections
Me, Myself and I
Body Awareness

Things to Talk About
1. Other than our hands, what other body parts can you open and shut?

Curriculum Extension

For Art: Finger Puppets

Agea
3,4,5,6

Materials
Finger paints, finger paint paper

Procedure
1. Allow the children to create designs using their fingers and finger paint.
2. If the children paint directly on the table, they can change designs a number of times.

3. When a final design is chosen, transfer it to a piece of paper by placing a sheet over their design, rubbing lightly and gently lifting the paper.

Developmental Bonus
Creative expression

Curriculum Extension

For Fine Motor: Marbles

Ages
3,4,5,6

Materials
Marbles, masking tape or chalk

Procedure
1. Use masking tape or chalk to make a circle two feet in diameter on the floor.
2. Place several marbles in the circle.
3. The children "shoot" a marble to knock other marbles outside the circle.

4. Talk about how to flick your index finger against your thumb to "shoot" the marbles.

Developmental Bonus
Hand-eye coordination
Fine motor development

Curriculum Extension
For Gross Motor: Drop the Clothespin

Ages
4,5

Materials
Bucket, clothespin

Procedure
1. Ask one child to stand.
2. Place the bucket at his feet.
3. He holds the clothespin vertically and drops it into the bucket.

Developmental Bonus
Hand-eye coordination

Curriculum Extensions
For Language: Finger Puppets

Ages
3,4,5,6

Materials
Oval-shaped cardboard pieces with two finger-size holes cut in one end, markers, yarn, ribbon, construction paper

Procedure
1. The children decorate the cardboard pieces to create finger puppets.
2. Encourage the children to put on a puppet show.

Developmental Bonus
Creative expression

Curriculum Extension
For Math: Finger Patterns

Ages
4,5,6

Materials
Pieces of cardboard shaped like hands with a different color line on each finger in ring position, small colored rubber bands

Procedure
1. The children look at the hand-shaped pattern cards and copy the pattern on their own hand using the rubber bands.

2. Encourage children to create new patterns.

Developmental Bonus
Patterning
Visual discrimination

Related Bibliography

Baer, Edith. *The Wonder of Hands*. Macmillan, 1992. A look at all we do with our hands.

Mariotti, Mario. *Hands Off!* Kane-Miller, 1990. This book uses hand prints and illustrations, cleverly turning fingers into soccer players.

Martin, Bill, Jr. and John Archambault. *Here Are My Hands*. Holt, 1987. A rhyme about ways we use different parts of our bodies.

Showers, Paul. *Find Out by Touching*. Ty Cromwell, 1961. A story of all the things we can explore with our hands.

Weiss, Nicki. *If You're Happy and You Know It*. Greenwillow, 1987. Eighteen songs told in story form with illustrations.

Related Records and Tapes

Scelsa, Greg and Steve Millans. "Hand Jive" from *We All Live Together, Vol. 4*. Youngheart Records, 1979.

Stewart, Georgiana Liccione. *Toes Up, Toes Down*. Kimbo.

"Count My Fingers" from *Songs About Me*. Kimbo.

Finger Play and Hand Exercises. Kimbo.

Put Your Finger in the Air. Kimbo.

Where Is the Table?

Tune: Where Is Thumbkin?

Where is the table, where is the table?
There it is, there it is.
I can touch the table, I can touch the table,
With my hand, with my hand.

Where is the chair, where is the chair?
There it is, there it is.
I can touch the chair, I can touch the chair,
With my hand, with my hand.

Where is the floor, where is the floor?
Under my feet, under my feet.
I can march around, I can march around,
On my toes, on my toes.

Where is the ceiling, where is the ceiling?
Over my head, over my head.
Oh, I cannot touch it, oh, I cannot touch it,
It's too high, it's too high.

Thematic Connections
Me, Myself and I
Home

Things to Talk About
1. What other things can we touch with our hands? What things are we not able to reach with our hands?
2. What other things do we walk on?

Curriculum Extension
For Art: Footprint Art

Ages
3, 4, 5, 6

Materials
Tempera paint, bulletin board paper, towels, two large shallow pans—one for paint and one for soapy water, marker

Procedure
1. Arrange items on the floor in this order: a pan of tempera paint, a large piece of bulletin board paper (about 8 feet long) laid lengthwise, a pan of slightly soapy water and a towel.
2. This activity requires two adults, one stationed by the pan of tempera and the other by the pan of soapy water.
3. The children take off their shoes and socks. (You may want to label shoes with masking tape.)
4. One at a time, let the children step into the paint and then step out and walk down the bulletin board paper before stepping into the soapy water waiting at the other end.
5. Dry their feet and help them put their shoes back on.
6. Label at least one footprint for each child.
7. Compare foot sizes and shapes.

Developmental Bonus
Fun
Visual discrimination

For Creative Movement: Musical Chairs

Ages
4,5,6

Materials
Chairs, recorded music

Procedure
1. Divide the class into groups of seven.
2. Give each group six chairs (three sets back to back).
3. Each group of children walks around their chairs when the music plays.
4. When the music stops, the children sit down in the chairs. One child will not get a chair. This child sits out and assists the teacher by acting as a judge.
5. Remove one chair from each group.
6. Repeat until one child is left in each group.

Developmental Bonus
Auditory discrimination

Gross Motor: Follow Me

Ages
3,4,5

Materials
None needed

Procedure
1. One child demonstrates walking, tiptoeing and crawling.
2. The other children copy the first child.

Developmental Bonus
Motor development

For Language: I Spy

Ages
3,4,5,6

Materials
None needed

Procedure
1. Appoint one child as "it."
2. This child secretly selects an item in the room and says, "I spy something _____ (red, big, tall, etc.)." The child gives clues until the item is guessed.

Developmental Bonus
Listening
Critical thinking

For Math: How High Can You Reach?

Ages
4,5,6

Materials
Masking tape, pen, ruler

Procedure
1. Ask each child to reach as high as she can on a wall.
2. Place masking tape at each place and label with the child's name.
3. Compare reaches.
4. Use a ruler to measure the highest and lowest reach.

Developmental Bonus
Measurement concepts

Related Bibliography

Aruego, José. *Look What I Can Do.* Macmillan, 1988. Two lively carabao romp through a game of copycat frightening their neighbors and themselves.

Hughes, Shirley. *Alfie's Feet.* Lothrop, 1983. The story of boots that end up on the wrong feet.

Kraus, Robert. *Leo the Late Bloomer.* HarperCollins, 1971. A young tiger seems to develop later than his peers and his mother and father are quite anxious.

McPhail, David. *Pig Pig Grows Up.* Dutton, 1985. A pig finds advantages to growing up.

Martin, Bill, Jr. and John Archambault. *Here Are My Hands.* Holt, 1987. A delightful chant about how we use our body.

Related Records and Tapes

Moore, Thomas. "Stand Up, Sit Down" from *Singing, Moving, and Learning* and "High, Low" from *I Am Special.* Thomas Moore Records.

Palmer, Hap. *Learning Basic Skills Through Music: Volume 2.* Activity Records, 1969.

We're So Glad You're Here

Tune: "Mulberry Bush"

This is <u>Tiffany</u> over here,
She has on a <u>bright</u> <u>blue</u> <u>dress</u>,
This is <u>Tiffany</u> our <u>new</u> friend,
We're so glad <u>she's</u> here.

Directions: Fill in the underlined words to fit each child in the class.

Thematic Connections
Me, Myself and I
Family

Things to Talk About
1. What makes each person special?
2. Name something that is blue, something that is red, something short, something tall.

<u>Curriculum Extension</u>
For Art: Special Drawing

Ages
3,4,5,6

Materials
Drawing paper, crayons

Procedure
1. Ask the children to draw something or someone that is special to them.
2. The children decorate the drawings with their favorite crayon(s).

Developmental Bonus
Creative expression

<u>Curriculum Extension</u>
For Dramatic Play: Dress Up

Ages
3,4,5,6

Materials
Lots of dress-up clothes, accessories and costumes

Procedure
1. Ask the children to dress as a person who is special to them.
2. Come together as a group and ask the children to tell why the person they chose is special to them.

Developmental Bonus
Creative expression

For Gross Motor: Special Dances

Ages
3,4,5,6

Materials
Optional—recorded music

Procedure
1. Ask the children to perform a special dance or walk.
2. Encourage the children to be creative.
3. If desired, allow the children to select music from classroom favorites to dance to.

Developmental Bonus
Creativity

For Language: Sharing Books

Ages
4,5,6

Materials
Books from home, masking tape, pen

Procedure
1. Invite the children to bring their favorite books from home to share with the other children.
2. Use a piece of masking tape to label each child's book.
3. Be sure to provide books at school for those children who don't have books at home or forget to bring one from home.

Developmental Bonus
Concept development

For Math: Measuring/Graphing

Ages
4,5,6

Materials
Tape, marker, paper, pencil

Procedure
1. With the tape and marker, label something tall and something short in the classroom.
2. Classify children in the classroom by the length of their hair. Predict the results first, then graph the results.
3. Classify children by skin color, light or dark. Predict first, then graph the results. Remember to be sensitive to the differences among the children.

Developmental Bonus
Measurement concepts
Predicting

Related Bibliography

Andersen, Hans Christian. *The Ugly Duckling*. Macmillan, 1987. An ugly duckling shunned by everyone develops into a magnificent swan.

Carle, Eric. *The Mixed-Up Chameleon*. HarperCollins, 1984. A chameleon wishes to be something other than himself. As he wishes for parts of other animals, his wishes come true.

LeSieg, Theo. *I Wish That I Had Duck Feet*. Random Books, 1965. A boy imagines what it would be like to have useful parts of various animals—an elephant's trunk, duck's feet, etc. He finally decides he is perfect just the way he is.

Hoffman, Mary. *Amazing Grace*. Dial, 1991. With the support of a loving mother and wise grandmother, a little black girl named Grace proves she can be anything she wants to be.

Sharmat, Marjorie Weinman. *I'm Terrific*. Holiday, 1977. Jason tries many ways of being different until he accepts himself.

Related Records and Tapes

Moore, Thomas. *I Am Special*. Thomas Moore Records.

Palmer, Hap. *Getting to Know Myself*. Educational Activities, 1972.

2

▼▼▼▼▼▼▼▼▼▼▼▼▼

OCTOBER

Farmer in the Dell
Gray Squirrel
I'm a Little Acorn Brown
The Old Gray Mare
Old MacDonald Had a Farm
Jack-O-Lantern

Farmer in the Dell

The farmer in the dell,
The farmer in the dell,
Hi, ho, the derry-o,
The farmer in the dell.

The farmer takes a wife....

The wife takes a child....

The child takes a nurse....

The nurse takes a dog....

The dog takes a cat....

The cat takes a mouse....

The mouse takes the cheese....

The cheese stands alone....

Thematic Connections
Farm
Animals
Family

Things to Talk About
1. What is a dell?
2. Why did each person or animal choose to take the person or animal that they chose?

Curriculum Extensions

For Art: Crayon Rubbings

Ages
3, 4, 5

Materials
Scissors, tagboard or poster-board, crayons, drawing paper, animal template

Procedure
1. Cut patterns of animal shapes from tagboard or posterboard.
2. The children place the patterns under their drawing paper and rub a crayon across the top of the paper to create an impression of the animal.
3. If desired, the children can add to their pictures.

Developmental Bonus
Visual discrimination

Curriculum Extensions

For Cooking: Making Butter

Ages
3, 4, 5

Materials
Whipping cream, baby food jars, salt, tablespoon, crackers

Procedure
1. Provide each set of two children with a baby food jar.
2. Pour two tablespoons of room temperature whipping cream in each jar. (One pint of whipping cream is enough for 12 jars.)

3. Instruct the children to take turns shaking the jar until a soft ball of butter is formed.
4. Taste the butter, salted and unsalted.
5. Discuss where milk, butter and cheese come from.
6. Spread the butter on crackers and enjoy!

Developmental Bonus
Concept development

Curriculum Extension
For Gross Motor: Dramatic Play

Ages
4,5,6

Materials
Barnyard animals, oatmeal and shoe boxes, blocks

Procedure
1. Turn the block center into a barnyard by bringing in an assortment of props.
2. Make a silo from an oatmeal box.
3. An old shoe box makes a great barn.
4. Ask the children to bring in plastic farm animals.
5. Model the kind of dramatic play that you wish to encourage, for example, the construction of a barnyard, recreation of the song, etc.

Developmental Bonus
Concept development

Curriculum Extension
For Language: Sequencing

Ages
4,5,6

Materials
Paper plates, scraps of construction paper, yarn, glue

Procedure
1. With the children, create a paper plate mask for each character in the song.
2. Ask the children to sequence the characters.
3. Talk about the relationships between the characters.

Developmental Bonus
Sequencing

Curriculum Extension
For Science: Animal Foods

Ages
3,4,5

Materials
Various seeds and grains—oats, corn, alfalfa, barley, etc.; small jars; magnifying glass

Procedure
1. Place grains and seeds in small jars.
2. Provide a magnifying glass for observation.

Developmental Bonus
Observation

Related Bibliography

Brown, Craig. *Patchwork Farmer*. Greenwillow, 1989. A farmer tears his clothes a number of times, but he is quick to repair his tears with patches.

Brown, Margaret Wise. *Big Red Barn*. HarperCollins, 1989. A rhyming tale about a farm with no people.

McPhail, David. *Farm Morning*. Harcourt, 1985. A wonderful description of early morning happenings on the farm.

Parkinson, Kathy. *The Farmer in the Dell*. Albert Whitman, 1988. The storybook of the song.

Related Records and Tapes

Lucky, Sharron. "The Farmer in the Dell" from *Sing Along with Lucky*. Melody House.

Weissman, Jackie. "I Had a Rooster" and "I See a Horse" from *Miss Jackie and Her Friends Sing About Peanut Butter, Tarzan and Roosters*. Miss Jackie, 1981.

Gray Squirrel

Gray squirrel, gray squirrel,
Swish your bushy tail.
Gray squirrel, gray squirrel,
Swish your bushy tail.
Wrinkle up your funny nose.
Hold an acorn in your toes.
Gray squirrel, gray squirrel,
Swish your bushy tail.

Thematic Connections
Animals
Fall
Nature

Things to Talk About
1. Name ways squirrels use their bushy tails.
2. What other animals have unusual tails?

Curriculum Extension
For Art: Acorn Roll

Ages
3,4,5,6

Materials
Drawing paper, cookie sheet, acorns, tempera paints, spoons

Procedure
1. Place a sheet of drawing paper on the cookie sheet.
2. Drop acorns in the tempera paint.
3. Remove the acorns with a plastic spoon and place them on the drawing paper.
4. Encourage the children to roll the acorns on the paper.
5. Watch the resulting designs.

Developmental Bonus
Creative expression

Curriculum Extension
For Fine Motor: Acorn Transfer

Ages
5,6

Materials
Acorns, two shallow boxes

Procedure
1. Put acorns in one of the boxes.
2. The children take off their shoes and socks, then transfer the acorns from one box to the next using their toes.

Developmental Bonus
Small muscle development
Coordination

For Math: Counting Acorns

Ages
4,5,6

Materials
Ten 6-inch squirrels cut from construction paper, paper cups, stapler, markers, acorns

Procedure
1. Staple a paper cup to each squirrel so the squirrels stand up.
2. Number the squirrels from 1 to 10.
3. The children count the appropriate number of acorns into each cup.

Developmental Bonus
Numeral recognition
Counting

For Outdoors: Tape the Tail on the Squirrel

4,5,6

Materials
Posterboard drawing of a squirrel with no tail, construction paper tails, tape, blindfold

Procedure
1. Play this game like Pin the Tail on the Donkey.
2. One at a time, blindfold a child and give her a tail. Then she tries to place the tail in the appropriate place on the posterboard squirrel.

Developmental Bonus
Coordination

For Science: Squirrel Watch

Ages
3,4,5,6

Materials
None needed

Procedure
1. In areas of the country where appropriate, take children to a park or a wooded area where squirrels live.
2. Sit quietly and watch the daily routine of squirrels.
3. If nuts or acorns are available, place a handful nearby so the children can watch the nut gathering that will surely follow.

Developmental Bonus
Concept development

Related Bibliography

Burton, Marileen Robin. *Tails Toes Eyes Ears Nose*. HarperCollins, 1988. Children must identify different animals by looking only at tails, toes, eyes, ears or nose.

Drummond, V.H. *Phewtus the Squirrel*. Lothrop, 1987. A stuffed orange toy squirrel comes to life in this story of a boy who loses his favorite toy.

Gardner, Beau. *Guess What?* Lothrop, 1985. Animals are identified by looking at only part of the animal.

Kroll, Steven. *The Squirrels' Thanksgiving*. Holiday House, 1991. A brother and sister squirrel learn what being thankful is all about.

Shannon, George. *The Surprise*. Greenwillow, 1983. The story of a squirrel who gives his mother himself as a birthday present.

Related Records and Tapes

Weissman, Jackie. *Sniggles, Squirrels and Chicken Pox, Vol. 1*. Miss Jackie, 1984.

I'm a Little Acorn Brown

I'm an little acorn brown,
Lying on the cold, hard ground,
Someone came and stepped on me,
Now I'm cracked as I can be.

I'm a nut. (clap, clap)
I'm a nut. (clap, clap)
I'm a dog gone nut.

Thematic Connections
Fall
Nature
Trees

Things to Talk About
1. What does the saying "Tall oaks from little acorns grow" mean?
2. Which animals like to eat acorns?

Curriculum Extension
For Art: Acorn Paints

Ages
3,4,5,6

Materials
Several acorns, nutcracker or hammer, bowl, cooking oil, measuring spoon, drawing paper

Procedure
1. Crack several acorns (at least a dozen) and collect the yellow meal from inside. Mix with 1/2 teaspoon of cooking oil to create a paste.
2. Allow children to paint with the acorn paint.

Developmental Bonus
Concept development
Creative expression

Curriculum Extension
For Creative Movement: Acorn Maracas

Ages
3,4,5

Materials
Large plastic eggs, acorns, masking tape

Procedure
1. Place several acorns inside a large plastic egg and seal with masking tape.
2. The children use the acorn "maracas" to keep time to the music.

Developmental Bonus
Creative expression

For Fine Motor: Playdough Creations

Ages
3,4,5

Materials
Playdough, acorns

Procedure
1. Ask the children to combine playdough and acorns to make exotic creations, for example, a decorated cake, funny people with acorn eyes.
2. Suggest that the children use the acorns to make imprints in the playdough.

Developmental Bonus
Creative expression

For Language: Nut Sort

Ages
3,4, 5

Materials
A variety of shelled nuts (acorns, pecans, walnuts, almonds, etc.), muffin tin

Procedure
1. Ask the children to sort the nuts into the muffin pan by color, shape, size or type of nut.

Developmental Bonus
Hand-eye coordination
Visual discrimination

For Science: Acorn Observation

Ages
3,4,5

Materials
Acorns, nutcracker or hammer, magnifying glass

Procedure
1. Provide cracked and whole acorns for the children to observe.
2. Look at the acorns first without the magnifying glass, then with the glass.
3. Ask what differences they notice between the cracked and whole acorns and between using and not using the magnifying glass.

Developmental Bonus
Observation skills

Related Bibliography

Galdone, Paul. *Henny Penny.* Clarion, 1979. A hen struck on the head by a falling acorn is convinced the sky is falling.

Hopkins, Lee Bennet. *Moments: Poems About the Seasons.* Harcourt, 1980. Fifty poems about the seasons.

Kellogg, Steven. *Chicken Little.* Morrow, 1985. A tongue-in-cheek version of Henny Penny.

Lyon, George Ella. *A B Cedar: An Alphabet of Trees.* Orchard Books, Watts, 1989. A tree for each letter of the alphabet with fruit and leaf samples for each.

Udry, Janice May. *A Tree is Nice.* HarperCollins, 1987. This book presents many reasons why trees are nice.

Related Records and Tapes

For Everything a Season. Melody House.
Hug the Earth. Tickle Tune Typhoon, 1985.

The Old Gray Mare

Oh, the old gray mare, she
Ain't what she used to be,
Ain't what she used to be,
Ain't what she used to be.
Oh, the old gray mare, she
Ain't what she used to be,
Many long years ago.

Chorus:
Many long years ago,
Many long years ago,
The old gray mare, she
Ain't what she used to be,
Many long years ago.

Oh, the old gray mare, she
Kicked on the whiffletree,
Kicked on the whiffletree,
Kicked on the whiffletree.
Oh, the old gray mare, she
Kicked on the whiffletree,
Many long years ago.

Thematic Connections
Animals
Farm

Things to Talk About
1. Talk about and define the differences between mares, colts and stallions.
2. List things a young mare might be able to do that an old mare probably can't do.

Curriculum Extension
For Art: Cup Horse Puppets

Ages
4,5,6

Materials
Paper cup, construction paper, crayons, glue, scissors, yarn

Procedure
1. Turn a paper cup on its side to look like a horse snout, and make a hole in the underside of the cup big enough for a finger to go through.
2. The children cut construction paper ears and glue them onto the edge of the cup.
3. Next, the children can draw eyes on their horse.
4. Yarn can be added for a mane.
5. The puppet is now ready for play.

Developmental Bonus
Creative expressions

For Cooking: Haystacks

Ages
3,4,5,6

Materials
One 6-ounce bag of butter-scotch morsels, margarine, Chinese noodles, mixing spoon, electric frying pan or crock pot or hot plate and pan, wax paper

1. Melt one 6-ounce bag of butterscotch morsels and two tablespoons of margarine in an electric frying pan.
2. Stir in Chinese noodles.
3. Drop by spoonfuls onto wax paper and allow to cool.
4. Eat and enjoy!

Developmental Bonus
Measurement concepts
Changes of state

For Language: Puppet Show

Ages
4,5,6

Materials
Puppets from art activity, index cards, pen

Procedure
1. Use the cup puppets from the art activity to create a puppet show.
2. Ask the children to name their horses. Print the horses' names on an index card.

Developmental Bonus
Creative expression

For Outdoors: Horseshoes

Ages
3,4,5,6

Materials
Stick, heavy cardboard, markers, scissors, tape and metal washers, if needed

Procedure
1. Cut horseshoes from heavy cardboard. If the horseshoes need to be weighted, tape on a couple of washers.
2. Push a stick into the ground.
3. Encourage the children to toss the horseshoes, trying to ring the stick.

Developmental Bonus
Hand-eye coordination
Large muscle development

For Science: Hoof Vibrations

Ages
3,4,5,6

Materials
Pencil

Procedure
1. Ask the children to place their heads on the table with one ear flat on the table surface.
2. Tap on the table with a pencil so the children can hear the sound vibrations.
3. Talk about how this technique was used to hear horses coming from a distance.

Developmental Bonus
Science concept

Related Bibliography

Anderson, C.W. *Lonesome Little Colt.* Aladdin, 1961. The other colts won't play with the orphaned colt, making him very sad. He finally finds a mother who loves him.

Brett, Jan. *Fritz and the Beautiful Horses.* Houghton Mifflin, 1987. Fritz, a pony separated from the other horses, becomes a hero when he rescues the children of the city.

Honda, Tetsuya. *Wild Horse Winter.* Chronicle Books, 1992. A herd of horses, including a newborn calf, makes it through a raging blizzard.

Isenbart, Hans-Heinrich. *Baby Animals on the Farm.* Putnam, 1984. An introduction to fifteen common farm animals.

Patent, Dorothy Hinshaw. *Baby Horses.* Carolrhoda, 1991. The life of horses from birth to life on their own.

Related Records and Tapes

Moore, Thomas. "The Pig and the Pony" from *I Am Special.* Thomas Moore Records.

Old MacDonald Had a Farm

Old MacDonald had a farm,
E—I—E—I—O.
And on his farm he had some cows,
E—I—E—I—O.
With a moo-moo here and a moo-moo there,
Here a moo, there a moo, everywhere a moo-moo,
Old MacDonald had a farm,
E—I—E—I—O.

Continue with other animals:
Sheep...baa-baa....
Pigs...oink-oink....
Ducks...quack-quack....
Horses...neigh-neigh....
Donkeys...hee-haw....
Chickens...chick-chick...., etc.

Thematic Connections
Farm
Animals
Plants

Things to Talk About
1. If Old MacDonald had an elephant on his farm, what noise would it make?
2. What noise do you think Old MacDonald himself makes?

Curriculum Extension
For Fine Motor: Corn Transfer

Ages
3,4,5

Materials
Tweezers, corn kernels, two bowls

Procedure
1. Provide the children with tweezers, one bowl of corn kernels and one empty bowl.
2. Ask the children to transfer the corn from one bowl to another with the tweezers.

Developmental Bonus
Hand-eye coordination

Curriculum Extension
For Gross Motor: Pretend Farms

Ages
3,4,5,6

Materials
Farm props—barn, plastic farm animals, tractors, trucks, etc.

Procedure
1. Provide the children with the props.
2. After helping set up the farm, leave them to play creatively on their own.

Developmental Bonus
Creative expression

For Language: Animal Puppets

Ages
3,4,5,6

Materials
Animal puppets (bought or teacher-made)

Procedure
1. Encourage the children to tell the story of "Old MacDonald Had a Farm" with the puppets.

Developmental Bonus
Creative expression

For Math: Farm Animal Count

Ages
4,5,6

Materials
Plastic farm animals, plastic strawberry cartons, number cards (from 1 to 10)

Procedure
1. Turn strawberry containers upside down and place a number card on top of each one.
2. The children count the proper number of plastic farm animals into each cage (strawberry container).

Developmental Bonus
Numeral recognition
Counting

For Outdoors: Old MacDonald

Ages
3,4,5,6

Materials
Props from the gross motor activity, sand box or sand pile, farm vehicles, leaves, acorns, etc.

Procedure
1. Bring the props used in the gross motor activity outdoors to the sand pile.
2. Supplement with farm vehicles, leaves, acorns, etc.
3. With the children, set up a farm in the sand box.
4. Construct a barn and lay out roads and fields.
5. Encourage the children to play "Old MacDonald" with the farm.

Developmental Bonus
Concept development

Related Bibliography

Brown, Margaret Wise. *Big Red Barn*. HarperCollins, 1989. The story of a farm filled with animals but no people.

Jones, Carol. *Old MacDonald Had a Farm*. Houghton, 1989. The story and illustrations of the traditional song.

Martin, Bill Jr. *Barn Dance!* Holt, 1986. The old barn dance comes to life with a party where animals dance.

Rounds, Glen. *Old MacDonald Had a Farm*. Holiday, 1989. The traditional song illustrated with goofy looking critters.

Tafuri, Nancy. *Early Morning in the Barn*. Greenwillow, 1983. The barn comes to life with the morning sun and sounds of the waking animals.

Related Records and Tapes

Beall, Pamela Conn and Susan Hagen Nipp. "Old MacDonald" from *Wee Sing Children's Songs and Fingerplays*. Price Stern Sloan, 1979.

Jenkins, Ella. "I Like the Way That They Stack the Hay" from *This-A-Way, That-A-Way*. Folkways, 1973.

Jenkins, Ella. "Did You Feed My Cow?" from *You'll Sing a Song, and I'll Sing a Song*. Folkways, 1989.

Rosenshontz. "The Garden Song" from *Rosenshontz Tickles You*. RS Records, 1980.

"Old MacDonald" from *Sing-A-Long*. Peter Pan, 1989.

Jack-O-Lantern

Tune: "Clementine"

Jack-O-Lantern, Jack-O-Lantern,
You are such a funny sight.
As you sit there in my window,
Looking out into the night.

You were once a yellow pumpkin,
Growing on a sturdy vine.
Now you are my Jack-O-Lantern,
Let your candlelight shine.

Thematic Connections

Halloween
Nature
Plants
Farm

Things to Talk About

1. Where do pumpkins come from?
2. What makes a pumpkin different from a Jack-O-Lantern?
3. What do you think is inside a pumpkin?

Curriculum Extension

For Art: Giant Pumpkins

Ages
3,4,5,6

Materials
Easel paper, scissors, tempera paint, brushes

Procedure
1. Cut easel paper into pumpkin shapes.
2. Ask the children to paint pictures on the pumpkin-shaped paper.

Developmental Bonus
Creative expression

Curriculum Extension

For Fine Motor: Play-dough Pumpkins

Ages
3,4,5

Materials
Flour, salt, water, bowl, red and yellow food coloring

Procedure
1. With the children, mix the ingredients in a bowl, then knead for 10 minutes.
2. Add red and yellow food coloring to create orange play-dough.
3. The children create Jack-O-Lanterns from the orange play-dough.

4. Encourage them to fashion different faces on the play-dough Jack-O-Lanterns.

Developmental Bonus
Creative expression

Curriculum Extension
For Math: Pumpkin Seriation

Ages
4,5

Materials
Orange construction paper, markers, scissors

Procedure
1. Cut out several pumpkins ranging in size from very small to large.
2. The children place the pumpkins in order from smallest to largest.

Developmental Bonus
Sequencing

Curriculum Extension
For Outdoors: Back to Nature

Ages
4,5,6

Materials
Pumpkin from the science activity

Procedure
1. When the children are finished using the Jack-O-Lantern for decoration, bury it outside or in a terrarium and observe the decaying process.

Developmental Bonus
Concept development

Curriculum Extension
For Science: Pumpkin Carving

Ages
3,4,5,6

Materials
Pumpkin, chalk or markers, knife, spoon, bowl

Procedure
1. Bring a pumpkin into the classroom.
2. Discuss what type of face to carve.
3. Use chalk or non-permanent markers to show alternatives.
4. Let the class select the face.
5. Older children may want to estimate the number of seeds inside the pumpkin.
6. Carve the pumpkin.
7. Reserve the seeds for toasting and to use for counting activities.

Developmental Bonus
Concept development

Related Bibliography

Bunting, Eve. *Scary, Scary Halloween*. Clarion, 1988. A cat and her kittens watch a parade of trick-or-treaters in their ghoulish disguises.

Johnston, Tony. *The Vanishing Pumpkin*. Putnam, 1983. A stolen pumpkin makes a very old man and lady pretty sad as they think about the pumpkin pie they were going to enjoy.

Martin, Bill, Jr. and John Archambault. *The Magic Pumpkin*. Holt, 1989. A jack-o-lantern comes to life and creates havoc on Halloween night.

Prelutsky, Jack. *It's Halloween*. Greenwillow, 1977. A collection of 12 poems all about Halloween from carving pumpkins to bobbing for apples.

Williams, Linda. *The Little Old Lady Who Was Not Afraid of Anything*. Crowell, 1986. An old lady meets some scary things on her way home.

Related Records and Tapes

Finkelstein, Mark and Carol. *Everyday's a Holiday*. Melody House. Activity Records, 1971.

Palmer, Hap. *Witches Brew*. Educational Activities.

Palmer, Hap. *Holiday Songs and Rhythms*. Educational Activities.

3

▼▼▼▼▼▼▼▼▼▼▼▼▼

NOVEMBER

B—I—N—G—O

There was a farmer had a dog,
And Bingo was his name-o.
B—I—N—G—O,
B—I—N—G—O,
And Bingo was his name-o.

There was a farmer had a dog,
And Bingo was his name-o.
Clap—I—N—G—O,
Clap—I—N—G—O,
And Bingo was his name-o.

Continue the song, substituting a clap for each consecutive letter with each verse.

Thematic Connections
Animals
Pets
Farm
Family

Things to Talk About
1. Who has a dog? What is the dog's name?
2. Brainstorm some good names for dogs.
3. How would a different dog's name change the song?

Curriculum Extension
For Art: My Favorite Pet

Ages
4,5, 6

Materials
Drawing paper, crayons

Procedure
1. Encourage students to draw a picture of their favorite pet or a make-believe pet and give it a name.

2. Transcribe the names onto their pet pictures.

Developmental Bonus
Creative expressions
Fine motor development

Curriculum Extension
For Fine Motor: Playdough Creations

Ages
4,5,6

Materials
Playdough

Procedure
1. Encourage the children to make the letters represented in the song with the playdough.
2. Also create playdough dogs or bones.

Developmental Bonus
Visual discrimination
Ordering and sequencing
Vocabulary

For Language: Bingo

Ages
3, 4, 5,6

Materials
Teacher-made bingo cards, beans or buttons

Procedure
1. Create a bingo game using color squares, letters, animal pictures or whatever you would like.
2. Play bingo.
3. Ask the children if they think the farmer named his dog after the game.

Developmental Bonus
Visual discrimination

For Math: Ordinal Position

Ages
5,6

Materials
Alphabet letters B, I, N, G and O

Procedure
1. With the children, discuss the ordinal position of the letters in the name Bingo, for example, "B" is first and "O" is last.
2. Be sure to use letters (bulletin board letters are great), so children can actually see you place the letters in proper order.
3. Let children play with the letters and place them in the appropriate position.

Developmental Bonus
Ordering and sequencing

For Science: Animal Sort

Ages
3,4,5

Materials
Pictures of animals, boxes for sorting

Procedure
1. Collect pictures of various animals.
2. Ask the children to sort the animals into those that live on a farm and those that don't.
3. Sort by other characteristics.

Developmental Bonus
Concept awareness

Related Bibliography

Bridwell, Norman. *Clifford the Big Red Dog.* Scholastic, 1988. A lovable, big red dog that gets into lots of trouble doing what every child would love to do.

Day, Alexandra. *Good Dog, Carl.* Green Tiger, 1991. A large dog plays baby sitter to an infant while the child's mother goes out.

Keats, Ezra Jack. *Whistle for Willie.* Puffin, 1977. A little boy struggles with learning to whistle so he can call his dog.

Keats, Ezra Jack. *Pet Show!* Macmillan, 1974. An unusual entry into the pet show wins Peter a prize.

Kellogg, Steven. *Can I Keep Him?* Dial, 1971. A little boy is determined to have a pet. He takes home lots of "possibilities" until finally his mother consents.

Related Records and Tapes

Beall, Pamela Conn and Susan Hagen Nipp."BINGO" from *Wee Sing Children's Songs and Fingerplays.* Price Stern Sloan, 1979.

Moore, Thomas."The Pig and the Pony" and "Alphabet Boogie" from *I Am Special.* Thomas Moore Records.

Thumb, Tom. *Animals Are Wonderful.* Tom Thumb.

Go Tell Aunt Rhody

Go tell Aunt Rhody,
Go tell Aunt Rhody,
Go tell Aunt Rhody,
Her old gray goose is dead.

The one we've been saving,
The one we've been saving,
The one we've been saving,
To make a feather bed.

She died on Friday,
She died on Friday,
She died on Friday,
With an aching in her head.

Old gander's weeping,
Old gander's weeping,
Old gander's weeping,
Because his wife is dead.

Goslings are mourning,
Goslings are mourning,
Goslings are mourning,
Because their mother's dead.

Go tell Aunt Rhody,
Go tell Aunt Rhody,
Go tell Aunt Rhody,
Her old gray goose is dead.

Thematic Connections
Family
Death
Animals

Things to Talk About
1. In different parts of the country this song might be "Aunt Nancy" or something else.
2. Do you think Aunt Rhody was glad to get the feathers?
3. Talk about different ways to talk to people. How do we tell people things like the goose died?

Curriculum Extension

For Art: Feather Crayon Rubbings

Ages
3,4,5,6

Materials
Different-sized feathers, crayons, drawing paper

Procedure
1. Place feathers under the drawing paper and rub with crayon to create a rubbing.
2. Add designs to the rubbings if desired.

Developmental Bonus
Creative expression

Curriculum Extension

For Language: Communication

Ages
4,5,6

Materials
Chart tablet paper, marker

Procedure
1. Talk about ways we communicate to others, for example, writing, body language, voice, signs, etc.
2. Make a list of all the communication methods the children can think of.

Developmental Bonus
Concept development
Creative thinking

Curriculum Extension
For Outdoors: Feather Hunt

Ages
3,4,5

Materials
Feather

Procedure
1. Hide the feather without the children seeing.
2. Ask the children to look for it.
3. After it is found, ask a child to hide it.

Developmental Bonus
Problem-solving skills

Curriculum Extension
For Science: Making Gray

Ages
3,4,5,6

Materials
Black and white tempera paint, brushes, paper

Procedure
1. Ask the children to mix black and white paint on their papers to create gray.
2. The children think of things they can paint that are gray and then paint those pictures.

Developmental Bonus
Concept development

Curriculum Extension
For Social Studies: Family Tree

Ages
3,4,5,6

Materials
Pictures children bring from home, tape

Procedure
1. Draw a large tree on the bulletin board.
2. Attach the pictures to the tree, making a class family tree.
3. Talk about different kinds of families, being sensitive to many possible family situations.

Developmental Bonus
Social awareness
Concept development

Related Bibliography

Aliki. *Go Tell Aunt Rhody.* Macmillan, 1986. Brightly colored illustrations help tell the story of the song.

Duvoisin, Roger. *Petunia.* Knopf, 1962. A silly duck thinks she can get smarter just by carrying a book.

Galdone, Joanna. *Gertrude and the Goose Who Forgot.* Franklin Watts, 1975. An absent-minded goose loses her keys, and when she retraces her steps across the farmyard, she finds a number of other articles she had left behind.

Gerstein, Mordicai. *Follow Me!* Morrow, 1983. Seven ducks and a goose are lost until a duck herd leads them home.

Ryder, Joanne. *Catching the Wind.* Morrow, 1989. Humans become birds and take flight in a V formation. Great illustrations!

Related Records and Tapes

Moore, Thomas. "The Mail Carrier" from *Songs for the Whole Day.* Thomas Moore Records.

Hush, Little Baby

Hush, little baby, don't say a word,
Papa's going to buy you a mockingbird.

If that mockingbird won't sing,
Papa's going to buy you a diamond ring.

If that diamond ring turns brass,
Papa's going to buy you a looking glass.

If that looking glass gets broke,
Papa's going to buy you a billy goat.

If that billy goat won't pull,
Papa's going to buy you a cart and bull.

If that cart and bull turn over,
Papa's going to buy you a dog named Rover.

If that dog named Rover won't bark,
Papa's going to buy you a horse and cart.

If that horse and cart fall down,
You'll still be the sweetest little baby in town.

Thematic Connections
Family
Money
Siblings

Things to Talk About
1. Substitute Mama, Grandma, Grandpa, Uncle or Aunt for Papa, and sweetest little baby can be prettiest girl or handsomest boy.
2. Talk about things that can be bought as opposed to things you can't buy.
3. Talk about the sounds babies make.

Curriculum Extension
For Language: Mock Actions

Ages
3,4,5,6

Materials
None needed

Procedure
1. Explain how mockingbirds imitate other birds.

2. Divide children into pairs.
3. Each pair takes turns mocking (imitating) each other.

Developmental Bonus
Coordination

Curriculum Extension
For Language: Song Substitution

Ages
3,4,5,6

Materials
None needed

Procedure
1. Sing the song, leaving off the last word in each line and substituting a clap. For example, "Hush, little baby, don't say a (clap), Mama's going to buy you a mocking (clap), etc."
2. Next try clapping for the first word in each line.

Developmental Bonus
Patterning

For Math: Using Money

Ages
3, 4, 5, 6

Materials
Play money, objects to buy (perhaps items from the song—ring, looking glass, etc.), masking tape, marker

Procedure
1. Use masking tape and a marker to price the various items. Use simple or more complicated prices depending on the ages of the children in your class.
2. One child acts as the "seller" and the other children "purchase" the items.
3. Take turns being the "seller."

Developmental Bonus
Money concepts
Counting

For Science: Looking Glasses

Ages
3, 4, 5, 6

Materials
Looking glasses—sunglasses, binoculars, mirrors, magnifying glasses, etc.

Procedure
1. Provide different types of looking glasses for the children.
2. The children look through the various types of glasses and discuss the differences.

Developmental Bonus
Concept development
Analytical skills

For Social Studies: Stand-ins

Ages
3, 4, 5, 6

Materials
Pictures of different family members (be sure to include a variety of cultures), pictures of objects

Procedure
1. As the children sing the song, hold up a picture of a family member, for example, mama, papa, brother, sister, grannies, or grandpas. The children substitute that person's name or relationship as they sing the song.
2. Hold up a picture of an object. Substitute that object for the one in the song. For example, "Hush, little baby, don't say a word, (Grannie's) going to buy you a (big red car), etc."
3. Using only the first two lines of the song, continue to change people and objects.

Developmental Bonus
Creative expression
Critical thinking
Visual discrimination

Related Bibliography

Caseley, Judith. *Silly Baby*. Greenwillow, 1988. Lindsey's mother has a baby even though Lindsey didn't want it. When the baby cries a lot, Lindsey's mother shows her baby pictures to prove she was just as silly.

Hoban, Russell. *Baby Sister for Frances*. HarperCollins, 1964. Frances feels unloved with the new baby in the house, and she runs away.

Keats, Ezra Jack. *Peter's Chair*. HarperCollins, 1967. Peter doesn't want to give up his old baby furniture to his new baby sister.

Scott, Ann Herbert. *On Mother's Lap*. Houghton Mifflin, 1992. A little Eskimo boy is upset when a new baby joins his family. He is sure that there is not enough room on mother's lap for both him and the new baby.

Winter, Jeanette. *Hush, Little Baby*. Pantheon, 1984. Traditional English song beautifully illustrated in a storybook.

Related Records and Tapes

Beall, Pamela Conn and Susan Hagen Nipp. "Hush Little Baby" from *Wee Sing Children's Songs and Fingerplays*. Price Stern Sloan, 1979.

Moore, Thomas. "Hush Little Baby" from *Sleepy Time*, Educational Record Center, 1980.

"Hush Little Baby" from *Sing-a-Long*, Peter Pan.

My Grandfather's Clock

My Grandfather's clock was too tall for the shelf,
So it stood ninety years on the floor.
It was taller by far than the old man himself,
And it weighed, not a penny, weighed more.

It was bought on the morn of the day that he was born,
It was always his treasure and pride.
But it stopped short never to go again,
When the old man died,
When the old man kicked the bucket and died.

Ninety years without slumbering,
Tick-tock, tick-tock.
Life second numbering,
Tick-tock, tick-tock.

It stopped short never to go again,
When the old man died,
When the old man kicked the bucket and died.

Thematic Connections

Time
Family
Days of the week

Things to Talk About

1. Discuss the phrase "weighed not a penny." Explain that a penny weight is a colloquialism used in Great Britain to describe something that does not weigh much.

2. What is meant by "the old man kicked the bucket"?

Curriculum Extension

For Art: Paper Plate Clocks

Ages
4, 5, 6

Materials
Paper plates, crayons, brads, construction paper, scissors

Procedure
1. Help the children make clocks, using paper plates for the clock face.

2. Younger children may only want to put 12, 3, 6, and 9 on their clock faces.
3. Cut minute and hour hands from construction paper and attach to the clock face with brads.

Developmental Bonus
Time concepts

Curriculum Extension

For Math: Telling Time

Ages
5, 6

Materials
Margarine tub with lid, tagboard or posterboard, scissors, brad, marker, paper

Procedure
1. Using the posterboard, cut out a circle slightly larger than the margarine tub lid. Draw a clock face on the posterboard and glue to the top of the lid.

2. Make clock hands out of cardboard. Attach both hands to the clock face with the brad.
3. Write different times (on the hour only) on small pieces of paper and place them inside the tub.
4. The children take turns picking a piece of paper from the margarine tub. The teacher tells the child what time the paper says and the child moves the hands to illustrate that time.

Developmental Bonus
Time concepts

Curriculum Extension
For Outdoors: Sundial

Ages
4,5,6

Materials
Six-foot-long broomstick or dowel, compass, rocks

Procedure
1. Draw a circle four to five feet in diameter in a sunny area of the playground.
2. Poke a broomstick or dowel into the center of the circle.
3. Use a compass to determine which direction is North. North represents 12:00 noon on the clock.
4. Watch the shadow of the dowel throughout the day. Ask children to place a rock at different points of the circle.
5. Explain to the children that ancient cultures used the sundial to tell time.
6. Use the sundial to keep track of time for a couple of days.

Developmental Bonus
Concept development
Observation skills

Curriculum Extension
For Science: Hour Glass

Ages
5,6

Materials
Three-minute egg timer, puzzles

Procedure
1. Challenge the children to complete puzzles, racing the three-minute timer.
2. Find other activities and tasks to "race" against the timer. For example, setting the table for snack, picking up blocks, etc.

Developmental Bonus
Concept development

Curriculum Extension
For Social Studies: Counting Rope

Ages
4,5,6

Materials
Rope

Procedure
1. Explain to children that some Native Americans used knots on a rope to keep track of time.
2. Each day, place one knot in the rope.
3. Use the counting rope for a week to keep track of the passing days.

Developmental Bonus
Concept development

Related Bibliography

Allen, Jeffery. *Mary Alice, Operator Number Nine*. Little, 1976. When Mary Alice (a duck) gets sick, it's impossible to find a replacement to provide the time.

Balian, Lorna. *Amelia's Nine Lives*. Humbug, 1986. Nora loses her cat for a week.

Carle, Eric. *The Very Hungry Caterpillar*. Putnam, 1981. A caterpillar eats its way through the week.

Carle, Eric. *The Grouchy Ladybug*. HarperCollins, 1986. A grouchy ladybug spends from 6:00 a.m. to 6:00 p.m. looking for a fight.

Hutchins, Pat. *Clocks and More Clocks*. Macmillan, 1970. With every clock in the house showing a different time, the clock maker is called in to ascertain which one gives the correct time.

Related Records and Tapes

Bram, Sharon and Lois. "Rock Around the Clock" from *Stay Tuned*, A&M, 1987.
Arco Iris de Colores. Melody House.

Oh Where, Oh Where Has My Little Dog Gone?

Oh where, oh where has my little dog gone?
Oh where, oh where can he be?
With his ears cut short and his tail cut long,
Oh where, oh where can he be?

Thematic Connections
Animals
Pets
Circus

Things to Talk About
1. What does the song mean when it says "his ears cut short and his tail cut long"?
2. Many animals have different names for babies and adults. Can you think of baby animal names? What are baby dogs called?

Curriculum Extension
For Art: Origami Paper Dog

Ages
5,6

Materials
White construction paper, scissors, crayons

Procedure
1. Cut the construction paper into a perfect square.

2. Fold diagonally to create a triangle.
3. Fold two sides of the triangle down.
4. Fold the bottom angle of the triangle up.
5. Use crayons to draw features on the dog.

Developmental Bonus
Hand-eye coordination
Fine motor development

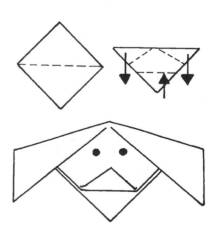

For Dramatic Play: A Home for Puppy

Ages
3, 4, 5, 6

Materials
Large cardboard box (washing machine or dryer box would be great), scissors or box cutter, tempera paint, paintbrushes

Procedure
1. Cut a door in one side of the box.
2. With the children's help, paint and decorate the box to create a dog house.
3. Use the home for dramatic play.

Developmental Bonus
Creative expression

For Language: Pet Stories

Ages
3, 4, 5, 6

Materials
Paper, pencil, crayons

Procedure
1. Ask the children to dictate stories about their favorite pet or about the pet they wish they had.
2. Transcribe the stories onto paper, then let the children illustrate them.

Developmental Bonus
Creative expression

For Outdoors: Dog and Bone

Ages
4, 5, 6

Materials
A construction paper bone

Procedure
1. The children sit in a circle with their eyes closed.
2. One child is "it." This child hides the bone somewhere.
3. After the bone is hidden, the other children look for it.
4. The child who finds the bone becomes "it."

Developmental Bonus
Problem-solving skills

For Science: Who Am I?

Ages
3, 4, 5, 6

Materials
One-half sheet of posterboard, laminated animal and pet pictures, velcro, scissors

Procedure
1. Cut a small circle (the size of a child's face) on one-half of the posterboard.
2. Glue a velcro strip on the other half of the posterboard and on the back of each of the animal pictures.
3. One child holds up the board and places her face through the hole.
4. Without letting the first child see, another child places an animal on the velcro strip on the board.
5. The child holding the board asks her classmates yes/no questions about the animal on the board.
6. Repeat with another child and another animal.

Developmental Bonus
Critical thinking

Related Bibliography

Day, Alexandra. *Good Dog, Carl.* Green Tiger, 1985. Carl, a large Rottweiler, babysits a human baby.

dePaola, Tomie. *The Comic Adventures of Old Mother Hubbard and Her Dog.* Harcourt, 1981. An updated rendition of the traditional nursery rhyme.

Keats, Ezra Jack. *Whistle for Willie.* Viking, 1964. Peter wants to learn to whistle so he can call his dog.

Thayer, Jane. *The Puppy Who Wanted a Boy.* Morrow, 1986. A puppy named Petey spends Christmas Eve looking for an owner and ends up finding a home in a home for boys.

Zion, Gene. *Harry the Dirty Dog.* HarperCollins, 1956. Harry gets so dirty his family doesn't recognize him.

Related Records and Tapes

Moore, Thomas. "The Pig and the Pony" from *I am Special.* Thomas Moore Records.

Stewart, Giorgiana Liccione. Walk Like the Animals. Kimbo, 1976.

Thumb, Tom. *Animals Are Wonderful.* Tom Thumb.

Five Fat Turkeys Are We

Five fat turkeys are we.
We slept all night in a tree.
When the cook came around,
We couldn't be found and,
That's why we're here you see!

Oh, five fat turkeys are we.
We spent the night in a tree.
It sure does pay on Thanksgiving day,
To sleep in the tallest tree.

Thematic Connections

Thanksgiving
Fall
Animals

Things to Talk About

1. How do turkeys get up into the trees?
2. List other places turkeys could hide.

Curriculum Extension

For Art: Turkey Hand Prints

Ages
3,4,5,6

Materials
Drawing paper, crayons

Procedure
1. Trace a child's hand onto a piece of paper.
2. Draw an eye on the thumb.
3. Ask the child to color the other fingers like feathers.
4. Add legs and the turkey is complete.

Developmental Bonus

Creative expression
Concept development

Curriculum Extension

For Cooking: No-Bake Pumpkin Custard

Ages
3,4,5,6

Materials
Canned pumpkin pie filling, marshmallow creme, whipped topping, cinnamon, mixing bowl and spoon, measuring spoons, bowls and spoons

Procedure
1. With the children's help, mix together two tablespoons of pumpkin pie filling, one tablespoon of marshmallow creme, and one tablespoon of whipped topping for an individual portion. Place in a serving bowl.
2. Repeat for each child in the class.
3. Sprinkle cinnamon on top.

4. Eat. Yum!

Developmental Bonus
Measurement concepts

Curriculum Extension
For Language: Thanksgiving Dinner Menu

Ages
4,5,6

Materials
Paper, pencil, crayons

Procedure
1. Ask the children to describe their Thanksgiving menus. Transcribe what they say onto drawing paper.
2. Then the children illustrate their dictated menus.

Developmental Bonus
Creative expression
Vocabulary development

Curriculum Extension
For Math: Feather Match

Ages
3,4,5

Materials
Manilla folder; red, blue, yellow, green, purple and orange construction paper; scissors; glue

Procedure
1. Cut two feathers from each sheet of construction paper.
2. Glue one feather of each color inside the manilla folder.
3. Ask the children to match the other feathers to those glued in the folder.

Developmental Bonus
One-to-one correspondence
Color matching

Curriculum Extension
For Science: Turkey Bones

Ages
4,5,6

Materials
Cleaned and dried turkey bones—leg, wishbone, neck, etc.

Procedure
1. Place the bones in the science center for the children to examine them.
2. Other animal bones can be included for comparisons.

Developmental Bonus
Concept development

Related Bibliography

Brown, Marc. *Arthur's Thanksgiving*. Little, Brown, 1984. Arthur volunteers to be the turkey in the school's Thanksgiving play. The results are humorous.

Child, Lydia Maria. *Over the River and Through the Wood*. Morrow, 1992. A story of the traditional song—a trip to the grandparents for Thanksgiving.

Kroll, Steven. *Oh, What a Thanksgiving! Scholastic, 1988. A little boy imagines what the first Thanksgiving was like.*

Prelutsky, Jack. *It's Thanksgiving*. Greenwillow, 1982. A collection of Thanksgiving poems.

Schatell, Brian. *Farmer Goff and His Turkey Sam. HarperCollins, 1982.* A goofy story of a pie-loving prize turkey who pigs out at the County Fair.

Related Records and Tapes

Palmer, Hap. *Holiday Songs and Rhythms*. Educational Records, 1971.

Finkelstein, Marc and Carol. *Every Day's a Holiday*. Melody House.

The More We Get Together

Tune: "Did You Ever See a Lassie?"

The more we get together,
Together, together,
The more we get together,
The happier are we.

For your friends are my friends,
And my friends are your friends,
The more we get together,
The happier are we.

Thematic Connections
Thanksgiving
Family
Friends
Celebrations

Things to Talk About
1. When families get together, what do they do? At meal time? In the car, etc.?
2. What things do you do with other people?
3. What things do we do together in a community (parades, ball games, etc.)?

Curriculum Extensions
For Art: Parade Hats

Ages
3,4,5,6

Materials
Paper plates, streamers, ribbons, paint, paintbrushes, construction paper, scissors

Procedure
1. Using the paper plates as a base, the children create their own parade hats.
2. Younger children may need help designing their hats and with any necessary cutting.
3. The children can wear their hats for the parade described in the dramatic play activity.

Developmental Bonus
Creative expression

Curriculum Extensions
For Cooking: Fruit Salad

Ages
3, 4,5,6

Materials
Fruit, bowl, knife, cutting board, bowls, spoons, optional —salad dressing or mayonnaise

Procedure

1. Ask each child to bring a piece of fruit from home. (Be sure to bring extra for those children who forget.)
2. With the children's help, cut the fruit for salad and mix them up in the bowl.
3. Mix with salad dressing or mayonnaise, if desired.
4. Serve and eat.

Developmental Bonus
Fine motor development

Curriculum Extensions
For Dramatic Play: Parade

Ages
3,4,5,6

Materials
Streamers, paper sacks, paints, paper, rhythm instruments

Procedure
1. Ask the children to help you plan a parade.
2. Use bicycles, costumes, rhythm instruments.
3. Use a wagon as a "float."
4. The children can wear the hats from the art activity.
5. Parade through the classroom and the school.

Developmental Bonus
Creative expression

Curriculum Extensions
For Gross Motor: Make Friendship Circles

Ages
3,4,5,6

Materials
Butcher paper, crayons

Procedure

1. Ask each child to select a partner.
2. Each pair takes one piece of paper and crayons.
3. Ask the pairs of children to make interlocking circles on the butcher paper.

Developmental Bonus
Coordination

Curriculum Extensions
For Language: Parent Tea

Ages
3,4,5,6

Materials
Paper and crayons, ingredients for cookies or sandwiches, tea, plates and cups

Procedure

1. Discuss the origin of tea parties.
2. Plan and prepare a menu with the children.
3. The children design invitations for their parents with the paper and crayons.
4. Have a great party!

Developmental Bonus
Concept development

Related Bibliography

Aliki. *We Are Best Friends*. Greenwillow, 1982. When a boy's best friend moves, he finds a new friend.

Delton, Judy. *Two Good Friends*. Crown, 1986. Two animal friends use their talent to help each other.

Kherdian, David and Nonny Hogrogian. *The Cat's Midsummer Jamboree*. Philomel, 1990. A roaming mandolin playing cat encounters a number of other musical animals.

Tsutsui, Yoriko. *Anna's Secret Friend*. Viking, 1987. When Anna, a little Japanese girl, moves to a new house, she receives gifts from a secret someone who wants to be her friend.

Wolkstein, Diane. *Banza*. Dial, 1981. A little tiger gives his banjo to a goat for protection. Two natural enemies create a great model for friendship.

Related Records and Tapes

Beall, Pamela Conn and Susan Hagen Nipp. "The More We Get Together" from *Wee Sing Sing-Alongs*. Price Stern Sloan, 1990.

Moore, Thomas. *The Family*. Thomas Moore Records.

Palmer, Hap. *Marching*. Educational Activities.

She'll Be Comin' 'Round the Mountain

She'll be comin' 'round the mountain when she comes,
She'll be comin' 'round the mountain when she comes,
She'll be comin' 'round the mountain,
She'll be comin' 'round the mountain,
She'll be comin' 'round the mountain, when she comes.

She'll be drivin' six white horses when she comes,
She'll be drivin' six white horses when she comes,
She'll be drivin' six white horses,
She'll be drivin' six white horses,
She'll be drivin' six white horses, when she comes.

We'll all have chicken and dumplin's when she comes,
We'll all have chicken and dumplin's when she comes,
We'll all have chicken and dumplin's,
We'll all have chicken and dumplin's,
We'll all have chicken and dumplin's, when she comes.

Thematic Connections
Celebrations
Family
Transportation

Things to Talk About
1. Talk about the ways people travel.
2. How is a road through the mountains different from a road on flat land?
3. How are things different at your house when a relative comes to visit?

Curriculum Extension
For Art: Family Pictures

Ages
3, 4, 5, 6

Materials
Drawing paper, crayons

Procedure
1. Ask the children to draw pictures of their families.
2. Label the people in each drawing and display the pictures on the bulletin board.

Developmental Bonus
Creative expression
Fine motor development

Curriculum Extension
For Gross Motor: Building

Ages
3, 4, 5, 6

Materials
Blocks, small people

Procedure
1. Ask the children to build mountains with the blocks.
2. Add people for dramatic play.
3. Urge the children to play out the story of the song.

Developmental Bonus
Creative expression

For Language: Song Writing

Ages
4,5,6

Materials
Chart tablet, pen or crayon

Procedure
1. Make up a new song using the same language pattern, for example, "He'll be coming down the chimney when he comes."
2. Write the song on chart tablet paper so the children see the relationship of their words and written text.

Developmental Bonus
Creativity
Practice with language patterns

For Math: Measurements

Ages
4,5,6

Materials
Modeling clay or playdough, ruler

Procedure
1. Provide the children with playdough or modeling clay.
2. Suggest that they make a mountain.
3. Compare the sizes of the mountains by measuring with a ruler.
4. Think of other ways to measure the mountains.

Developmental Bonus
Fine motor development
Size concepts
Vocabulary

For Science: Yummy Dumplin's

Ages
3,4,5,6

Materials
Ten flour tortillas, two 8-ounce cans of chicken broth, deep fryer or crock pot

Procedure
1. Make dumplin's by tearing flour tortillas into quarter sections and dropping in hot chicken broth for ten minutes. *NOTE:* When using a deep frying or crock pot, remember to supervise the children closely.
2. Boil, cool and serve. Yum! Yum!

Developmental Bonus
Observation of change of state

Related Bibliography

Allard, Harry. *The Stupids Have a Ball.* Houghton, 1978. The Stupids are a funny and unusual family. In this book, they plan a costume party to celebrate their children's bad report cards.

dePaola, Tomie. *Watch Out for the Chicken Feet in Your Soup.* S&S Trade, 1974. A little boy takes a friend to visit his Italian grandmother's house and is pleasantly surprised when his friend's appreciation of her heritage affects his own.

Munsch, Robert. *David's Father.* Annick, 1983. David's father is a very unusual person, but if you think he's strange, wait until you meet his grandmother.

Shaw, Nancy. *Sheep in a Jeep.* Houghton Mifflin, 1986. A funny tale of sheep driving a jeep and having plenty of troubles.

Kovalski, Maryann. *The Wheels on the Bus.* Little Brown, 1987. Grandma, Jenny and Joanna miss the bus because they're so involved in singing the title song that they don't notice the bus come and go.

Related Records and Tapes

Beall, Pamela Conn and Susan Hagen Nipp. "She'll Be Comin' 'Round the Mountain" from *Wee Sing Children's Songs and Fingerplays.* Price Stern Sloan, 1979.

Beall, Pamela Conn and Susan Hagen Nipp. "She'll Be Comin' 'Round the Mountain" from *Wee Sing Sing-Alongs.* Price Stern Sloan, 1990.

Scruggs, Joe. "Swing Low Sweet Chariot" from *Deep in the Jungle.* Rabbit Shadow Records, 1987.

"She'll Be Comin' 'Round the Mountain" from *Sing-A-Long.* Peter Pan, 1987.

"She'll Be Comin' 'Round the Mountain" from *Bert and Ernie Sing-A-Long.* Sesame Street, 1975.

▼▼▼▼▼▼▼▼▼▼▼▼▼

4

DECEMBER

Jingle Bells

Hanukkah Song

Christmas Is Coming

My Dreidel

O Christmas Tree

We Wish You a Merry Christmas

Jingle Bells

Dashing through the snow,
In a one-horse open sleigh.
O'er the fields we go,
Laughing all the way.

Bells on bobtail ring,
Making spirits bright.
What fun it is to ride and sing,
A sleighing song tonight.

Jingle bells, jingle bells,
Jingle all the way.
Oh, what fun it is to ride
In a one-horse open sleigh.

Jingle bells, jingle bells,
Jingle all the way.
Oh, what fun it is to ride
In a one-horse open sleigh.

Thematic Connections

Christmas
Winter

Things to Talk About

1. This song was written more than 100 years ago.
2. Help children understand phrases such as "bells on bobtail ring" and "making spirits bright."

Curriculum Extension

For Art: Snowy Picture

Ages
3,4,5,6

Materials
Golf ball, white tempera paint, dark blue construction paper, rectangular cake pan or shallow rectangular box

Procedure
1. Put a piece of construction paper in the pan or box. Place a golf ball in white paint.

2. Remove the golf ball from the paint and place it in the box or pan.
3. The children roll the ball around in the pan to create a snowy effect on the paper.

Developmental Bonus
Creative expression
Curriculum Extension

Curriculum Extension

For Dramatic Play: Homemade Sleigh

Ages
3,4,5,6

Materials
Large cardboard box (about 12 x 18 inches in size), scissors, rope, optional—bells

Procedure
1. Cut the top flaps off of the box. If the box is deep, cut it down so that it is no more than 4 to 6 inches high.

2. Make a hole in each of the long sides of the box about 2 inches from one corner. Insert a rope through each hole and knot it to make a pulling strap. Add bells if desired.

3. A few stuffed animals or dolls to pull in the sleigh will add to the fun.

Developmental Bonus
Concept development

Curriculum Extension

For Fine Motor: Snowflakes

Ages
4, 5,6

Materials
Paper plates or paper, scissors

Procedure
1. Give each child a paper plate or a round piece of paper.
2. Show the children how to fold the plate and make scissor cuts.
3. Open the plate to reveal a "snowflake."

Developmental Bonus
Fine motor development
Creative expressions

Curriculum Extension

For Gross Motor: Ring the Bell

Ages
3,4,5,6

Materials
Two or three counter bells (available at office supply stores), two or three pieces of white felt, scissors, beanbags

Procedure
1. Cut the felt into circles 10 inches in diameter. These are "snowflakes."

2. Place the counter bells on the floor and cover with felt "snowflakes."
3. The children throw the beanbags at the snowflakes. They will know they hit the correct spot when they hear the bell ring.

Developmental Bonus
Hand-eye coordination

Curriculum Extension

For Math: Counting Bags

Ages
4,5,6

Materials
Felt, 15 jingle bells (available at craft or hobby stores), stick-on numbers, glue gun, velcro

Procedure
1. Cut two 3-inch squares of felt.
2. Use a glue gun to glue the two pieces together on three sides, creating a pocket or bag.
3. Attach a 1-inch piece of Velcro just inside the top of each pocket/bag.
4. Place stick-on numbers from 1 to 5 onto each bag.
5. The children place the appropriate number of bells into each bag.
6. The children can also place the bags into appropriate order by weight (lightest to heaviest), sound (lowest to highest) or in numerical sequence.

Developmental Bonus
Seriation

Related Bibliography

Brown, Margaret Wise. *The Little Fir Tree*. Harper, 1979. The story of a little lame boy and a fir tree that is brought to him.

Dr. Seuss. *How the Grinch Stole Christmas*. Random House, 1957. The wicked greedy Grinch steals all the Christmas gifts and almost ruins Christmas.

Keats, Ezra Jack. *The Snowy Day*. Viking, 1962. A little boy has a great experience on a snowy afternoon in the city. Afraid the snow won't last, he tries to keep a snowball in his pocket.

Moore, Clement C. *The Night Before Christmas*. Knopf, 1985. A New York version of the famous Christmas verse.

Van Allsburg, Chris. *The Polar Express*. Houghton Mifflin, 1985. A man remembers a mysterious Christmas Eve when he rode the polar express to the North Pole and was selected by Santa to receive the first Christmas gift.

Related Records and Tapes

Palmer, Hap. *Holidays and Rhythms*. Educational Activities, 1971.
Raffi. *Raffi's ChristmasAlbum*. Shoreline, 1983.

Hanukkah Song

O Hanukkah, O Hanukkah,
Come light the menorah.
Let's have a party,
We'll all dance the horah.
Gather 'round the table,
We'll give you a treat.
Dreidels to play with,
And latkes to eat;

And while we are playing,
The candles are burning low.
One for each night,
They shed a sweet light
To remind us of days long ago.
One for each night,
They shed a sweet light,
To remind us of days long ago.

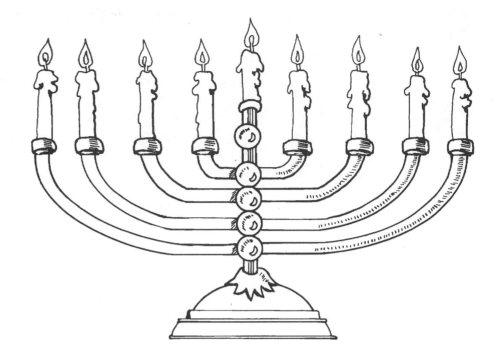

Thematic Connections
Hanukkah
Holidays

Things to Talk About
1. Hanukkah commemorates the recapturing of the temple in Jerusalem. To the Jewish people, it represents their religious freedom.
2. Explain that the menorah is a symbol of Hanukkah.

Curriculum Extension
For Art: Star of David

Ages
4,5,6

Materials
Construction paper triangles (two for each child), glue, paper

Procedure
1. Demonstrate to the children how to place the two triangles together to form a Star of David.

2. The children create their star and glue it onto another piece of paper.

Developmental Bonus
Concept development

Curriculum Extension
For Cooking: Latkes (Potato Pancakes)

Ages
3,4,5,6

Materials
Grater, measuring spoons, mixing bowl and spoon, 1 grated onion, 1 teaspoon salt, 1 egg, 6 medium potatoes (washed, pared and grated), 3 tablespoons flour, 1/2 teaspoon baking powder, cooking oil, electric frying pan, paper towels, applesauce, spoons and bowls

Procedure
1. Mix the onion, salt and egg with the potatoes.

2. Add flour and baking powder.
3. Drop by spoonfuls into the hot oiled frying pan.
4. Brown on both sides.
5. Drain on paper towels.
6. Serve with applesauce. Enjoy!

Developmental Bonus
Cultural experience

Curriculum Extension
For Fine Motor: Dreidel

Ages
4,5,6

Materials
Dreidels; tokens—raisins, nuts, toothpicks, pennies, etc.; bowl (pot)

Procedure
1. Show the children how to play dreidel.
2. Each player puts one token in the pot.
3. One player spins the dreidel.
4. If the dreidel lands on "N," the player receives nothing. If it lands on "G," the player receives all the tokens in the pot. If it lands on "H," the player gets half. If it lands on "S," the player adds two tokens to the pot.
5. The game continues until one player has won all the tokens.

Developmental Bonus
Hand-eye coordination
Fine motor development

Curriculum Extension
For Language: Menorah Flannel Pieces

Ages
3,4,5,6

Materials
Menorah base, candles and flames cut from felt

Procedure
1. Encourage the children to assemble the menorah on the flannel board.

Developmental Bonus
Concept development

Curriculum Extension
For Math: Eight

Ages
4,5,6

Materials
Paper plates, odds and ends—bottle caps, paper clips, crayons, candles, pennies, marbles, etc.

Procedure
1. Remind the children about the significance of the number eight to Hanukkah.
2. The children count eight items into each plate.

Developmental Bonus
Cultural experience

Related Bibliography

dePaola, Tomie. *My First Chanukah.* Putnam, 1989. All the symbols of Chanukah from the candles on the menorah to the dreidel to the delicious potato latkes are vividly portrayed in this book on Chanukah.

Hirsh, Marilyn. *Hanukkah Story.* Bonim Books, 1977. An easy to understand version of the Hanukkah story.

Kimmel, Eric A. *The Chanukka Guest.* Holiday, 1990. An aging woman mistakes a bear for a rabbi. She makes the best potato latkes in the whole village, and the bear, as well as the villagers, is very pleased.

Manushkin, Fran. *Latkes and Applesauce: A Hanukkah Story.* Scholastic, 1990. A dog and a kitten lost in a blizzard during Hanukkah manage to survive the storm. They come up with a potato and an apple, thus providing the ingredients for the traditional latkes and applesauce.

Schotter, Roni. *Hanukkah.* Little, Brown, 1990. Five children and their parents and grandmother spend Hanukkah enjoying all its rich traditions.

Related Records and Tapes

Gallina, Jill. *Holiday Songs for All Occasions.* Kimbo, 1978.

Christmas Is Coming

Christmas is coming,
The goose is getting fat.
Please put a penny
In the old man's hat.
Please put a penny
In the old man's hat.

If you don't have a penny,
A ha' penny will do,
If you don't have a ha' penny,
Then God bless you,
If you don't have a ha' penny,
Then God bless you.

Thematic Connections
Celebrations
Christmas
Holidays

Things to Talk About
1. Discuss the origin of Christmas (as factually as possible).
2. Brainstorm all the things you see that help you know Christmas is coming.

Curriculum Extension
For Cooking: Sugar Cookies

Ages
3,4,5,6

Materials
Sugar cookie dough, sprinkles, Christmas cookie cutters, cookie sheets, oven, optional—decorations

Procedure
1. Help the children cut shapes from the cookie dough and decorate as desired.
2. Bake and eat.

Developmental Bonus
Creative expression
Concept development

Curriculum Extension
For Dramatic Play: Wrapping Presents

Ages
4,5,6

Materials
A variety of boxes, recycled wrapping paper, bows, tape

Procedure
1. Set up a gift wrapping section in the dramatic play center.
2. Let the children experiment with different wraps and bows.

Developmental Bonus
Coordination
Creative expression

For Language: Mystery Package

Ages
4,5,6

Materials
Wrapping paper; boxes; tape; ribbon; several small inexpensive items—pieces of gum, plastic car, marbles

Procedure
1. For several days, without the children seeing, wrap a small item and place it in the language center.
2. Allow the children to shake the boxes.
3. Provide clues, one at a time, as to what is inside the package.
4. Keep each item wrapped until someone guesses what is inside.
5. Let the "guesser" open the package and keep its contents.

Developmental Bonus
Critical thinking

For Math: Counting Pennies

Ages
4,5,6

Materials
Pennies, construction paper, marker, scissors

Procedure
1. Draw and cut out five top hats on construction paper.
2. Write the numbers 1 to 5 on the construction paper hats.
3. The children count the appropriate number of pennies and place them on the hat.

Developmental Bonus
Counting

For Social Studies: Tree of Hands

Ages
3,4,5,6

Materials
Green construction paper, crayons, scissors, stapler or tape

Procedure
1. Ask the children to trace around their hands (with fingers open) and then cut out their hand prints.
2. Staple or tape cutout hand prints to a bulletin board area to form a tree shape.
3. Place hands with fingers downward and staple the hands in rows with a descending number of hands in each overlapped row.

Developmental Bonus
Creative expression
Fine motor development
Concept development

Related Bibliography

Brett, Jan. *The Twelve Days of Christmas*. Putnam, 1990. This storybook tells the stories of the unique gifts given each of the twelve days preceding Christmas.

Delacre, Lulu. *Las Navidades: Popular Christmas Songs From Latin America*. Scholastic, 1990. A book of Latin American children's songs about Christmas with wonderful illustrations.

dePaola, Tomie. *Merry Christmas, Strega Nona*. Harcourt Brace Jovanovich, 1991. Strega Nona refuses to use her magic to fix Christmas dinner.

Dr. Seuss. *How the Grinch Stole Christmas*. Random House, 1957. The wicked greedy Grinch steals all the Christmas gifts and almost ruins Christmas.

Moore, Clement C. *The Night Before Christmas*. Knopf, 1985. A New York version of the famous Christmas verse.

Related Records and Tapes

Beall, Pamela Conn and Susan Hagen Nipp. "Christmas is Coming" from *Wee Sing Children's Songs and Fingerplays*. Price Stern Sloan.

Raffi. *Raffi's Christmas Album*. Shoreline, 1983.

My Dreidel

I have a little dreidel,
I made it out of clay;
And when it's dry and ready,
Then dreidel I shall play.

Oh dreidel, dreidel, dreidel,
I made it out of clay;
Oh dreidel, dreidel, dreidel,
Now dreidel I shall play.

It has a lovely body,
With legs so short and thin;
And when it is all tired,
It drops and then I win.

Oh dreidel, dreidel, dreidel,
With legs so short and thin;
Oh dreidel, dreidel, dreidel,
It drops and then I win.

My dreidel is always playful,
It loves to dance and spin;
A happy game of dreidel,
Come play, now, let's begin.

Oh dreidel, dreidel, dreidel,
It loves to dance and spin;
Oh dreidel, dreidel, dreidel,
Come play, now, let's begin.

Thematic Connections
Holidays
Customs
Hanukkah

Things to Talk About

1. The dreidel is a four-sided top stamped with Hebrew letters on each side. The letters N (nun), G (gimmel), H (heh), and S (shin) represent Hebrew words which mean "a great miracle happened." This is a reference to the sacred oil that burned for eight days, even though there was only enough oil to burn for one day—the miracle that Hanukkah celebrates. The dreidel is a traditional Hanukkah gift.

2. Explain how the dreidel game is played (see the fine motor activity in this section). Ask children if they can think of other games similar to this game.

Curriculum Extension

For Art: Making Dreidels

Ages
4,5,6

Materials
A 4-inch cardboard square, pencil

Procedure
1. Draw a line diagonally from one corner to the opposite one. Repeat for the other two corners.
2. Put dreidel letters G, H, S and N on each of the four resulting sections.
3. Poke a hole in the middle of the square large enough to fit a pencil snugly.
4. Poke a pencil into the hole to create a spinning top.

Developmental Bonus
Concept development

For Fine Motor: Dreidel

Ages
3,4,5,6

Materials
Dreidel; tokens—nuts, raisins, marbles, toothpicks, pennies, etc.; bowl (pot)

Procedure
1. Each player puts one token in the pot.
2. One player spins the dreidel.
3. If the dreidel lands on "N," the player receives nothing. If it lands on "G," the player receives all the tokens in the pot. If it lands on "H," the player gets half. If it lands on "S," the player adds two tokens to the pot.
4. The games continues until one player has won all the tokens.

Developmental Bonus
Coordination
Fine motor development

For Language: Concentration

Ages
4,5,6

Materials
Index cards, markers or crayons, scissors

Procedure
1. Print the Hebrew letters from the dreidel on index cards. Print two symbols on each card.
2. Cut each card in half.
3. The children play concentration (memory) with the cards.

Developmental Bonus
Visual discrimination
Visual memory

For Language: Menorah Game
5,6

Materials
Cards with a menorah drawn on them, eight orange flames for each child

Procedure
1. Give each child a card.
2. Ask the children questions about Hanukkah (see the related bibliography).
3. For every right answer, the children place a flame on one of the candles on the menorah.

Developmental Bonus
Concept development

For Science: Balancing & Spinning

Ages
4,5,6

Materials
A collection of items—tops, coins, spools, etc.; a straw

Procedure
1. Show the children how to balance a straw across the tip of their finger. Explain that when the top is spinning, it is balanced on its tip.
2. Let the children try to balance a straw across a finger.
3. Next give the children various items—tops, coins, spools—to spin.

Developmental Bonus
Balancing concepts

Related Bibliography

Aleichem, Sholem. *Hanukah Money*. Morrow, 1991. How Motl and his brother celebrate a much-loved Jewish holiday.

dePaola, Tomie. *My First Chanukah*. Putnam, 1989. All the symbols of Chanukah from the candles on the menorah to the dreidel to the delicious potato latkes are vividly portrayed in this book about Chanukah.

Grossman, Roz and Gladys Gewirtz. *Let's Play Dreidel*. KarBen Copies, 1989. The words of the song "Let's Play Dreidel!" describe how the game is played.

Schotter, Roni. *Hanukkah!* Little, Brown, 1990. Five children and their parents and grandmother spend Hanukkah enjoying all its rich traditions.

Simon, Norma. *Hanukkah*. Crowell, 1966. A simple explanation of Hanukkah, a holiday that has meaning for people of all faiths.

Related Records and Tapes

Palmer, Hap. "Hanukkah" from *Holiday Songs and Rhythms*. Activity Records, 1971.

Gallina, Jill. *Holiday Songs for All Occasions*. Kimbo, 1978.

O Christmas Tree

O Christmas tree, O Christmas tree,
How lovely are your branches.
Not only green when summer glows,
But in the winter when it snows,
O Christmas tree, O Christmas tree,
How lovely are your branches.

Thematic Connections
Holidays
Christmas
Trees

Things to Talk About
1. Discuss all the ways people use trees for their well-being.
2. Discuss using live trees for Christmas that are in buckets and can be planted outside after Christmas.

Curriculum Extension
For Art: Sponge Trees

Ages
3,4,5,6

Materials
Sponges cut into Christmas tree shapes, drawing paper, green tempera paint

Procedure
1. Place the paint, sponges and paper out for the children to use.
2. The children dip the tree sponges in the green paint and create designs on their paper.
3. Older children can add details to the pictures when the paint is dry.

Developmental Bonus
Creative expression

Curriculum Extension
For Fine Motor: Popcorn and Cranberry Chains

Ages
4,5,6

Materials
Popped popcorn, cranberries, needles, thread

Procedure
1. String popcorn and cranberries to make garlands for an indoor or outdoor tree.
2. Create different patterns for the children to follow—popcorn, cranberry, popcorn, cranberry, etc.; cranberry,

cranberry, popcorn, cranberry, cranberry, etc.

3. Use more complicated patterns with older children.

Developmental Bonus
Fine motor development
Sequencing

Curriculum Extension
For Math:
Tree Seriation

Ages
3,4,5

Materials
Construction paper trees cut in a variety of sizes

Procedure
1. The children arrange trees from smallest to largest.
2. Differences in size can be more subtle for older children.

Developmental Bonus
Sequencing

Curriculum Extension
For Outdoor:
Christmas Bird Feeder

Ages
3,4,5,6

Materials
Peanut butter, bird seed, pine cones, cookie sheet, wax paper, pipe cleaners

Procedure
1. Spread bird seed on a cookie sheet.
2. Place peanut butter on a sheet of wax paper.
3. The children roll the pine cones first in the peanut butter, then in bird seed.
4. Place pipe cleaners around the cone for hanging.
5. Hang bird feeders outdoors for winter birds.

Developmental Bonus
Environmental awareness

Curriculum Extension
For Science:
Christmas Potpourri

Ages
3,4,5

Materials
Christmas tree needles, cinnamon sticks cut into 1/2-inch pieces, nutmeg, small pine cones, netting, ribbon

Procedure
1. The children place a mixture of pine needles, cinnamon sticks, nutmeg and pine cones on a piece of netting. Bundle together and tie.
2. Hang potpourri around the classroom for Christmas smells.
3. Explain to the children that this is a natural way to create a pleasant smell without harming the environment.

Developmental Bonus
Fine motor development
Environmental awareness

Related Bibliography

Brett, Jan. *The Twelve Days of Christmas*. Putnam, 1990. This storybook tells the stories of the unique gifts given each of the twelve days preceding Christmas.

Brown, Margaret Wise. *Christmas in the Barn*. HarperCollins, 1979. A beautifully illustrated story of the nativity.

Brown, Margaret Wise. *The Little Fir Tree*. HarperCollins, 1979. The story of a little lame boy and a fir tree that is brought to him.

Dr. Seuss. *How the Grinch Stole Christmas*. Random House, 1957. The wicked greedy Grinch steals all the Christmas gifts and almost ruins Christmas.

Moore, Clement C. *The Night Before Christmas*. Knopf, 1985. A New York version of the famous Christmas verse.

Related Records and Tapes

Raffi. *Raffi's Christmas Album*. Shoreline, 1983.
Gallina, Jill. *Holiday Songs for All Occasions*. Kimbo, 1978.

We Wish You a Merry Christmas

We wish you a Merry Christmas,
We wish you a Merry Christmas,
We wish you a Merry Christmas,
And a Happy New Year.

Now bring us some figgy pudding,
Now bring us some figgy pudding,
Now bring us some figgy pudding,
And a cup of good cheer.

We won't go until we get some,
We won't go until we get some,
We won't go until we get some,
So bring it out here.

We wish you a Merry Christmas,
We wish you a Merry Christmas,
We wish you a Merry Christmas,
And a Happy New Year.

Thematic Connections

Holidays
Christmas

Things to Talk About

1. "Merry Christmas" is a greeting. What are other holiday greetings?
2. If you could make a special wish, what would it be?

Curriculum Extension

For Art: Making Greeting Cards

Ages

3,4,5,6

Materials

Sponges cut into Christmas shapes, paper, tempera paint, crayons

Procedure

1. Fold paper in half to form cards.
2. Encourage the children to use the sponges to create a Christmas design for the front of their cards.

3. The children dictate their greeting to you. Transcribe it onto the inside of their cards.

Developmental Bonus

Creative expression

Curriculum Extension

For Fine Motor: Greeting Card Puzzles

Ages

3,4,5,6

Materials

Old greeting cards, scissors, plastic sandwich bags

Procedure

1. Cut the fronts of old greeting cards into puzzle pieces.
2. Place the pieces to each card in a separate plastic bag.
3. The children put puzzle pieces together.
4. Cut more complicated puzzle pieces for older children.

Developmental Bonus

Visual discrimination
Hand-eye coordination

For Gross Motor: Santa's Workshop

Ages
3, 4, 5, 6

Materials
Scraps of wood, nails, small hammers, pliers

Procedure
1. Set up a woodworking area in the classroom or outdoors.
2. Encourage the children to create objects using nails, hammers, pliers, etc.
3. Be sure to supervise closely and limit the number of children using the woodworking area.

Developmental Bonus
Gross motor development
Hand-eye coordination

For Language: Writing Letters to Santa

Ages
3, 4, 5, 6

Materials
Paper and pencils

Procedure
1. The children dictate their letters to Santa. Transcribe them onto paper.
2. Older children should be encouraged to use inventive spelling and do their own writing.
3. Be aware of and sensitive to those children who do not celebrate Christmas.

Developmental Bonus
Concept development

For Math: Paper Chains

Ages
3, 4, 5, 6

Materials
Red and green construction paper, scissors, glue

Procedure
1. Cut construction paper into 1 x 9 inch strips.
2. Loop a strip into a circle and glue it at the seam.
3. Place a second loop through first and continue the chain.
4. The children can create their own color patterns.

Developmental Bonus
Patterning
Fine motor development

Related Bibliography

Brown, Margaret Wise. *Christmas in the Barn*. HarperCollins, 1961. A beautifully illustrated story of the nativity.

Dr. Seuss. *How the Grinch Stole Christmas*. Random House, 1957. The wicked greedy Grinch steals all the Christmas gifts and almost ruins Christmas.

Pearson, Tracey Campbell. *We Wish You A Merry Christmas*. Dial, 1986. Eight little carolers proceed through the snow until they reach the home of an elderly couple who invite them in. They demand figgy pudding!

Moore, Clement C. *The Night Before Christmas*. Knopf, 1985. A New York version of the famous Christmas verse.

Hyman, Trina Schart. *How Six Found Christmas*. Holiday House, 1991. A story of a little girl, a cat, a dog, a hawk, a fox, and a mockingbird who join in the search to find the meaning of Christmas.

Related Records and Tapes

Beall, Pamela Conn and Susan Hagen Nipp. "We Wish You a Merry Christmas" from *Wee Sing Children's Songs and Fingerplays*. Price Stern Sloan, 1979.

Palmer, Hap. *Holiday Songs and Rhythms*. Activity Records, 1971.

Raffi. *Raffi's Christmas Album*. Shoreline, 1983.

Richman, Trudie. *I Love a Holiday*. Melody House.

5

▼▼▼▼▼▼▼▼▼▼▼▼▼

JANUARY

Boom, Boom Ain't It Great to Be Crazy?
Are You Sleeping?
Peanut Butter
Polly Wolly Doodle
Color Song
The Fox

Boom, Boom, Ain't It Great to Be Crazy?

A horse and a flea and three blind mice,
Sat on a curbstone shooting dice,
The horse he slipped and fell on the flea,
"Whoops," said the flea, "There's a horse on me!"

Chorus:
Boom, boom, ain't it great to be crazy?
Boom, boom, ain't it great to be crazy?
Giddy and foolish the whole day through,
Boom, boom, ain't it great to be crazy?

Way down South where bananas grow,
A flea stepped on an elephant's toe.
The elephant cried with tears in this eyes,
"Why don't you pick on someone your size?"
(Chorus)

Way up North where's there's ice and snow,
There lived a penguin and his name was Joe.
He got so tired of black and white,
He wore pink slacks to the dance last night.
(Chorus)

Thematic Connections
Me, Myself and I
Circus

Things to Talk About
1. Talk about how much fun it can be to do things that are a little crazy.
2. What is crazy? Is it crazy to do things differently from others?

Curriculum Extension
For Art: Funny Drawings

Ages
3,4,5,6

Materials
Drawing paper, crayons, masking tape

Procedure
1. Tape drawing paper on the underside of the table.
2. The children lie on their backs under the table to create their drawings.

3. Talk about how this feels different from the "normal" way to draw.

Developmental Bonus
Creative expression
Critical thinking

Curriculum Extension
For Cooking: Crazy Corn

Ages
3,4,5,6

Materials
Popcorn popper, popcorn, cooking oil, salt, butcher paper

Procedure
1. Overlap two or three 8-foot-long sheets of butcher paper on the floor. Place the popcorn popper in the middle.
2. The children sit around the outside of the paper. NOTE: Caution the children to remain seated while the corn is popping.

3. Measure the appropriate amount of oil and corn into the popper.

4. Pop the popcorn in the popper without the lid.

5. Popcorn will fall to the floor. Ask the children not to eat the popcorn until all the corn has popped. Use caution because the popcorn will still be hot when it lands on the paper.

Developmental Bonus
Measurement concept
Change of state

Curriculum Extension
For Dramatic Play: Silly Clothes

Ages
3,4,5,6

Materials
Old clothes, hats, scarves, costumes, sunglasses, etc.

Procedure
1. The children use the clothes and props to create funny costumes.

2. Have a style show.

Developmental Bonus
Creative expression

Curriculum Extension
For Fine Motor: Stringing Bead Challenge

Ages
3,4,5,6

Materials
Stringing beads, shoelaces, string

Procedure
1. Hang the string from the ceiling.

2. Attach the shoelace to the string.

3. The children string beads going up instead of the "normal" method.

4. What makes this way more difficult?

Developmental Bonus
Fine motor development
Hand-eye coordination
Critical thinking

Curriculum Extension
For Fine Motor: Upside Down Puzzles

Ages
3,4,5,6

Materials
Puzzles

Procedure
1. Turn puzzle pieces over and have the children put the puzzle together looking only at the backs of the pieces.

2. Use simple puzzles with the younger children and complicated ones with the older children.

Developmental Bonus
Hand-eye coordination
Visual discrimination

Related Bibliography

Cohen, Caron Lee. *Bronco Dogs*. Dutton, 1991. Six Gun Gus and Cannonball Clyde, a couple of outlandish outlaws, get themselves into real trouble. Trouble for Gus and Clyde means plenty of laughs for the reader.

Dr. Seuss. *The Cat in the Hat*. Random House, 1957. A crazy cat pays a visit to two children whose mother is away from home. Zany and wacky, the cat's activities delight every child.

LeSieg, Theodore. *Wacky Wednesday*. Bergin & Garvey, 1974. A little boy wakes up to a day of everything out of place.

Small, David. *Imogene's Antlers*. Crown, 1988. A little girl wakes up with antlers on her head and spends a humorous day trying to adjust.

Townson, Hazel. *Terrible Tuesday*. Morrow, 1986. Terry's mother's prediction of a terrible Tuesday is wilder than imagined.

Related Records and Tapes

Beall, Pamela Conn and Susan Hagen Nipp. "Boom, Boom Ain't It Great to Be Crazy?" from *Wee Sing Silly Songs*. Price Stern Sloan, 1986.

Sharon, Lois and Bram. "Silly Names and Crazy Gibberish" from *In the Schoolyard*. Elephant Records, 1981.

Are You Sleeping?

Are you sleeping,
Are you sleeping,
Brother John, Brother John?
Morning bells are ringing,
Morning bells are ringing,
Ding, ding, dong!
Ding, ding, dong!

Thematic Connections
Me, Myself and I
Family

Things to Talk About
1. Who or what wake you up in the morning?
2. How do you feel when you first wake up?

Curriculum Extension
For Art: Bells!

Ages
4,5,6

Materials
Egg carton, scissors, tempera paints, paintbrushes, glitter, confetti, sequins, glue

Procedure
1. Cut an egg carton apart, creating 12 bell shapes. (Each individual section of the egg carton when cut apart and turned upside down looks like a bell.)

2. The children paint and decorate their bells with glitter, confetti, sequins, etc.

Developmental Bonus
Creative expression

Curriculum Extension
For Language: Name Substitutions

Ages
3,4,5,6

Materials
None needed

Procedure
1. Substitute the names of classmates in the song. For example, "Are you sleeping, are you sleeping, my friend (Gayla), my friend (Gayla)."
2. Change "morning bells" to "evening bells."
3. Change the words "Brother John" to "Sister Michelle."
4. Ask the children if changing any of these words changes the song's meaning.

Developmental Bonus
Concept development

Curriculum Extension
For Math: Bell Seriation

Ages
3,4,5

Materials
Several different sizes of bells cut from construction paper

Procedure
1. Have children arrange the bells from largest to smallest and from smallest to largest.
2. Ask them to accomplish this activity vertically and horizontally.

Developmental Bonus
Visual discrimination

Curriculum Extension
For Science:Ring That Bell

Ages
3,4,5,6

Materials
A variety of bells, gloves

Procedure
1. Allow the children to experiment with ringing the bells.
2. Have the children put on gloves and see if the sounds of the bells are altered.

Developmental Bonus
Auditory discrimination

Curriculum Extension
For Social Studies: Lullabies

Ages
3,4,5,6

Materials
Several records of lullabies

Procedure
1. Have children lie on the rug or put their heads down on a table and listen to lullabies.

2. Include lullabies from a variety of other countries.
Ireland—Tooraloora
Germany—Brahm's lullaby
Africa—Kumbayah
France—Claire de Lune
Austria—Edelweiss

Developmental Bonus
Auditory discrimination

Related Bibliography

Aragon, Jane Chelsea. *Lullaby.* Chronicle, 1989. The tune to a mother's lullaby carries all through the night, over farms and towns, meadows and woods, from sea to the moon to the whales and back to mother and child.

Miles, Sally. *Alfi & the Dark.* Chronicle, 1988. When Alfie wakes up in the middle of the night, he wonders out loud where the dark goes when the lights are turned on.

Field, Eugene. *Wynken, Blynken, and Nod.* Putnam, 1986. The wonderful poem about three sleepy children sailing in a sea of star.

Waber, Bernard. *Ira Sleeps Over.* Houghton Mifflin, 1973. Ira spends the night away from home for the first time and worries that his friend will laugh at him for bringing his teddy bear.

Woods, Audrey. *The Napping House.* Harcourt Brace Jovanovich, 1984. A cumulative tale of a house where everyone is peacefully sleeping until a flea bites the cat and starts a chain reaction.

Related Records and Tapes

Beall, Pamela Conn and Susan Hagen Nipp. "Are You Sleeping?" from *Wee Sing-Alongs.* Price Stern Sloan, 1990.

Moore, Thomas. *Sleepy Time.* Educational RecordCenter, 1980.

Scelsa Greg and Steve Millang. *Quiet Moments with Greg and Steve.* Youngheart Records, 1983.

Let's Visit Lullaby Land. Kimbo.

Sweet Dreams. Kimbo.

Peanut Butter

Chorus:
Peanut, peanut butter—Jelly,
Peanut, peanut butter—Jelly!

First you take the peanuts and you dig
'em, dig 'em
Dig 'em, dig 'em, dig 'em
Then you smash 'em, smash 'em,
Smash 'em, smash 'em, smash 'em,
Then you spread 'em, spread 'em,
Spread 'em, spread 'em, spread 'em.

(Chorus)
Then you take the berries and you pick
'em, pick 'em
Pick 'em, pick 'em, pick 'em,
Then you smash 'em, smash 'em,
Smash 'em, smash 'em, smash 'em,
Then you spread 'em, spread 'em,
Spread 'em, spread 'em, spread 'em.

(Chorus)
Then you take the sandwich and you bite
it, bite it
Bite it, bite it, bite it
Then you chew it, chew it,
Chew it, chew it, chew it
Then you swallow it, swallow it, swallow it,
Swallow it, swallow it, swallow it.

(Hum chorus)
Peanut, peanut butter—jelly,
Peanut, peanut butter—jelly!

Thematic Connections
Cooking
Nutrition

Things to Talk About
1. Where do peanuts come from?
2. Which do you like better, peanut butter or jelly?
3. What are other kinds of sandwiches?

Curriculum Extension
For Art: Peanut Collage

Ages
3,4,5

Materials
Peanut shells, glue, drawing paper, scissors—optional

Procedure
1. Use the shells from the shelled peanuts (see the fine motor activity) to make textured collages.
2. If desired, the paper can be cut into the shape of a peanut.

Developmental Bonus
Creative expression

Curriculum Extension
Cooking: Making Peanut Butter

Ages
3, 4,5,6

Materials
Peanuts, blender, measuring cups and spoons, cooking oil, salt, crackers, knife

Procedure
1. Place one cup of peanuts in a blender or food processor.
2. Add a teaspoon of cooking oil.
3. Blend.
4. If you didn't use salted peanuts, you may want to add one-quarter teaspoon salt.
5. Spread on crackers, eat and enjoy!

Developmental Bonus
Concept development

For Fine Motor: Shelling

Ages
3,4

Materials
Peanuts in the shell

Procedure
1. Let the children shell enough peanuts to make their own peanut butter (see the cooking activity).

Developmental Bonus
Fine motor development

For Language: Recipe Collection

Ages
3,4,5

Materials
Paper, pencil

Procedure
1. Have students dictate their recipes for their favorite sandwich.
2. Transcribe their dictation onto paper, creating a class recipe book. (This will be a humorous collection, one that parents will love!)

Developmental Bonus
Sequencing
Vocabulary Development

For Math: Graphing

Ages
5,6

Materials
Peanuts, graph, marker or stickers

Procedure
1. Give each child an unshelled peanut.

2. Have the child open the peanut and count the nuts inside.
3. Make a graph. Let each child illustrate on the graph (make an "x" or place a sticker in the correct square) how many nuts were in his shell.

Developmental Bonus
Comparison

1 nut	2 nuts	3 nuts
X		
	X	
X		
		X
	X	
	X	

Related Bibliography

Degen, Bruce. *Jamberry*. HarperCollins, 1983. Berryland fruit pickers go on an unforgettable rhyming jamboree.

Hoban, Russell. *Bread and Jam for Frances*. Harper, 1986. Frances doesn't want to try any new foods, so her mother gives her bread and jam for every meal.

Lord, John V. and Janet Burroway. *The Grand Jam Sandwich*. Houghton Mifflin, 1990. Poem story about a wasp-filled town and the sandwich made to trap them.

Silverstein, Shel. "Peanut Butter Sandwich" from *Where the Sidewalk Ends*. Harper, 1974. A poem about a king who loves peanut butter sandwiches so much that even after his mouth gets stuck closed from peanut butter, he's still not ready to give it up.

Westcott, Nadine Bernard. *Peanut Butter and Jelly: A Play Rhyme*. Dutton, 1987. A rhyme that follows the song.

Related Records and Tapes

Weissman, Jackie. "Peanut Butter" from *Miss Jackie and Her Friends Sing About Peanut Butter, Tarzan and Roosters*. Miss Jackie, 1981.

Scruggs, Joe. "Peanut Butter" from *Late Last Night*. Educational Graphics Press, 1984.

"Peanuts" from *Bert and Ernie Sing Along*. Sesame Street, 1975.

Polly Wolly Doodle

Oh, I went down South to see my Sal,
Sing Polly wolly doodle all the day.
My Sally is a spunky gal,
Sing Polly wolly doodle all the day.

Chorus:
Fare thee well, fare thee well,
Fare thee well, my fairy fay.
For I'm going to Louisiana for to see my Susyanna,
Singing Polly wolly doodle all the day.

My Sally is a maiden fair,
Sing Polly wolly doodle all the day.
With curly eyes and laughing hair,
Sing Polly wolly doodle all the day.

(Chorus)

Behind the barn, down on my knees,
Sing Polly wolly doodle all the day.
I thought I heard a chicken sneeze,
Sing Polly wolly doodle all the day.

(Chorus)

He sneezed so hard with whooping cough,
Sing Polly wolly doodle all the day.
He sneezed his head and tail right off,
Sing Polly wolly doodle all the day.

(Chorus)

Thematic Connections
Tall tales

Things to Talk About
1. What does "Fare thee well!" mean?
2. How many ways can you think of to say goodbye? (wave, hug, pat, speak)
3. Can you think of ways people say goodbye in other languages?

Curriculum Extension

For Art: Doodles

Ages
3, 4,5,6

Materials
Drawing paper, crayons

Procedure
1. Make a crayon mark on a piece of paper for each child.
2. The children create a picture using your mark or doodle.
3. Have a "show and tell" about the pictures.

Developmental Bonus
Creative expression
Problem-solving skills

Curriculum Extension

For Cooking: New Orleans Biscuits

Ages
3,4,5,6

Materials
Deep frying pot, biscuits, cooking oil, powdered sugar, slotted spoon, paper towels

Procedure
1. Explain to the children that fried biscuits (donuts) are popular in Lousiana.
2. With careful supervision, heat the cooking oil.
3. Cut the biscuits in half and give one half to each child.
4. Allow the children to put the biscuits in the oil using the slotted spoon.
5. Fry the donuts until they rise to the top of the oil.

6. Remove from the cooker, drain on paper towels and then sprinkle with powdered sugar.

Developmental bonus
Concept development

Curriculum Extension
For Language: Rhyming Words

Ages
5,6

Materials
Magazine pictures of words that rhyme with Polly—holly, trolley, collie, dolly, etc—and those that don't rhyme with Polly; magazines

Procedure
1. The children sort through the pictures to find the items that rhyme with Polly.
2. Then the children look through magazines to find pictures of things that rhyme with their names.

Developmental Bonus
Auditory discrimination

Curriculum Extension
For Math: Chicken Puzzles

Ages
4,5,6

Materials
Simple chicken pattern, scissors, paper, marker

Procedure
1. Use a simple chicken pattern to trace and cut out eight chicken shapes.
2. Cut the heads from the chickens using a variety of zigzag lines.
3. Put numerals from 1 to 8 on the chicken heads, and make the corresponding number of dots on the matching bodies.
4. The children match the heads to the correct bodies.

Developmental Bonus
Numeral recognition
Counting

Curriculum Extension
For Science: Homemade Compass

Ages
5,6

Materials
Saucer, water, cork, needle, magnet, paper clips, knife, square sheet of paper two inches larger than the saucer, magnetic compass

Procedure
1. Fill the saucer with water.
2. Stroke the needle in one direction with the magnet to magnetize it. Test it with a compass.
3. Trim a slice of cork and float it in the water.
4. Place the needle across the cork.
5. Mark the four corners of the paper with N for North, S for South, W for West and E for East.
6. Set the saucer of water on the paper and allow the needle to come to rest.
7. Lift the saucer without disturbing the needle and move the paper so that the needle points to North.

Developmental Bonus
Concept development

Related Bibliography

Kellogg, Steven. *Pecos Bill.* Morrow, 1986. The anecdotes of Texas' fabled cowboy hero come to life.

Kellogg, Steven. *Paul Bunyan.* Morrow, 1988. The legend of the lumberjack, Paul Bunyan, retold by Kellogg.

Kellogg, Steven. *Johnny Appleseed.* Morrow, 1988. The larger-than-life story of a true American hero, John Chapman, who planted apple trees across the American frontier.

Nelson, Esther L (ed.) . *The Fun-to-Sing Song Book.* Sterling, 1984. A collection of 60 wild and crazy songs.

Strauss, Barbara and Helen Friedland. *See You Later Alligator.* Price Stern Sloan, 1987. An amusing collection of rhyming phrases.

Related Records and Tapes

Sharon, Lois and Bram. "Silly Names and Crazy Gibberish" from *In the Schoolyard.* Elephant, 1981.

"Polly Wolly Doodle" from *Sing-A-Long.* Peter Pan, 1987.

Color Song

Tune: "I've Been Working on the Railroad"

Red is the color for an apple to eat.
Red is the color for cherries, too.
Red is the color for strawberries,
I like red, don't you?

Blue is the color for the big blue sky.
Blue is the color for baby things, too.
Blue is the color of my sister's eyes,
I like blue, don't you?

Yellow is the color for the great big sun.
Yellow is the color for lemonade, too.
Yellow is the color of a baby chick,
I like yellow, don't you?

Green is the color for the leaves on the trees.
Green is the color for green peas, too.
Green is the color of a watermelon,
I like green, don't you?

Orange is the color for oranges.
Orange is the color for carrots, too.
Orange is the color of a jack-o-lantern,
I like orange, don't you?

Purple is the color for a bunch of grapes.
Purple is the color for grape juice, too.
Purple is the color for a violet,
I like purple, don't you?

Thematic Connections
Colors
Self-Concept

Things to Talk About
1. What would it be like if everything in the world were only one color?
2. What color would you use to paint the whole world?

Curriculum Extension
For Art: Easel Creations

Ages
3,4,5

Materials
Easel, primary color paints, easel paper, paintbrushes

Procedure
1. Allow children to experiment with one color of paint each day of the week.
2. Use different-sized brushes and different shapes and textures of paper.

Developmental Bonus
Creative expression

Curriculum Extension
For Language: Tracing Color Words

Ages
5,6

Materials
Index card with color words (red, blue and yellow) written in the appropriate color, onion skin paper or tracing paper, paper clips, crayons

Procedure
1. Place onion skin paper or tracing paper over the index cards and secure with paper clips.
2. The children trace the color words onto the onion skin paper.

Developmental Bonus
Hand-eye coordination
Fine motor development

For Math: Color Classification

Ages
3,4,5,6

Materials
Inch cubes or colored beads, paper, markers

Procedure
1. The children separate beads or cubes by color.
2. The older children can graph the results.

Developmental Bonus
Classification
Concept of more or less

For Outdoors: Invisible Paint

Ages
3,4,5

Materials
Buckets, water, brushes

Procedure
1. The children use the water and brushes to "paint" the fence, wall or other appropriate surface.
2. Ask them why the water disappears.

Developmental Bonus
Gross motor development
Concept development

For Science: Color Mixing

Ages
4,5,6

Materials
Yellow, blue and red paint; paintbrushes; paper

Procedure
1. The children experiment with mixing the primary colors to make secondary colors.
2. Use the new colors to paint a picture.

Developmental Bonus
Concept development

Related Bibliography

Carle, Eric. *The Mixed Up Chameleon.* HarperCollins, 1984. The story of a mixed-up chameleon whose wishes come true as he wishes to be other animals.

Lionni, Leo. *Little Blue and Little Yellow.* Astor-Honor, 1959. A story of blue and yellow make green. Two children as colors, one blue, one yellow, make green when they hug.

Lobel, Arnold. *The Great Blueness and Other Predicaments.* Harper Collins, 1968. The story of how colors came into existence via a wizard.

Peek, Merle. *Mary Wore Her Red Dress and Henry Wore His Green Sneakers.* Clarion, 1985. Eight animals on their way to a birthday party are described in simple color-coded verse.

Serfozo, Mary. *Who Said Red?* Macmillan, 1988. A little farm girl and her brother describe red, yellow, blue, and green through simple rhymes.

Related Records and Tapes

Moore, Thomas. "At the Easel" from *I Am Special.* Thomas Moore Records.

Palmer, Hap. "This is a Song About Colors" from *Learning Basic Skills Through Music: Volume 1.* Activity Records, 1969.

Palmer, Hap. *Getting to Know Myself.* Educational Activities, 1972.

Color Me a Rainbow. Melody House.

The Fox

The fox went out in the chilly night,
He prayed for the moon to give him light;
He'd many a mile to go that night
Before he reached the town-o, town-o,
town-o,
He'd many a mile to go that night
Before he reached the town-o.

He ran till he came to a great big bin,
The ducks and the geese were kept
therein;
A couple of you will grease my chin
Before I leave this town-o...

So he grabbed a gray goose by the neck
And threw a duck across his back;
He didn't mind their "quack, quack,
quack"
And their legs dangling down-o...

Then old Mother Flipper-flopper jumped
out of bed
And out of the window she stuck her
head;
Said, "John, John, the gray goose is
gone,
And the fox is in the town-o...

So John he ran to the top of the hill
And he blew his horn both loud and shrill;
The fox he said, "I'd better flee with my
kill
Or they'll soon be on my trail-o...

He ran till he came to his cozy den
And there were his little ones, eight, nine,
and ten;
They said, "Daddy, you better go back
again
'Cause it must be a mighty fine town-o...

So the fox and wife, without any strife,
They cut up the goose with a fork and a
knife;
They never had such a supper in their
lives
And the little ones chewed on the
bones-o...

Thematic Connections
Animals
Hunting

Things to Talk About
1. What did the fox mean by "grease my chin"? What do foxes generally eat?
2. The fox is on a hunt. Can you think of times when the fox is hunted?
3. What time of the year do you think it is in the song?

Curriculum Extension
For Art: Ice Painting

Ages
3,4,5,6

Materials
Ice tray, popsicle sticks, powdered tempera paint, paper

Procedure
1. Put water in an ice tray and stick a popsicle stick in each cubicle.
2. Freeze.

3. Sprinkle powdered tempera paint on drawing paper.

4. Encourage children to use the ice cube and stick like a paintbrush.

Developmental Bonus
Creative expression

Curriculum Extension
For Gross Motor: Town-O

Ages
3,4,5,6

Materials
White paper sacks, brown paper sacks, markers, blocks, cars, people, animals

Procedure
1. Create a miniature town by opening paper sacks and decorating them with markers.

2. Encourage children to add other props to create a town.

Developmental Bonus
Creative expression

Curriculum Extension
For Language: Footprint Concentration

Ages
3,4,5

Materials
Index cards, markers or crayons

Procedure
1. Draw animal footprints on the index cards. Make two fox footprint cards, two ducks and two chickens.

2. The children turn the cards face down.

3. They take turns trying to turn up a matched set.

Developmental Bonus
Visual memory

Curriculum Extension
For Outdoors: Duck, Duck, Fox

Ages
3,4,5,6

Materials
None needed

Procedure
1. Children sit in a circle.

2. One child is "it."

3. "It" goes around the outside of the circle, tapping each child on the head saying "duck" and eventually "fox."

4. When "it" says "fox," that child gets up and chases "it" around the circle.

5. If "it" gets back to the fox's place in the circle, "it" is safe.

6. If the fox tags "it" before "it" gets back around the circle, "it" has to go into the chicken pen in the center of the circle.

7. The fox becomes "it" and the game starts again.

Developmental Bonus
Social development
Social concepts

Curriculum Extension
For Science: Fox Food

Ages
5,6

Materials
Various pictures from magazines of things a fox might eat and things a fox would not eat, for example, chickens, candy, cookies, horse, goat, etc.

Procedure
1. Have children sort through pictures, separating those items that might be dinner for the fox from those that would not.

Developmental Bonus
Concept development

Related Bibliography

Fox, Mem. *Hattie and the Fox*. Bradbury, 1988. A chicken spies a nose, two eyes, two ears, a body, four legs, and a tail in the bushes.

Giffard, Hannah. *Red Fox*. Dial, 1991. Red Fox sets out to find food for his mate, Rosie, and himself.

Hogrogian, Nonny. *One Fine Day*. Macmillan, 1971. An Armenian folktale about a sly fox who steals milk from an old woman and loses his tail in the process.

Spier, Peter. *Fox Went Out On a Chilly Night*. Doubleday, 1961. The picture book of the traditional song.

Tejima, Keizaburo. *Fox's Dreams*. Philomel, 1987. A lone fox goes out on a snowy winter's night in search of his dream.

Related Records and Tapes

Beall, Pamela Conn and Susan Hagen Nipp. "Fox Went Out on a Chilly Night" from *Wee Sing Silly Songs*. Price Stern Sloan, 1986.

6

▼▼▼▼▼▼▼▼▼▼▼▼

FEBRUARY

A Tisket, A Tasket
The Bus Song
Down by the Station
Jim Along Josie
Michael Finnegan
Muffin Man

A Tisket, a Tasket

A tisket, a tasket,
A green and yellow basket.
I wrote a letter to my love,
And on the way I lost it,
I lost it, I lost it,
And on the way I lost it.
A little boy picked it up,
And put it in his pocket.

Thematic Connections
Post Office
Community Helpers
Friends
Mail

Things to Talk About
1. What do you think the little boy did with the letter? What could he have done to get it back to is owner?
2. Sing the song again, substituting a little girl for the little boy.
3. Ask the children what they know about letter carriers. How does mail get to your house?

Curriculum Extension
For Art: Basket Making

Ages
3,4,5,6

Materials
Scraps of cardboard, paper plates, scissors, stapler, tape, lace, pipe cleaners, margarine tubs, junk jewelry, beads, ribbon, lace and trims

Procedure
1. With the children, use the cardboard and paper plates to construct baskets.
2. Use other materials to decorate the baskets.

Developmental Bonus
Creative expression

Curriculum Extension
For Dramatic Play: Post Office

Ages
3,4,5,6

Materials
Envelopes, pencils, boxes for mail sorting, papers, stamps, boxes

Procedures

1. Talk to children about how a post office works. Take a field trip to a post office, if possible, or invite a letter carrier to come into the classroom and tell about his/her job.

2. Encourage the children to set up a post office and role play situations related to mail sorting and delivery.

Developmental Bonus
Concept development

Curriculum Extension

For Language: Letter Writing

Ages
3,4,5,6

Materials
Paper, pencils, envelopes, stamps

Procedure

1. The younger children dictate letters to a family member. The teacher transcribes the letters for them.

2. Encourage older children to use inventive spelling to write their own letters.

3. Mail the letters.

Developmental Bonus
Concept development

Curriculum Extension

For Outdoors: Lost and Found

Ages
3,4,5

Materials
Six or eight letters (use junk mail)

Procedure

1. Hide letters outside.

2. The children try to find the letters.

3. After all the letters are found, let a few children hide them again. Then the other children find them.

Developmental Bonus
Visual awareness

Curriculum Extension

For Science: Secret Messages

Ages
5,6

Materials
Lemon, toothpick, shallow dish, paper, heat source (light bulb or warming tray)

Procedure

1. Squeeze the juice from one lemon into a shallow dish.

2. Dip a toothpick into the lemon juice and write or draw a message on paper.

3. Allow the message to dry. It will disappear.

4. Then hold the paper next to the light or place it on a warming tray and watch the message reappear.

5. The heat causes a chemical change in the lemon juice that makes it turn brown.

Developmental Bonus
Concept development

Related Bibliography

Gibbons, Gail. *The Post Office Book.* Crowell, 1982. A nonfiction account of what goes on in a modern post office.

Keats, Ezra Jack. *Letter to Amy.* HarperCollins, 1968. Peter worries that his friend Amy won't come to his birthday party. He writes an invitation.

Payne, Emmy. *Katy No-Pocket.* Houghton Mifflin, 1973. A pouchless kangaroo searches for a suitable pocket.

Rylant, Cynthia. *Mr. Grigg's Work.* Orchard, 1989. A story about a man who runs a country post office and really loves his work.

Tsutsui, Yoriko. *Anna's Secret Friend.* Viking, 1987. When Anna, a little Japanese girl, moves to a new neighborhood, she receives flowers, a paper doll, and a letter from a mysterious someone who wants to be friends.

Related Records and Tapes

Moore, Thomas. The Letter Carrier. Thomas Moore Records.

"A Tisket, A Tasket" from *Singing Games For Little People.* Kimbo.

"A Tisket, A Tasket" from *Sing-A-Long.* Peter Pan, 1987.

The Bus Song

The people in the bus go up and down,
Up and down, up and down.
The people in the bus go up and down,
All around the town.

The wiper on the bus goes, "Swish,
swish, swish,
Swish, swish, swish, swish, swish,
swish...."

The brake on the bus goes, "Roomp,
roomp, roomp,
Roomp, roomp, roomp, roomp, roomp,
roomp...."

The money in the bus goes, "Clink, clink,
clink,
Clink, clink, clink, clink, clink, clink...."

The wheels on the bus go round and
round,
Round and round, round and round...."

The baby on the bus goes, "Wah, wah,
wah,
Wah, wah, wah, wah, wah, wah...."

Thematic Connections
Community Helpers
Transportation

Things to Talk About
1. How do wheels make work easier?
2. Demonstrate, or have a child demonstrate, moving a stack of blocks one at a time from one location to another. Then use a play truck to move the blocks.

Curriculum Extension

For Art: Spool Painting

Ages
3,4,5

Materials
Spools, (those with spoked tops are best), tempera paint, yellow construction paper cut into simple bus shapes

Procedure
1. Encourage the children to use the spools to print wheels all over the bus-shaped paper.

Developmental Bonus
Concept development

Curriculum Extension

For Dramatic Play: Pretend Bus

Ages
3,4,5,6

Materials
Bus props—bus driver cap, pretend money, a bowl or pan for the money; chairs arranged in rows of two; newspaper; baby dolls; etc.

Procedure
1. Provide the props and encourage the children to act out the situations in the song.

Developmental Bonus
Creative expression

For Gross Motor: Sand Table Tracks

Ages
3,4,5,6

Materials
Sand, water, several different cars with tires of different patterns and widths

Procedure
1. Dampen the sand in the sand table or remove some sand from the table and place it in a baking pan.
2. Encourage children to make tracks in the sand and then examine the tracks for differences.

Developmental Bonus
Visual discrimination

For Language: New Words

Ages
4,5,6

Materials
Chart tablet paper, crayon

Procedure
1. Talk about other sounds that could go with the song, for example, the wipers on the bus go squeak, squeak, squeak or the money on the bus goes jingle, jingle, jingle.
2. Write the new sounds on the chart tablet paper.
3. Sing the song with the new verses.

Developmental Bonus
Creative thinking

For Outdoors: Tire Rolling

Ages
3,4,5,6

Materials
Old tires (small ones are best)

Procedure
1. Allow the children to roll the tires on the playground.
2. Set up races, relays and distance contests.

Developmental Bonus
Large motor development

Related Bibliography

Alexander, Martha. *Move Over, Twerp*. Dial, 1989. Jeffrey is old enough to take the bus to school, but he has to figure out a way to keep the big kids out of his seat. Great example of problem solving.

Kovalski, Maryann. *The Wheels on the Bus*. Little, 1987. Grandma and Jimmy and Joanna are singing the title song while they wait for the bus to come, but they are so involved they miss the bus.

Raffi. *Wheels on the Bus*. McKay, 1990. An illustrated version of the song.

Sheldon, Dyan. *A Witch Got On at Paddington Station*. Dutton, 1987. A conductor tries to throw a loudly singing witch off the bus, and in the process spills her handbag of magic which makes the rest of the trip exciting.

Zelinsky, Paul. *The Wheels on the Bus*. Dutton, 1990. A story encompassing the song.

Related Records and Tapes

Jenkins, Ella. "The Jolly Bus Line" and "I Love to Ride the Bus" from *This-A-Way and That-A-Way*. Folkways, 1973.

Scelsa, Greg and Steve Millang. "Believe in Yourself" from *Kidding Around with Greg and Steve*. Youngheart Records, 1985.

Moore, Thomas. "The Bus Driver" from Singing, Moving and Learning. Thomas Moore Records.

Raffi. *Wheels on the Bus*. Crown, 1988.

Rosenshontz. *The Wheels on the Bus*. Kimbo.

Hammett, Carol Totsky and Elain Bueffel. "Wheels on the Bus" from *Toddlers on Parade*. Kimbo.

Down by the Station

Down by the station
Early in the morning,
See the little puffer bellies
All in a row.

See the engine driver
Pull the little throttle,
Puff, puff. Toot! Toot!
Off we go.

Thematic Connections
Transportation
Trains
Community Helpers

Things to Talk About
1. What are puffer bellies?
2. How is traveling on a train different from traveling in the car?

Curriculum Extension

For Art: Shoe Box Train

Ages
3, 4, 5, 6

Materials
Shoe boxes, tempera paints, paintbrushes, construction paper, scissors, glue

Procedure
1. Ask the children to bring shoe boxes from home. Be sure to have extras for those children who forget to bring a box.
2. The children paint their shoe boxes.
3. When the boxes are dry, the children cut out construction paper windows and wheels.
4. Glue the windows and wheels to the shoe box train.

Developmental Bonus
Creative expression

Curriculum Extension

For Dramatic Play: Train Station

Ages
3, 4, 5, 6

Materials
Construction paper, scissors, crayons, conductor hat, chairs, large boxes

Procedure
1. Read books about trains to the children (see the bibliography). Discuss how trains and train stations work.
2. Cut construction paper into tickets and decorate with crayons.

3. Allow the children to role play various situations related to trains, for example, engineer, ticket taker, ticket seller, etc.

Developmental Bonus
Concept development
Creative expression

Curriculum Extension
For Fine Motor: Shape Train

Ages
3,4,5,6

Materials
A variety of felt shapes, flannel board

Procedure
1. Demonstrate how combining shapes can create a variety of objects. For example, a rectangle and a triangle make a house, a triangle and a circle make a clown head, etc.
2. Encourage the children to create a train using the various shapes.

Developmental Bonus
Creative expression

Curriculum Extension
For Language: Vehicles

Ages
3,4,5

Materials
Several kinds of toy vehicles; photos or pictures that relate to each vehicle, for example, train/tracks, rocket/moon, car/garage, boat/ocean, etc.

Procedure
1. Encourage the children to match vehicles to related pictures.

Developmental Bonus
Concept development

Curriculum Extension
For Math: Train Sequence

Ages
4,5,6

Materials
Construction paper train cars, construction paper engine and caboose, sticky dots or marker

Procedure
1. Place dots or numerals on train cars.
2. The children arrange the cars from smallest numeral or number of dots to largest numeral or number of dots.

Developmental Bonus
Number recognition
Sequencing

Related Bibliography

Crews, Donald, *Freight Train*. Greenwillow, 1978. ?Brightly colored train moves through tunnels, across trestles and through cities and countryside.

Gibbons, Gail. *Trains*. Holiday, 1988. Passenger and freight trains are fun to watch.

Merriam, Eve. *Train Leaves the Station*. Holt, 1992. A country poem rich in details about a train leaving the station.

Piper, Watty. *The Little Engine That Could*. Platt and Monk, 1984. The story of a little engine who learned to believe in herself.

Van Allsburg, Chris. *The Polar Express*. Houghton Mifflin, 1985. A steam locomotive appears at a little boy's door on Christmas Eve and carries him on a mysterious trip to the North Pole.

Related Records and Tapes

Beall, Pamela Conn. "Down By the Station" from *Wee Sing Children's Songs and Fingerplays*. Price Stern Sloan, 1979.

Beall, Pamela Conn and Susan Hagen Nipp. "Down by the Station" from *Wee Sing Sing-Alongs*. Price Stern Sloan, 1990.

Sharon, Lois and Bram. "Train Is A-Comin'" from *Singing 'n Swinging*. Elephant Records, 1980.

Sharon, Lois and Bram. "Pufferbellies" from *One, Two, Three, Four, Live!*. Elephant Records, 1982.

Jim Along Josie

Hey, Jim along, Jim along Josie,
Hey, Jim along, Jim along Jo,
Hey, Jim along, Jim along Josie,
Hey, Jim along, Jim along Jo.

Walk, Jim along, Jim along Josie,
Walk, Jim along, Jim along Jo,
Walk, Jim along, Jim along Josie,
Walk, Jim along, Jim along Jo.

Hop, Jim along, Jim along Josie,
Hop, Jim along, Jim along Jo,
Hop, Jim along, Jim along Josie,
Hop, Jim along, Jim along Jo.

Add other verses—crawl, roll, swing, etc.

Thematic Connections
Me, Myself and I
Body Awareness

Things to Talk About
1. Can you think of other names like Jo and Josie that have long and short versions like Eric and Erica?
2. What names have you heard used for both girls and boys?

Curriculum Extension
For Gross Motor: Tunnel

Ages
3,4,5

Materials
Sheets, tables

Procedure
1. Place several square or rectangular tables together, not necessarily in a straight line. A zigzag arrangement will be more fun.
2. Drape a sheet or sheets over the tables.
3. Invite the children to crawl through the tunnel.
4. Have them try crawling through with their eyes shut.

Developmental Bonus
Large muscle development

Curriculum Extension
For Language: Movement Collage

Ages
4,5,6

Materials
Magazines, paper, scissors, glue

Procedure
1. Ask the children to look through magazines to find people walking, crawling, running, etc.
2. The children cut out pictures and glue them onto paper to make a movement collage.

Developmental Bonus
Concept development
Fine motor development

Curriculum Extension
For Math: Jump and Measure

Ages
4,5,6

Materials
Ruler, masking tape, block, paper, marker

Procedure
1. Place a line of masking tape on the floor. This is the starting line.
2. The children hold a block in one hand and jump as far as they can from the starting line.
3. After they jump, they place the block where they landed.
4. Measure the jump.
5. Help children record their distances.

Developmental Bonus
Gross motor development
Measurement concepts

Curriculum Extension
For Outdoors: Hopscotch

Ages
4,5,6

Materials
Chalk, stone

Procedure
1. Draw a hopscotch pattern on a sidewalk or blacktop area outside.
2. Invite children to play hopscotch.
3. Draw a simple hopscotch pattern for the younger children and a more complex one for the older children.

Developmental Bonus
Hand-eye coordination
Large muscle development

Curriculum Extension
For Science: Animal Movements

Ages
4,5,6

Materials
Pictures of various animals— snake, frog, kangaroo, horse, dog, centipede, etc.

Procedure
1. Ask the children to sort the animals according to movement, for example, the snake crawls, the frog jumps, the horse runs, the elephant walks, etc.
2. Notice that some animals could go into more than one category.

Developmental Bonus
Concept development

Related Bibliography

Aesop. *The Tortoise and the Hare*. Worlds Wonder, 1988. A jazzed-up race between a tortoise and a hare with a surprise ending.

Hutchins, Pat. *Rosie's Walk*. Aladdin, 1971. A hen named Rosie takes a stroll through the barnyard and is oblivious to the fox who keeps botching his attempts to catch her.

Kalan, Robert. *Jump Frog Jump*. Morrow, 1989. A cumulative sequence story where a frog narrowly escapes from a fish, turtle, snake and kids.

Stadler, John. *Hooray for Snail!*. Harper, 1984. A snail hits a home run and must circle the bases.

Sivulich, Sandra Stroner. *I'm Going on a Bear Hunt*. Dutton, 1973. A call and response story where children pattern your motions and repeat each sentence as you walk through the grass, climb a tree, swim across a lake, trudge through a swamp, and feel your way into a cave.

Related Records and Tapes

Moore, Thomas. "The Family" from *The Family*. Thomas Moore Records.

Palmer, Hap. "Sammy" from *Getting To Know Myself*. Educational Activities, 1972.

Michael Finnegan

There was an old man named Michael Finnegan,
He had whiskers on his chin-again,
They fell out and then grew in again,
Poor old Michael Finnegan,
Begin again.

There was an old man named Michael Finnegan,
He went fishing with a pin-again,
Caught a fish and dropped it in again,
Poor old Michael Finnegan,
Begin again.

There was an old man named Michael Finnegan,
He grew fat and then grew thin again,
Then he died and had to begin again,
Poor old Michael Finnegan,
Begin again.

Thematic Connections
Community Helpers

Things to Talk About
1. Michael Finnegan had whiskers on his chin. What animals have whiskers?
2. Substitute animals into the song. For example, "There was a cat (dog, mouse) named Michael Finnegan, He had whiskers on his chin-again...."

Curriculum Extension
For Art: Michael Finnegan Faces

Ages
4,5,6

Materials
Drawing paper, crayons, glue, yarn or string, scissors

Procedure
1. Encourage the children to draw their versions of Michael Finnegan.
2. Use cut-up yarn or string to create whiskers.
3. Glue the whiskers on the pictures.

Developmental Bonus
Creative expression

Curriculum Extension
For Dramatic Play: Barber Shop

Ages
3,4,5,6

Materials
Barber shop props—chair, combs, drape, shaving cream, pretend razor, barber shop pole made from cardboard tube and red and white crepe paper, etc.

Procedure
1. Place all items in the dramatic play center.
2. Encourage the children to dramatize events in the barber shop.

Developmental Bonus
Creative expression

For Fine Motor: Shaving Cream Fun

Ages
3,4,5,

Materials
Shaving cream, sponges, water

Procedure
1. Spray shaving cream on a table.
2. The children create pictures or designs in the cream.
3. The children can help clean up with sponges and water. (This is often as much fun as making the pictures.)

Developmental Bonus
Fine motor development

For Language: Begin Again Patterns

Ages
4,5,6

Materials
8 x 8 inch squares of white construction paper, 1 inch squares of red, blue and yellow construction paper

Procedure
1. Place the 8 x 8 inch white sheet of paper on the table.
2. Starting at the upper left-hand corner of the paper, create a pattern, using one square of each color.
3. Ask the children to continue the pattern.
4. Point out to the children that the resulting pattern is continuous—it does not always start at the left side of the paper.
5. This patterning exercise replicates the way words make up sentences and paragraphs, and shows that sentences do not always begin at the left margin.

Developmental Bonus
Patterning

For Science: Finnegan Hair

Ages
3,4,5,6

Materials
White paper cups, markers, potting soil, rye grass seed

Procedure
1. Draw a face on one side of the cup.
2. Place potting soil in the cup and sprinkle rye grass seeds on top of the soil.
3. Water.
4. In about a week, the grass will sprout and begin to look like hair.
5. Children can trim the "hair" a couple of times if desired.

Developmental Bonus
Concept of growth

Related Bibliography

Davis, Gibbs. *Katy's First Haircut*. Houghton Mifflin, 1985. Katy gets a haircut and now must get used to having short hair.

Freeman, Don. *Dandelion*. Puffin, 1977. A lion gets a haircut.

Freeman, Don. *Mop Top*. Viking, 1955. A little boy is afraid of his first trip to the barber and finds a number of excuses not to go.

Galdone, Paul. *The Three Little Pigs*. Clarion, 1979. The whole story from huffing and puffing and "not by the hair of my chinny chin chin" to the boiling pot.

Lobel, Arnold. *Whiskers and Rhymes*. Greenwillow, 1985. Original nursery rhymes about a variety of topics, including whiskers.

Related Records and Tapes

Beall, Pamela Conn and Susan Hagen Nipp. "Michael Finnegan" from *Wee Sing Silly Songs*. Price Stern Sloan, 1986.

Beall, Pamela Conn and Susan Hagen Nipp. "Father's Whiskers" from *Wee Sing Silly Songs*. Price Stern Sloan, 1986.

Sharon, Lois and Bram. "Michael Finnegan" from *Smorgasbord*. Elephant Records, 1980.

Muffin Man

Oh, do you know the muffin man,
The muffin man, the muffin man?
Oh, do you know the muffin man,
Who lives in Drury Lane?

Oh, yes, we know the muffin man,
The muffin man, the muffin man.
Oh, yes, we know the muffin man,
Who lives in Drury Lane.

Thematic Connections
Community Helpers
Nutrition

Things to Talk About
1. What kind of job do you think the muffin man has?
2. What other kinds of foods do you think he might sell?

Curriculum Extension

For Art: Muffin Holder Flowers

Ages
3,4,5,6

Materials
Paper muffin/cupcake holders, construction paper, glue, crayons

Procedure
1. Use paper muffin/cupcake holders for flower faces. Different-sized cupcake holders make different-sized flowers.
2. Glue them on construction paper and use crayons to add stems, leaves and backgrounds.

Developmental Bonus
Creative expression

Curriculum Extension

For Dramatic Play: Bakery

Ages
3,4,5,6

Materials
Props for a bakery—pots, pans, cookie sheets, muffin tins, baker's hat, playdough, pretend money, cookie cutters, etc.

Procedure
1. Set up a bakery in the dramatic play center using any props you can gather.
2. Encourage the children to role-play activities that might happen at the bakery.

Developmental Bonus
Concept development
Creative expression

Curriculum Extension
For Fine Motor: Muffin Tin Button Toss

Ages
4,5,6

Materials
Masking tape, muffin tin, buttons

Procedure
1. Place a line of masking tape on the floor. Place the muffin tin 18 inches from the line. Younger children toss buttons from this line into the muffin tin sections.
2. Older children can flip buttons from a line farther away or use one button to flip another (like Tiddly Winks).

Developmental Bonus
Hand-eye coordination

Curriculum Extension
For Math: Muffin Patterns

Ages
3,4,5,6

Materials
Paper cupcake/muffin holders of at least two different colors, muffin tin

Procedure
1. The children create a pattern in the muffin tin using the different colors of cupcake/muffin holders.
2. Ask the older children to create a pattern for the younger children to follow.

Developmental Bonus
Patterning

Curriculum Extension
For Science: Can You Tell by Looking?

Ages
4,5,6

Materials
Salt, sugar, flour, baking soda, wax paper, magnifying glass

Procedure
1. Place a small amount of sugar, salt, flour and baking soda on separate pieces of wax paper.
2. The children look at the four substances and try to identify what they are.
3. Look again using a magnifying glass.
4. Invite the children to taste a small mount of each as a final check.

Developmental Bonus
Concept development

Related Bibliography

Degen, Bruce. *Jamberry*. HarperCollins, 1983. Berryland fruit pickers go on an unforgettable rhyming jamboree.

Galdone, Paul. *The Little Red Hen*. Clarion, 1979. A lazy dog, cat and mouse refuse to help the hen bake her cake and they pay the consequences.

Hoban, Lillian. *Arthur's Christmas Cookies*. HarperCollins, 1972. Arthur mistakes salt for sugar and ruins the recipe.

Robart, Rose. *The Cake That Mack Ate*. Little, Brownand Company, 1987. A cumulative tale about a dog and a cat.

Related Records and Tapes

Scelsa, Greg and Steve Millang. "Muffin Man" from *We All Live Together*, Volume 2, Youngheart Records.

Moore, Thomas. "Make Myself Some Cookies" from *I Am Special*. Thomas Moore Records.

Sharon, Lois and Bram. "Muffin Man" from *Singing 'n Swinging*. Elephant Records, 1980.

7

▼▼▼▼▼▼▼▼▼▼▼▼▼

MARCH

Baby Bumblebee
The Green Grass Grows All Around
We Are Going to Sing About the Sky
Over in the Meadow
The Little Skunk's Hole
The Frog Went A-Courtin'

Baby Bumblebee

I'm bringing home a baby bumblebee,
Won't my mommy be so proud of me.
I'm bringing home a baby bumblebee,
"Ouch! It stung me!" (spoken)

I'm squishing up the baby bumblebee,
Won't my mommy be so proud of me.
I'm squishing up the baby bumblebee,
"Ooh! It's yucky!" (spoken)

I'm wiping off the baby bumblebee,
Won't my mommy be so proud of me.
I'm wiping off the baby bumblebee,
"Now my mommy won't be mad at me."
(spoken)

Thematic Connections

Insects
Bees
Spring

Things to Talk About

1. How are bees different from
ants? How are they alike?
2. Are all bees alike? How are
wasps different from bees?

Curriculum Extension

For Art: Painting

Ages
3,4,5,6

Materials
Yellow and black tempera
paint, easel paper, paintbrushes, recording of "Flight of
the Bumblebee"

Procedure
1. Invite the children to paint
bees on the easel paper.
2. Play "Flight of the Bumblebee" for inspiration.

Developmental Bonus
Creative expression

Curriculum Extension

For Cooking: Honey Balls

Ages
3,4,5,6

Materials
1/2 cup peanut butter, 1/2
cup honey, 1/2 cup carob
powder, 1/2 cup toasted wheat
germ, 1 cup chopped peanuts,
1/2 cup sunflower nuts, coconut flakes, measuring cups,
bowl and mixing spoon, wax
paper

Procedure
1. Combine all ingredients
except the coconut flakes.
2. Roll into 1-inch balls.
3. Roll the balls in coconut
spread on wax paper.
4. Chill, then eat.

Developmental Bonus
Measurement concepts

For Fine Motor: Flower to Hive Bees

Ages
4,5,6

Materials
A teacher-made bee or decorative bee from florist shop, 10 x 10-inch white posterboard, crayons, magnet, 1/2-inch washer, glue

Procedure
1. Glue the washer to the back of bee.
2. Draw a flower at the bottom left-hand corner of the posterboard and a beehive at the top right-hand corner.
3. Make a wiggly pathway between the flower and the hive.
4. Place the bee on the flower.
5. The children move the magnet under the cardboard from flower to hive.

Developmental Bonus
Hand-eye coordination
Fine motor development

For Language: Bee Puppets

Ages
3,4,5,6

Materials
Paper cup, construction paper tulip, tongue depressor, construction paper bee, glue

Procedure
1. Glue the tulip to the ouside of the paper cup.
2. Glue the bee to the tongue depressor.
3. Make a slit in the bottom of the cup just large enough for the tongue depressor to go through.
4. The children pull the tongue depressor down to hide the bee and poke it up to expose the bee.
5. Ask the children to describe or make up a story about the actions of the bee.

Developmental Bonus
Vocabulary development
Creative expression

For Science: Bee Observation

Ages
3,4,5,6

Materials
Dead bee in a jar, bee hive (if available), honeycomb (in honey if possible), large picture of a bee, magnifying glass, paper, pen

Procedure
1. Place all items in the science center to stimulate the children's curiosity.
2. Provide a magnifying glass for close-up inspection.
3. Write down all the questions the children have about bees.
4. With the children, discuss possible answers to the questions.

Developmental Bonus
Concept development
Critical thinking

Related Bibliography

Barton, Byron. *Buzz, Buzz, Buzz!* Macmillan, 1973. A cause and effect tale of what happens when the bee stings the bull.

Carle, Eric. *The Honeybee and the Robber: A Moving Picture Book.* Philomel, 1981. A honeybee faces her biggest challenge when a bear attempts to steal honey from the hive.

Ernst, Lisa Campbell. *The Bee.* Lothrop, 1986. A simple text follows a bee as it leaves its dark hive to discover a world of colors.

Lord, John Vernon. *The Giant Jam Sandwich.* Houghton Mifflin, 1987. The clever residents of Itching Down rid themselves of an invasion of wasps.

Stockton, Frank. *The Bee-Man of Orn.* Harper, 1987. The Bee-man and his bees get along wonderfully. The bees never thought to sting him, and he loved their honey. Then one day a sorcerer tells the Bee-man he has been transformed, and the Bee-man is determined to find out from what.

Related Records and Tapes

Beall, Pamela Conn and Susan Hagen Nipp. "Baby Bumblebee" from *Wee Sing Children's Songs and Fingerplays.* Price Stern Sloan.

Beall, Pamela Conn and Susan Hagen Nipp. "Baby Bumblebee" from *Wee Sing Silly Songs.* Price Stern Sloan.

The Green Grass Grows All Around

There was a tree. (echo)
All in the wood. (echo)
The prettiest little tree. (echo)
That you ever did see. (echo)
The tree in a hole, and the hole in the ground
And the green grass grew all around, all around,
And the green grass grew all around.

And on that tree. (echo)
There was a limb. (echo)
The prettiest little limb. (echo)
That you ever did see. (echo)
The limb on the tree, and the tree in a hole,
And the green grass grew all around, all around,
And the green grass grew all around.

And on that limb...there was branch...

And on that branch...there was a nest...

And in that nest...there was an egg...

And in that egg...there was a bird...

And on that bird...there was a wing...
And on that wing...there was a feather...

And on that feather...there was a bug...

And on that bug...there was a germ...

Thematic Connections
Nature
Animals
Trees

Things to Talk About
1. How would the song be different if the tree was growing on a mountain in rocks?
2. How would the song be different if it was winter?

Curriculum Extension

For Art: Arm and Hand Tree

Ages
3,4,5,6

Materials
Brown and green tempera paint, paintbrushes, sponges, paper, crayons

Procedure
1. Paint the palms of the children with brown paint. Continue painting that side of the arm up to the elbow.
2. The children press their arms and hands onto the art paper to make a print that should look like the trunk and branches of a tree. Let the prints dry.
3. Dip the sponge in the green tempera paint. "Paint" with the sponge across the branches to make leaves. The children may also want to use the sponges to make grass.
4. Older children may wish to add details like a bird's nest, bird, bug, etc., with crayons.

Developmental Bonus
Creative expression

Curriculum Extension

For Cooking: Green Snacks

Ages
3,4,5,6

Materials

Green gelatin, green cherries, celery, green olives, broccoli, bowls

Procedure

1. Make the gelatin with the children's help.
2. When the gelatin is ready to serve, add cherries, olives, celery and broccoli to the menu.
3. The children taste the various green items and make comparisons.

Developmental Bonus

Vocabulary development
Critical thinking

Curriculum Extension
For Gross Motor: Hole in the Ground Toss

Ages
3,4,5

Materials
Basket or trash can, beanbag or sponge ball

Procedure
1. Encourage the children to toss the ball or beanbag into the basket.

Developmental Bonus
Hand-eye coordination
Large muscle development

Curriculum Extension
For Language: Sequencing

Ages
3,4,5,6

Materials
Flannel board pieces for each item in the song, flannel board

Procedure
1. Ask the children to place the items on the flannel board in the appropriate sequence.

2. Ask what happens if you change the sequence.

Developmental Bonus
Sequencing

Curriculum Extension
For Science: Bird Nest

Ages
3,4,5,6

Materials
A real bird nest or several pictures of bird nests and birds building a nest, magnifying glass

Procedure
1. Invite the children to examine the bird nest.
2. Call attention to the different types of materials used to build the nest.

Developmental Bonus
Observation skills

Related Bibliography

Alborough, Jez. *The Grass is Always Greener.* Dial, 1987. A little lamb loses his friends when they move to a greener pasture while he is preoccupied eating.

Romanova, Natalia. *Once There Was a Tree.* Dial, 1985. A tree is now a stump, and a whole array of animals claim it as home. An ecology lesson in a tree.

Schertle, Alice. *In My Treehouse.* Lothrop, 1983. A treehouse is a great place for reading, observation, pretending or spending the night.

Silverstein, Shel. *The Giving Tree.* HarperCollins, 1964. A tree gives its apples, branches, and trunk to his friend.

Udry, Janice. *A Tree is Nice.* HarperCollins, 1957. A book that praises trees and the things you can do in and around them.

Related Records and Tapes

Mr. Al. "Show Me Green" from *Mr. Al Sings Colors and Shapes.* Melody House.

Beall, Pamela Conn and Susan Hagen Nipp. "The Green Grass Grows All Around" from *Wee Sing Silly Songs.* Price Stern Sloan.

We Are Going to Sing About the Sky

Tune: "She'll Be Comin' Round the Mountain"

We're going to sing a song about the sky.
We're going to sing a song about the sky.
We're going to sing a song, we are going to sing a song,
We're going to sing a song about the sky.

There are white fluffy clouds in the sky ...

There are dark fluffy clouds in the sky ...

There are many shiny stars in the sky ...

There's a big yellow sun in the sky ...

There's a big, big moon in the sky ...

Thematic Connections
Weather
Sky

Things to Talk About
1. Talk about the things we see in the sky, for example, birds, planes, rain.
2. What other songs do we know that are about the sky?

Curriculum Extension
For Art: Funny Clouds

Ages
4,5,6

Materials
Drawing paper, optional—scissors

Procedure
1. Allow children to cut or tear drawing paper into odd shapes.
2. When they are finished, let them present their "cloud" to the group and have everyone guess what they are (see the outdoors activity).

Developmental Bonus
Creative expression
Fine motor development

Curriculum Extension
For Language: Cloud Descriptions

Ages
4,5,6

Materials
Clouds from art activity, paper, pen, glue

Procedure
1. Ask the children to dictate a descriptive sentence about their cloud.
2. Transcribe the sentences onto separate pieces of paper. The children glue their clouds to their paper.

Developmental Bonus
Language development

For Math: Classifying

Ages
3,4,5

Materials
Pictures of items found in the sky and items not found in the sky, sorting boxes

Procedure
1. Ask the children to sort the pictures into things that belong in the sky and things that do not belong in the sky.
2. They can ask a friend to check their work.

Developmental Bonus
Classification
Concept development

For Outdoors: Cloud Gazing

Ages
3,4,5,6

Materials
None needed

Procedure
1. Take the children outside. Ask them to lie on their backs and look at the clouds.
2. Let the children take turns finding clouds with shapes that look like something familiar.

Developmental Bonus
Creativity

For Science: Recording Weather

Ages
3, 4,5,6

Materials
Posterboard, construction paper, scissors, crayons, marker

Procedure
1. Prepare a chart in advance. Use a posterboard and divide it into three sections. In the first section, place a piece of blue construction paper with a gray cloud drawn on it. In the second section, place a piece of blue construction paper with a white cloud on it. In the third section, place a piece of blue construction paper without a cloud.
2. For a period of at least two weeks, have the children record the cloud conditions in the sky each day.
3. Place a tally mark on the chart to record the cloud status for each day.
4. At the end of the recording period, count the results.
5. Does anyone want to predict tomorrow's sky condition?

Developmental Bonus
Observation

Related Bibliography

Barrett, Judi. *Cloudy With a Chance of Meatballs.* Atheneum, 1978. The town of "Chewandswallow" has a crisis when its normally good weather turns bad.

Carle, Eric. *Papa, Please Get the Moon for Me.* Picture Book Studio, 1991. When Monica asks for the moon, her father gets it with a very long ladder.

Kellogg, Steven. *Chicken Little.* Morrow, 1985. A little chicken hit on the head by an acorn thinks the sky is falling.

Kent, Jack. *Little Peep.* Simon & Schuster, 1989. A new hatchling tries to call up the sun.

Shaw, Charles G. *It Looked Like Spilt Milk.* HarperCollins, 1947. Simple clouds all look like something other than a cloud, for example, a rabbit, an ice cream cone, a sheep, etc.

Related Records and Tapes

Beall, Pamela Conn and Susan Hagen Nipp. "We Are Going to Sing About the Sky" from *Wee Sing Children's Songs and Fingerplays.* Price Stern Sloan, 1979.

Scelsa, Greg and Steve Millang. "It's a Beautiful Day" from *We All Live Together*, Volume 4. Youngheart Records, 1980.

Over in the Meadow

Over in the meadow, in the sand, in the sun,
Lived an old mother frog and her little froggie one.
"Croak!" said the mother; "I croak," said the one,
So they croaked and they croaked in the sand, in the sun.

Over in the meadow, in the stream so blue,
Lived an old mother fish and her little fishies two.
"Swim!" said the mother; "We swim!" said the two,
So they swam and they swam in the stream so blue.

Over in the meadow, on a branch of the tree,
Lived an old mother bird and her little birdies three.
"Sing!" said the mother; "We sing!" said the three,
So they sang and they sang on a branch of the tree.

Thematic Connections

Nature
Animals
Numbers

Things to Talk About

1. Did you know the verse of the song about birds was also going to be about three? How did you know?

2. What other animals might live in the meadow? Where would they live? In the meadow, in the stream, in the tree, in the grass, in the sand?

Curriculum Extension

For Fine Motor: Sand Play

Ages
3,4,5

Materials
Sand table or pan filled with sand, funnels, cups, sifters, strainers, plastic animals, etc.

Procedure

1. Place the above items in a sand table or a pan filled with sand.

2. Encourage the children to play with materials in the sand.

3. Talk about animals and insects that hide in the sand like frogs, turtles and fleas.

Developmental Bonus

Fine motor development
Hand-eye coordination

Curriculum Extension

For Gross Motor: Fishing

Ages
3,4,5

Materials
Masking tape, 12-inch dowel, string, magnet, construction paper fish, paper clips

Procedure

1. Use tape to make a boat shape on the floor.

2. Tie one end of the string to the dowel and the other end to the magnet.
3. Put a paper clip on the nose of each fish.
4. Let the children fish from the boat by touching the magnet to the paper clip on the fish and lifting the fish into the boat.

Developmental Bonus
Hand-eye coordination

Curriculum Extension
For Language: Next Verse

Ages
4,5,6

Materials
Chart tablet paper, crayon or marker

Procedure
1. Ask the children to choose another animal that might live in the meadow.
2. Talk about where that animal might be in the meadow. (Remember, you'll have to rhyme with four, five, etc.)
3. Write this new verse on the chart tablet paper.
4. Sing the new verse with the children.

Developmental Bonus
Creative thinking

Curriculum Extension
For Math: Making Sets

Ages
4,5, 6

Materials
Numeral cards; cutouts of frogs, fish and birds or an assortment of objects—buttons, washers, pennies, bottle caps, crayons

Procedure
1. Provide the children with numeral cards for 1, 2 and 3 and either cutouts or assorted objects.
2. Encourage the children to make several sets of 1, 2 and 3 cutouts or objects.

Developmental Bonus
Numeration concepts

Curriculum Extension
For Social Studies: Where Do I Live?

Ages
4,5,6

Materials
Pictures of several animals; chart with columns for land, water and air

Procedure
1. Invite children to sort the animals according to habitat.
2. Sort by other characteristics—hair, no hair; lives in cold climate, lives in warm climate, etc.

Developmental Bonus
Concept development

Related Bibliography

Eastman, P.D. *Are You My Mother?* Random House, 1960. A baby bird falls from the nest and tries to find his mother.

Ets, Marie Hall. *Play With Me*. Puffin, 1976. A little girl tries repeatedly to get the forest animals to play with her, but they all run away. When she finally sits still, they all come near.

Kalan, Robert. *Jump Frog Jump*. Morrow, 1989. Cumulative sequence story of a frog's narrow escape from a snake, a turtle, a fish and kids.

Lionni, Leo. *Fish is Fish*. Pantheon, 1970. A curious fish learns about the world from his frog friend's eyes. He sees birds, cows, and people from a fish point of view.

Lionni, Leo. *Swimmy*. Knopf, 1987. Several small fish band together to escape a big fish.

Related Records and Tapes

Beall, Pamela Conn and Susan Hagen Nipp. "Over in the Meadow" from *Wee Sing Nursery Rhymes and Lullabies*. Price Stern Sloan.

Moore, Thomas. "The Frog Family" from *The Family*. Thomas Moore Records.

Wisher, Tom and Teresa Whitaker. "How Does It Feel to Be a Fish" from *We've Got to Come Full Circle*. Folkways.

The Little Skunk's Hole

Tune: "Turkey in the Straw"

*Oh, I stuck my head
In the little skunk's hole,
And the little skunk said,
"Well, bless my soul!
Take it out! Take it out!
Take it out! Remove it!"*

*Oh, I didn't take it out,
And the little skunk said,
"If you don't take it out,
You'll wish you had,
Take it out! Take it out!"
Pheew! I removed it!*

Thematic Connections
Animals
Trees

Things to Talk About
1. How would the song be different if it were a rabbit's hole instead of a skunk's hole?
2. Discuss the cause and effect relationship in the song.

Curriculum Extension
For Art:
Black and White

Ages
3,4,5

Materials
Black and white tempera paint, paintbrushes, easel paper

Procedure
1. Encourage the children to paint with the black and white paint.

2. They can paint skunks or just be creative. Black and white paints are fascinating to young children.

Developmental Bonus
Creative expression

Curriculum Extension
For Fine Motor:
Bean Sweep and Sort

Ages
3,4,5

Materials
Black beans, white beans, pastry brush, scoop, empty coffee can, two margarine tubs

Procedure
1. The children use a pastry brush to sweep beans into the scoop, then into the coffee can.
2. The children can also separate the beans by color and place each color in a designated margarine tub.

Developmental Bonus
Fine motor development
Hand-eye coordination

Curriculum Extension
Gross Motor: Skunk Hole Golf

Ages
3,4,5,6

Materials
Masking tape, empty half-gallon ice cream carton, ping pong ball, wrapping paper, cardboard tube

Procedure
1. Make a small "X" on the floor with the masking tape.
2. Cut the ice cream carton in half (vertically) to create a skunk's hole. Place one of the halves four to five feet from the "X".
3. Invite the children to place the ping pong ball on the "X" and use the wrapping paper tube to hit it into the skunk's hole.

Developmental Bonus
Hand-eye coordination

Curriculum Extension
For Language: In and Out

Ages
4,5,6

Materials
Chart tablet paper, marker

Procedure
1. Ask the children to list all the things we can go in and out of.
2. With the children, brainstorm ways skunks could make people stay away without spraying them.

Developmental Bonus
Critical thinking
Problem solving

Curriculum Extension
For Science: What's My Scent?

Ages
3,4,5,6

Materials
Six film canisters or pill canisters; six cotton balls; vanilla, peppermint and lemon extract; colored dots

Procedures
1. Dab the extracts on two cotton balls for each scent—two vanilla, two peppermint and two lemon.
2. Place each cotton ball in a canister and close.
3. Allow children to open the canisters, smell the cotton ball and then find the canister that matches the smell.
4. For self checking, place a color coded dot of the same color on the bottom of each pair of smells.

Developmental Bonus
Smell discrimination

Related Bibliography

Brett, Jan. *Annie and the Wild Animals*. Houghton Mifflin, 1985. Jan Brett's illustrations create a magical story.

Jonas, Ann. *Holes and Peeks*. Greenwillow, 1984. Holes are a lot less scary when you do something about them — mend them, plug them, or make them smaller.

Sharmat, Marjorie Weinman. *Bartholomew the Bossy*. Macmillan, 1984. Popularity and authority go to a skunk's head with interesting consequences.

Wells, Rosemary. *Fritz and the Mess Fairy*. Dial, 1991. Fritz, a young skunk, is very messy. He leaves towels on the floor, dirty laundry under the bed, and runs constant science experiments, but his mess is nothing to the one the Mess Fairy leaves behind. Fritz spends a frantic night cleaning.

Wells, Rosemary. *Hazel's Amazing Mother*. Penguin, 1985. A warm, triumphant story about the power of mother love.

Related Records and Tapes

Beall, Pamela Conn and Susan Hagen Nipp. "The Little Skunk's Hole" from *Wee Sing Silly Songs*. Price Stern Sloan, 1986.

The Frog Went A-Courtin'

The frog went a-courtin', he did ride,
unh-hunh, unh-hunh.
The Frog went a-courtin', he did ride,
With a sword and pistol by his side,
unh-hunh, unh-hunh.

He rode up to Miss Mousie's den,
unh-hunh, unh-hunh.
He rode up to Miss Mousie's den,
Said, "Please Miss Mousie, won't you let
me in, unh-hunh, unh-hunh.

First, I must ask my Uncle Rat, unh-hunh,
unh-hunh.
First, I must ask my Uncle Rat,
And see what he will say to that,
unh-hunh, unh-hunh.

"Miss Mousie, dear, won't you marry me?
unh-hunh, unh-hunh.
"Miss Mousie, dear, won't you marry me?
Way down under the apple tree?
unh-hunh, unh-hunh.

Where will the wedding supper be? unh-
hunh, unh-hunh.
Where will the wedding supper be?
Under the same old apple tree,
unh-hunh, unh-hunh.

What will the wedding supper be? unh-
hunh, unh-hunh.
What will the wedding supper be?
Hominy grits and a black-eyed pea, unh-
hunh, unh-hunh.

The first come in was a bumble bee,
buzz-buzz, buzz-buzz.
The first come in was a bumble bee,
With a big bass fiddle on his knee, buzz-
buzz, buzz-buzz.

The last come in was a mockingbird,
mock-mock, mock-mock,
The last come in was a mockingbird,
And said, "This marriage is too absurd,"
mock-mock, mock-mock.

Thematic Connections
Animals
Spring
Trees

Things to Talk About
1. List things from the song
that make Frog and Mousie
seem like people.
2. Where do you think Frog
and Mousie will live?
3. What does it mean when
people say "I have a frog in my
throat?"

Curriculum Extension

For Fine Motor: Feed the Frog

Ages
3,4,5

Materials
One meatball press sprayed
green, two wiggly eyes, glue,
pompoms, two bowls

Procedure

1. After spraying the meatball press green, glue the wiggly eyes on the ball part of the press. The result should look like a frog.

2. The children use the meatball press to pick up pompoms and move them from one bowl to another.

Developmental Bonus

Hand-eye coordination
Fine motor development

<u>Curriculum Extension</u>

For Gross Motor: Lily Pad Toss

Ages

3, 4,5,6

Materials

Three service bells (available at office supply stores), three pieces of green felt cut like lily pads, three beanbags

Procedure

1. Place the service bells on the floor. Cover each bell with a piece of green felt.

2. The children toss the beanbags at the pads, trying to ring the bell.

Developmental Bonus

Hand-eye coordination

<u>Curriculum Extension</u>

For Math: Frog and Lily Pad Match

Ages

3,4,5,6

Materials

Lima beans sprayed green, several lily pads cut from green paper

Procedure

1. Put eyes and mouth on each green lima bean to make them look like frogs.

2. The children match one lily pad to one frog.

3. For older children, put numerals on the lily pads and ask them to place the appropriate number of frogs on the lily pads.

Developmental Bonus

One-to-one correspondence

<u>Curriculum Extension</u>

For Outdoors: Leap Frog

Ages

4,5,6

Materials

None needed

Procedure

1. The children form a line, squatting on their hands and knees.

2. The child at the end of the line straddle-jumps over each child and takes his place at the front of the line.

3. Repeat with the next child at the back of the line.

Developmental Bonus

Coordination
Curriculum Extension

For Science: Tadpole Watch

Ages

3, 4,5,6

Materials

Tadpoles, fish bowl or aquarium, paper, crayons

Procedure

1. Put several tadpoles in a fish bowl or aquarium in the science center.

2. The children watch the tadpoles change into frogs.

3. Encourage the children to record the number of days needed for the entire process.

Developmental Bonus

Concept development
Observation skills

Related Bibliography

Conover, Chris. *Froggie Went A'Courtin'*. Farrar, Straus & Giroux, 1986. A nicely illustrated version of the song.

Kalan, Robert. *Jump Frog Jump*. Morrow, 1989. A chain of events is kicked off when a frog jumps after a fly.

Kellogg, Steven. *The Mysterious Tadpole*. Puffin, 1992. A tadpole given to a boy by his uncle turns into a Loch Ness monster.

Lobel, Arnold. *Frog and Toad Together*. Harper, 1972. Frog and toad are good friends.

Mayer, Mercer. *A Boy, Dog and a Frog*. Dial, 1985. A wordless picture book about a boy and his dog who are determined to catch a frog.

Related Records and Tapes

Jenkins, Ella. "The Green Frog Sits by the Stream" from *Hopping Around from Place to Place*. Educational Activities, 1983.

Lucky, Sharron. "Frog Went A-Courtin'" from *The Magic of Music, Movement and Make Believe*. DLM.

Moore, Thomas. "The Frog Family" from *The Family*. Thomas Moore Records.

"Froggy Went A-Courtin'." Melody House.

8
▼▼▼▼▼▼▼▼▼▼▼▼▼

APRIL

Five Little Ducks
Eensy Weensy Spider
Little Bunny Foo Foo
Raindrop Song
Rain, Rain Go Away
Six White Ducks
I'm a Little Flower

Five Little Ducks

Five little ducks
Went out to play.
Over the hill and far away,
Mama Duck called with a
Quack-quack-quack,
Four little ducks came
Swimming back.

Four little ducks
Went out to play.
Over the hill and far away,
Mama Duck called with a
Quack-quack-quack,
Three little ducks came
Swimming back.

Three little ducks....

Two little ducks....

One little duck
Went out to play
Over the hill and far away,
Papa Duck called with a
Quack-quack-quack,
Five little ducks
Came swimming back!
With all their friends.

Thematic Connections
Nature
Animals
Numbers

Things to Talk About
1. Where do you think the ducks were hiding?
2. Why did they come to the papa but not the mama?
3. Sing the song again switching the place of mama and papa.

Curriculum Extension
For Art:
Duck Rubbings

Ages
3,4,5,6

Materials
Posterboard duck cutouts of different sizes, art paper, crayons, optional—wallpaper

Procedures
1. The children place the posterboard cutouts under the art paper and rub with crayons.

2. Try using cutouts from textural wallpaper.
3. The older children can sequence the cutouts from large to small and small to large.

Developmental Bonus
Creative expression

Curriculum Extension
For Fine Motor:
Feed the Duck

Ages
4,5,6

Materials
Small box, duck cutout with open mouth, glue, scissors, goldfish crackers, tweezers

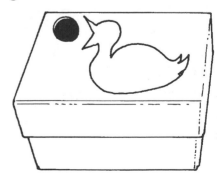

Procedure

1. Glue duck cutout to outside top of the box lid.
2. Cut a circle about the size of a penny by the duck's mouth.
3. Provide the children with goldfish and tweezers and invite them to use the tweezers to pick up the goldfish and put them in the duck's mouth.
4. When finished, the children can eat the goldfish they've placed in the box.

Developmental Bonus

Fine motor development
Hand-eye coordination

Curriculum Extension

For Language: Duck Pond

Ages
3,4,5,6

Materials
Eight rubber or plastic ducks; tub; water; colored tape (red, blue, green, yellow)

Procedure

1. Place a piece of colored tape on the bottom of each duck. Create pairs by using two pieces of each color tape.
2. Float the ducks in the tub.
3. The children name a color and then pick up two ducks in an attempt to find matching colors.

Developmental Bonus
Visual memory
Color recognition

Curriculum Extension

For Math: Variations of Five

Ages
4,5,6

Materials
Lima beans, sealable sandwich bag, marker

Procedure

1. Place five lima beans in a sealable sandwich bag.
2. Draw a vertical line down the middle of the bag (extending from the top to the bottom of the bag).
3. Encourage the children to manipulate the beans on either side of the line to see all the combinations of five.

Developmental Bonus
Numeration—Understanding of five

Curriculum Extension

For Outdoors: Find the Ducks

Ages
3,4,5

Materials
Five rubber ducks

Procedure

1. Hide five ducks on the playground.
2. Encourage the children to find the ducks.
3. Repeat the activity, letting a few children hide the ducks for their classmates.

Developmental Bonus
Problem-solving skills

Related Bibliography

Gerstein, Mordicai. *Follow Me!*. Morrow, 1983. Seven ducks and a goose lose their way home until the duck herd leads them back.

Ginsburg, Mirra. *Across the Stream*. Greenwillow, 1982. A bad dream and a rescue, with a hen and her chicks and a duck and her ducklings as characters.

McCloskey, Robert. *Make Way for Ducklings*. Viking, 1941. A family of ducklings search for a peaceful home in Boston.

Raffi. *Five Little Ducks*. Crown, 1988. A storybook that illustrates the words to the song.

Roy, Ron. *Three Ducks Went Wandering*. Seabury, 1979. Three ducks innocently and inadvertently avoid a dangerous bull, fox, hawk, and snake in a clever sequence story.

Related Records and Tapes

Raffi, Six Little Ducks. *More Singable Songs*. Shoreline, 1988.

Hammett, Carol Totsky and Elaine Bueffel "Little White Duck" from *Toddlers on Parade*. Kimbo, 1985.

Eensy Weensy Spider

The eensy weensy spider
Climbed up the water spout.
Down came the rain
And washed the spider out.

Out came the sun
And dried up all the rain,
And the eensy weensy spider
Climbed up the spout again.

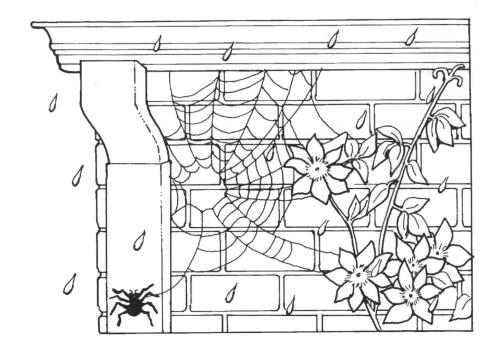

Thematic Connections

Insects
Nature
Self-Esteem

Things to Talk About

1. What is a water spout?
2. What did the spider do when the rain washed her out?
3. Did you ever have to try something many times before you were successful?
4. Do you see grown-ups who have to try something lots of times before they are successful?

Curriculum Extension

For Art: Straw Blowing

Ages
4,5,6

Materials
Drawing paper, straw (cut in half), tempera paint, teaspoon

Procedure
1. Provide each child with a straw and a piece of paper.
2. Put a teaspoon of paint on the paper and encourage children to blow the paint in all directions to create spider designs. NOTE: Instruct the children to hold the straw slightly away from the paint.

Developmental Bonus
Creative expression

Curriculum Extension

For Creative Movement: Spider Dance

Ages
3,4,5

Materials
Recordings of various types of music

Procedure
1. Play music and encourage the children to dance like spiders.
2. After a while, change to a different piece of music and ask the children to dance like spiders to it.

Developmental Bonus
Creative expression

Curriculum Extension
For Language: Spider Puppets

Ages
4,5,6

Materials
Pipe cleaners, elastic string

Procedure
1. The children create spider puppets from pipe cleaners by twisting four pipe cleaners together in the middle and spreading the eight resulting legs. Attach a piece of elastic string for a great effect.
2. Let the children create their own versions of movements for the song, or let them create their own story.

Developmental Bonus
Hand-eye coordination
Language development

Curriculum Extension
For Science: Scientific Observations

Ages
4,5,6

Materials
Spider and insect photos

Procedure
1. Display photographs of spiders in the science center along with photographs of other insects.
2. Encourage the children to look for differences and similarities between spiders and other insects.

Developmental Bonus
Visual discrimination
Concept development

Curriculum Extension
For Social Studies: Challenges

Ages
4,5,6

Materials
Chart paper or blackboard, pen or chalk

Procedure
1. Help the children make a list of everyday tasks that are difficult to achieve.
2. Discuss the struggle of the Eensy Weensy Spider. How does it apply to difficult tasks?

Developmental Bonus
Critical thinking

Related Bibliography

Carle, Eric. *The Very Busy Spider*. Putnam, 1989. A glimpse of the life of a spider as it spins its web.

Graham, Margaret B. *Be Nice to Spiders*. HarperCollins, 1967. A look at how the spider befriends man.

McDermott, Gerald. *Anansi the Spider: A Tale from the Ashanti*. Henry Holt, 1972. Anansi, the half-man and half-spider creature of African folklore, uses his wits instead of brawn to solve his problems.

Piper, Watty. *The Little Engine That Could*. Platt and Munk, 1984. A wonderful story of a little engine who learns to believe in herself.

Unknown. *Itsy Bitsy Spider*. DLM, 1991. A "full of personality" spider illustrates the song. The lesson she learns is then applied to everyday experiences in the lives of children like learning to tie a shoe, blow up a balloon, hit a ball, etc.

Related Records and Tapes

Beall, Pamela Conn and Susan Hagen Nipp. "Eentsy Weentsy Spider" from *Wee Sing Children's Songs and Fingerplays*. Price Stern Sloan, 1979.

.Moore, Thomas. "Spiders" from *Songs from the Whole Day*. Thomas Moore Records.

Moore, Thomas. "Itsy Bitsy Spider" from *Singing, Learning and Moving*. Thomas Moore Records.

Moore, Thomas. *Songs for the Whole Day*. Thomas Moore Records.

Richard, Little. "Itsy Bitsy Spider" from *For the Children*.

Weissman, Jackie. "Eensy Weensy Spider" from *Miss Jackie and Her Friends Sing About Peanut Butter, Tarzan and Roosters*. Miss Jackie, 1981

Hammett, Carol and Elaine Bueffel"Itsy Bitsy Spider" from *It's Toddler Time*. Kimbo, 1982.

Little Bunny Foo Foo

Little Bunny Foo Foo,
Hopping through the forest,
Scooping up the field mice
And boppin' 'em on the head.

(Spoken)
And down came the good fairy and she said:
"Little Bunny Foo Foo,
I don't want to see you
Scooping up the field mice
And boppin' 'em on the head.

(Spoken)
I'll give you three chances,
And if you don't behave
I'll turn you into a goon!"

The next day:

Same as before except,
"I'll give you two more chances..."

Next verse, say,
"I'll give you one more chance..."

Last verse, say,
"No more chances! Now you're a goon! POOF!!"

The moral of the story is: Hare Today, Goon Tomorrow

Thematic Connections
Easter
Animals
Mice
Rabbits

Things to Talk About
1. How are mice and rabbits alike? How are they different?
2. Why do you think Bunny Foo Foo caught the mice?

Curriculum Extension
For Art: Bunny Ears

Ages
3,4,5,6

Materials
White construction paper, scissors, stapler, crayons

Procedure
1. Cut 1 1/2-inch strips of paper to make a headband for each child.
2. Cut large ears from construction paper and staple them to each side of each child's headband.
3. The children decorate the ears with crayons, if desired.

Developmental Bonus
Creative expression

Curriculum Extension
For Creative Movement: Bunny Hop

Ages
3,4,5,6

Materials
Record with bunny hop music

Procedure
1. The children line up holding each other by the waist.
2. Follow the directions in the music, dancing the bunny hop.

Developmental Bonus
Large muscle development
Coordination

For Gross Motor: Scooping Field Mice

Ages
3,4,5,6

Materials
Two empty bleach bottles or gallon milk jugs, scissors, glue, grey felt squares, two wiggly eyes, 6-inch piece of grey yarn, beans

Procedure
1. Turn an empty bottle on its side and cut out top and three sides to create a scoop. Round the corners and bottom. Don't cut the handle. Repeat for the second bottle.
2. Cut the felt into two oval shapes 4 to 6 inches long.
3. To create a mouse, glue the two pieces of felt together around the edges, leaving a place to fill with beans.
4. Fill with beans.
5. Insert a yarn tail and finish gluing.
6. Glue on eyes and a pair of ears.
7. Encourage the children to toss the beanbag mouse back and forth and catch it with their scoops.

Developmental Bonus
Coordination

Curriculum Extension
For Language: Color Match

Ages
3,4,5

Materials
Manilla folder; bunny shapes without tails cut from red, blue, yellow, green, purple and orange construction paper; penny; marker; 1-inch pompoms in red, blue, yellow, green, purple and orange

Procedure
1. Glue bunny shapes inside the manilla folder, three on each side.
2. Use a penny to trace a tail for each bunny.
3. The children match the correct color tails (pompoms) to the corresponding bunnies.

Developmental Bonus
Visual discrimination

Curriculum Extension
For Math: Bunny Hop Numbers

Ages
4,5,6

Material
Five white floor tiles or pieces of laminated paper, marker

Procedure
1. Write numerals 1 to 5 on the tiles or paper.
2. Lay the tiles or paper on the floor, not necessarily in sequential order.
3. Invite the children to hop like a bunny from tile to tile or paper to paper, following the correct sequential order.

Developmental Bonus
Numeral recognition

Related Bibliography

Aardema, Verna. *Rabbit Makes a Monkey Out of Lion.* Dial, 1989. A rabbit, rat, and turtle outsmart a lion and steal his personal stash of honey.

Aardema, Verna. *Who's in Rabbit's House?* Dial, 1977. A music story of how rabbit and his friends got The Long One out of his house.

Grossman, Virginia. *Ten Little Rabbits.* Chronicle, 1991. A counting book that blends reality and fantasy in its portrayal of Native American bunnies.

Martin, Rafe. *Foolish Rabbit's Big Mistake.* Putnam, 1985. A rabbit thinks the earth is breaking up when he hears an apple fall, and he runs off to warn his friends.

Potter, Beatrix. *The Tale of Peter Rabbit.* Warne, 1991. Mrs. Rabbit warns all her children to stay away from Mr. MacGregor's garden, but Peter disobeys and the consequences are almost disastrous.

Related Records and Tapes

Beall, Pamela Conn and Susan Hagen Nipp. "Little Bunny Foo Foo" from *Wee Sing Silly Songs.* Price Stern Sloan, 1986.

Lucky, Sharron. "The Bunny Hop" from *The Hokey Pokey.* Melody House.

Sharon, Lois and Bram. "Rabbit Foo Foo" from *Mainly Mother Goose.* Elephant, 1984.

Raindrop Song

If all of the rain drops
Were lemon drops and gum drops,
Oh, what a rain it would be.
I'd stand outside
With my mouth open wide
I wouldn't care if I never went inside.

If all of the snow flakes
Were Hershey Bars and milk shakes
Oh, what a rain it would be.
I'd stand outside
With my mouth open wide
I wouldn't care if I never went inside.

Thematic Connections

Weather
Rain

Things to Talk About

1. What kind of cloud would rain lemon drops and gum drops?
2. What kind of rain drops would healthy eaters like to have?

Curriculum Extension

For Art: Fantasy Rain

Ages
4,5,6

Materials
Paper, paint, paintbrushes, markers, crayons, pastels

Procedure
1. Ask the children to draw pictures of their favorite kind of rainy day.
2. Provide a variety of art materials.

Developmental Bonus
Creative expression

Curriculum Extension

For Cooking: Making Candy

Ages
3,4,5,6

Materials
Evaporated milk, margarine, confectioner's sugar, food coloring, sifter, measuring cups, mixing bowl and spoon, wax paper

Procedure
1. With the children, mix 1/3 cup evaporated milk, 1/2 cup margarine and 2 1/2 cups confectioner sugar (sifted) in a bowl.
2. Separate into four parts. Add a few drops of food coloring to each part, creating a portion of pink, yellow, blue and green mixtures.
3. Roll the mixture into balls on wax paper.
4. Refrigerate for a couple of hours.

5. Eat and enjoy.

Developmental Bonus
Measurement concepts

Curriculum Extension
For Fine Motor: Gumdrop Sculpture

Ages
3,4,5,6

Materials
Gumdrops from the math activity, toothpicks

Procedure
1. Use the gumdrops from the math activity. Give each child several toothpicks.
2. Encourage the children to create a sculpture, using the toothpicks to connect gumdrops.

Developmental Bonus
Creative expression

Curriculum Extension
For Language: Umbrella Magic

Ages
4,5,6

Materials
Umbrella, chart tablet paper, markers

Procedure
1. Talk to the children about the uses of an umbrella.
2. Brainstorm with the children about other ways to use an umbrella.
3. List their ideas on chart tablet paper.

Developmental Bonus
Creative thinking

Curriculum Extension
For Math: Gumdrop Sorting

Ages
4,5,6

Materials
Gumdrops, optional—paper and markers

Procedure
1. Give each child a handful of gumdrops.
2. Ask the children to sort their gumdrops by color.
3. Older children can graph the results.

Developmental Bonus
Classification

Related Bibliography

Balian, Lorna. *The Sweet Touch.* Abingdon, 1976. A genie's spell causes everything Peggy touches to turn to candy.

Cooney, Nancy Evans. *The Umbrella Day.* Philomel, 1989. A little girl uses her imagination to turn an umbrella into a toadstool, a wild animal tent, and a boat.

Martin, Bill, Jr. and John Archambault. *Listen to the Rain.* Holt, 1988. A poem that describes rain from its whisper to its roar.

Polacco, Patricia. *Thunder Cake.* Philomel, 1990. A Russian tale of how a grandmother helps her granddaughter lose her fear of thunderstorms by baking a cake before the storm comes.

Prelutsky, Jack. *Rainy, Rainy Saturday.* Greenwillow, 1980. A collection of fourteen poems about rain and bad weather.

Related Records and Tapes

Sharon, Lois and Bram. "Candy Man" from *One, Two, Three, Four, Live!* Elephant Records, 1982.

Thumb, Tom. "Big Rock Candy Mountain" from *Fiddle-E-Fee.* Tom Thumb.

Rain, Rain Go Away

Rain, rain, go away,
Come again another day;

Rain, rain, go away,
Little (Johnny) wants to play.

Thematic Connections
Weather
Rain
Colors

Things to Talk About
1. Talk about the value of rain to the earth and to people.
2. What happens when it rains?

Curriculum Extension
For Art: Rainbows

Ages
3,4,5,6

Materials
Small squeegee (window washer tool); red, purple, blue, green and yellow tempera paints; drawing paper

Procedure
1. The children place a small amount of each color paint on the left edge of their paper in the following order top to bottom: red, purple, blue, green and yellow.
2. The children take turns smearing paint across their paper with the squeegee.

Developmental Bonus
Creative expression
Concept development

Curriculum Extension
For Cooking: Gelatin Rainbows

Ages
3,4,5,6

Materials
Three or four flavored gelatins, glass dish, bowls and spoons

Procedure
1. Prepare one gelatin at a time. Let it cool and set before preparing the next.
2. Layer gelatins to create a rainbow effect.
3. Serve, eat and enjoy!

Developmental Bonus
Measurement concepts
Color concepts

For Dramatic Play: Baby Bath Time

Ages
3,4,5,6

Materials
Baby bath props—small tub, baby doll, towel, washcloth, small bar of soap, empty baby powder bottle, doll clothes

Procedure
1. Provide the children with props and guidance.
2. Allow the children to pretend to bathe the baby.

Developmental Bonus
Sequencing
Creative expression

For Science: Raindrop Close-ups

Ages
5,6

Materials
Eye droppers, container of water, plate, magnifying glass

Procedure
1. The children use the eye dropper to place a drop of water on the plate.
2. Then they use the magnifying glass to look closely at the water.
3. Talk about the way the water holds its shape. Explain that water has a protective skin.
4. Have the children touch the drop of water, thus breaking the "skin." What happens?

Developmental Bonus
Observation
Concept development

For Social Studies: Saving Water

Ages
4,5,6

Materials
Chart tablet, marker

Procedure
1. Talk about the importance of using water conservatively.
2. Help the children brainstorm ways to save water.
3. Write their ideas down on the paper.
4. Incorporate as many ideas as possible into the classroom.

Developmental Bonus
Creative thinking

Related Bibliography

Aardema, Verna. *Bringing the Rain to Kapiti Plain*. Dial, 1981. A cumulative tale of how Ki-pat brings rain to the arid Kapiti Plain.

Blegvad, Lenore. *Rainy Day Kate*. McElderry, 1988. A little boy plans a full day of activities for when his friend comes to visit, but his plans are spoiled when it rains. He finds a solution by creating an imaginary friend.

Freeman, Don. *A Rainbow of My Own*. Viking, 1966. A little boy dressed in rainy-weather attire describes his real and imaginary search for a rainbow.

Martin, Bill and John Archambault. *Listen to the Rain*. Holt, 1988. A poem that describes rain from its whisper to its roar.

Skofield, James. *All Wet! All Wet!* HarperCollins, 1984. A little boy in a raincoat with a big umbrella spends a rainy day outside looking at animal and insect life.

Related Records and Tapes

Beall, Pamela Conn and Susan Hagen Nipp. "Rain, Rain, Go Away" from *Wee Sing Children's Songs and Fingerplays*. Price Stern Sloan, 1979.

Beall, Pamela Conn and Susan Hagen Nipp. "It Ain't Gonna Rain" from *Wee Sing Silly Songs*. Price Stern Sloan.

Moore, Thomas. "My Umbrella" from *Songs for the Whole Day*. Thomas Moore Records.

Peter, Paul and Mary. "It's Raining" from *Peter, Paul and Mommy*. Warner.

Scelsa, Greg and Steve Millang. "The World is a Rainbow" from *We All Live Together*, Vol. 2. Youngheart Records, 1978.

"It Ain't Gonna Rain" from *Sing-A-Long*. Peter Pan, 1987.

Six White Ducks

Six white ducks that I once knew
Fat ducks, skinny ducks, fair ones , too.
But the one little duck with a feather on
his back
He ruled the others with a quack, quack,
quack!
Quack, quack, quack, quack, quack,
quack.
He ruled the others with a quack, quack,
quack.

Down to the river they would go,
Wibble, wobble, wibble, wobble all in a
row.
But the one little duck with a feather on
his back
He ruled the others with a quack, quack,
quack!
Quack, quack, quack, quack, quack,
quack.
He led the others with a quack, quack,
quack!

Home from the river they would come,
Wibble, wobble, wibble, wobble,
ho-hum-hum!
But the one little duck with a feather on
his back,
He led the others with a quack, quack,
quack!
Quack, quack, quack, quack, quack,
quack
He led the others with a quack, quack,
quack.

Thematic Connections
Animals
Farm
Easter

Things to Talk About
1. What do ducks eat? Have you ever fed ducks?
2. Can you think of other ways to describe how ducks move?

Curriculum Extension
For Art: Feather Painting

Ages
4,5,6

Materials
Feathers, drawing paper, tempera paint

Procedure
1. The children paint a picture using a feather as a brush.
2. Provide a variety of feathers to obtain variation in pictures.

Developmental Bonus
Creative thinking
Creative expression

Curriculum Extension
For Gross Motor: Follow the Feather

Ages
3,4,5,6

Materials
Feather

Procedure
1. Give the feather to the child who is designated as the leader.
2. The rest of the children follow the actions of the leader.
3. Allow the leader to select a successor.

Developmental Bonus
Visual memory
Large muscle development

For Math: Variations of Six

Ages
5,6

Materials
Lima beans, sealable sandwich bag, marker

Procedure
1. Place six lima beans in a sealable sandwich bag.
2. Draw a vertical line down the middle of the bag (extending from the top to the bottom of the bag).
3. The children manipulate the beans on either side of the line to see all the combinations of six.

Developmental Bonus
Numeration—Understanding of six

For Outdoors: Duck Relay

Ages
4,5,6

Materials
Two feathers

Procedure
1. Divide the children into two teams. Place each team in a line.
2. Place two feathers about 15 feet away, one in front of each team.
3. The first child in each line squats on his heels, wobbles to the feather, picks it up and gives it to the next child on the team (relay style).
4. The team to complete the course first is the winner.

Developmental Bonus
Large muscle development

For Science: Feather Race

Ages
4,5,6

Materials
One-foot piece of yarn or string; feathers; objects—tissue, penny, paper cups, cotton ball, paper clip, etc.; paper, crayons

Procedure
1. Attach the piece of yarn or string to two objects in the classroom so that it is about 3 feet above the floor. This creates a line.
2. Select two children to play.
3. One child uses the feather and the other child chooses an object from those listed above.
4. Each child drops the "racer" from the yarn line at the same time.
5. Keep a record of which object wins the race.

Developmental Bonus
Critical thinking

Related Bibliography

Andersen, Hans Christian. *The Ugly Duckling.* Knopf. 1986. An ugly duckling rejected by all he sees eventually turns into a beautiful swan.

Ellis, Anne. L. *Dabble Duck.* HarperCollins, 1984. A pet duck isn't lonely anymore after his family adopts a stray dog.

Gerstein, Mordicai. *Follow Me!.* Morrow, 1983. Seven ducks and a goose, each a different color, are lost until a duck herd leads them home.

McCloskey, Robert. *Make Way for Ducklings.* Viking, 1941. A mama and papa mallard look for a suitable place to raise their babies.

LeSieg, Theo. *I Wish That I Had Duck Feet.* Random House, 1965. A little boy imagines what it would be like to have duck feet, long, long tail, antlers, long nose and whale spout, only to decide he likes himself as he is.

Related Records and Tapes

Hammett, Carol Totsky and Elaine Bueffel, "Six White Ducks" from *Toddlers on Parade.* Kimbo, 1985.

Raffi. "Six White Ducks" from *More Singable Songs.* A and M Records.

Scelsa, Greg and Steve Millang. "The Ugly Ducking" from *We All Live Together,* Vol. 4. Youngheart Records, 1980.

I'm a Little Flower

Tune: "I'm a Little Teapot"

I'm a little flower,
Green and red.
I grew up in a flower bed,
With a little rain and tender care,
Flowers, flowers, everywhere.

Thematic Connections
Colors
Nature
Plants

Things to Talk About
1. What do plants and flowers need to grow up healthy?
2. What do children need to grow up healthy?

Curriculum Extension

For Art: Sponge Painting

Ages
3,4,5

Materials
Sponges, scissors, tempera paints, construction paper, crayons

Procedure
1. Cut sponges into various petal shapes.
2. Provide each child with a piece of construction paper and green and red tempera paint.
3. The children create flowers using sponges and paint.
4. When the paintings are dry, use crayons for details.

Developmental Bonus
Creative expression

Curriculum Extension

For Language: Flower Talk

Ages
3,4,5

Materials
Flowers

Procedure
1. Ask the children to bring flowers from home. (Be sure to bring extras for children who forget.)
2. Ask the children to describe the flowers. A good beginning is to say, "Tell me about your flower."

3. Talk about how the flowers are alike and how they are different, how we use flowers (to cheer people up) and what they need to grow. Be creative. The object of this activity is to encourage the children to talk and, therefore, develop their language skills.

Developmental Bonus
Language development
Visual discrimination

Curriculum Extension
For Math: Classifying

Ages
4,5

Materials
Magazine pictures of flowers, teacher-made flowers

Procedure
1. Classify magazine pictures of flowers or the flowers from the language activity by color, size, type, group.
2. Use teacher-made flowers to extend classification. For example, "Put all the red flowers in the 'red flower' bed. Put all the tall flowers in the 'tall flower' bed."

Developmental Bonus
Visual discrimination
Vocabulary development

Curriculum Extension
For Science: Egg Carton Gardens

Ages
3, 4,5,6

Materials
Egg carton, potting soil, marigold seeds, popsicle stick, marker, ruler

Procedure
1. With the children, plant marigold seeds in an egg carton. Place potting soil in each crate of the carton. Then plant the seeds.
2. Put an unmarked popsicle stick in each crate to use as a measuring stick.
3. The children can use a marker to record weekly growth.
4. After several weeks, remove the popsicle stick and use a standard ruler to measure weekly growth.

Developmental Bonus
Observation skills
Measurement concepts

Curriculum Extension
For Social Studies: Flower Shop

Ages
3, 4,5,6

Materials
Flowers, vases, play money, etc.

Procedure
1. Talk about the beds children sleep in and the beds flowers sleep in.
2. Turn the dramatic play center into a flower shop.

Developmental Bonus
Critical thinking

Related Bibliography

Carle, Eric. *The Tiny Seed.* Picture Book Studio, 1991. The story of the birth of a plant.

dePaola, Tomie. *The Legend of the Bluebonnet.* Putnam, 1983. A little Indian girl makes a great sacrifice, but in doing so ends a drought and brings the flowers.

Lobel, Arnold. *The Rose in My Garden.* Greenwillow, 1984. A tale about garden flowers that include a mouse, a cat and a bee.

Spier, Peter. *Peter Spier's Rain.* Doubleday, 1982. It's a wordless picture book that illustrates the adventures of a brother and sister in a rainstorm.

Williams, Barbara. *Hello, Dandelions!* Henry Holt, 1979. A group of beautiful photos introduce young children to a number of flowers and plants.

Related Records and Tapes

Raffi. *Everything Grows.* Shoreline, 1987.

Rosenshontz. *"The Garden Song" from Rosenshontz Tickles You.* RS Records, 1980.

Hug the Earth. Tickle Tune Typhoons, 1985.

9

▼▼▼▼▼▼▼▼▼▼▼▼▼▼▼

MAY

Animal Fair
The Bear Wen Over the Mountain
Crocodile Song
Fiddle-I-Fee
One Elephant
The Three Bears
Three Little Monkeys

Animal Fair

I went to the animal fair,
The birds and the beasts were there,
The big baboon by the light of the moon
Was combing his auburn hair,
You should have seen the monk;
He sat on the elephant's trunk,
The elephant sneezed and fell on his knees,
And what became of the monk,
The monk, the monk, the monk?

Suggestion: "The monk, the monk" can be sung continuously by a few while others sing the song again.

Thematic Connections

Animals
Fairs
Celebrations

Things to Talk About

1. Have you ever been to a fair? What was it like?
2. Describe a fair that animals might like. How would it be different from a fair for people?

Curriculum Extension

For Art: Animal Mask

Ages
4, 5, 6

Materials
Paper plates, construction paper, glue, crayons, scissors, string or ribbon

Procedure
1. Create animal faces by using construction paper and crayons to decorate a paper plate face.
2. Cut out eyes and attach strings or ribbons so the children can wear the masks.

Developmental Bonus
Creative expression
Concept development

Curriculum Extension

For Cooking: Carousel Cookies

Ages
3, 4, 5, 6

Materials
Vanilla wafers, peanut butter, animal crackers

Procedure
1. Spread a little peanut butter on each vanilla wafer and stand an animal cookie up in the peanut butter to make a carousel.
2. Eat and enjoy!

Developmental Bonus
Creative expression

For Creative Movement: Let's Pretend

Ages
3,4,5

Materials
None needed

Procedure
1. Ask the children to act like various animals while their classmates attempt to guess which animal they are imitating.
2. They could use the animal masks they created in the art activity.

Developmental Bonus
Concept development

For Language: Animal Match

Ages
3,4,5

Materials
Sets of simple animal shapes, one cut from white paper and another cut from black paper

Procedure
1. The children match the animal shadows (black cutouts) with animal shapes (white cutouts).

Developmental Bonus
Visual discrimination

For Math: Animal Sort

Ages
3,4

Materials
Pictures of animals (some large, some small), two boxes or baskets for sorting

Procedure
1. Ask the children to sort animal pictures by size (elephants, hippos and giraffes are large; mice, dogs and monkeys are small).
2. Sort by other characteristics—water animals and land animals; animals with teeth and animals with no teeth; etc.

Developmental Bonus
Visual discrimination

Related Bibliography

Barrett, Judi. *Animals Should Definitely Not Wear Clothing.* Atheneum, 1970. This is a hilarious book depicting very humorous reasons why animals should not wear clothes.

Cole, William. *I Went to the Animal Fair, A Book of Animal Poems.* World, 1958. A collection of animal poems.

Maestro, Betsy and Giulio. *A Wise Monkey Tale.* Crown, 1975. A monkey outsmarts his friends to get out of a hole.

Merriam, Eve. *Where is Everybody? An Animal Alphabet.* Simon and Schuster, 1992. An alphabet alliteration poem describing where each animal is.

Thomas, Patricia. *"Stand Back," Said the Elephant, "I'm Going to Sneeze!"* Lothrop, 1990. The elephant's jungle friends all implore him not to sneeze because they all remember the last time he sneezed.

Related Records and Tapes

Beall, Pamela Conn and Susan Hagen Nipp. "Animal Fair" from *Wee Sing Silly Songs.* Price Stern Sloan, 1986.

Frost, Derrie. A Zippity Zoo Day. Melody House.

Animal Walks. Kimbo.

Stewart, Georgiana Liccione, Walk Like the Animals. Kimbo, 1976.

The Bear Went Over the Mountain

The bear went over the mountain,
The bear went over the mountain,
The bear went over the mountain,
To see what he could see.

To see what he could see,
To see what he could see,
The bear went over the mountain,
To see what he could see.

The other side of the mountain,
The other side of the mountain,
The other side of the mountain,
Was all that he could see.

Was all that he could see,
Was all that he could see,
The other side of the mountain,
Was all that he could see.

Thematic Connections
Bears
Animals

Things to Talk About
1. What do you think the bear expected to see on the other side of the mountain?
2. Brainstorm some things the bear might have seen and change the second verse, for example a rabbit in a pasture.

Curriculum Extension
For Art: Textured Bears

Ages
3,4,5

Materials
A cardboard bear-shaped pattern, glue, paintbrushes, coffee grounds, drawing paper, construction paper, scissors, crayons

Procedure
1. The children use the bear-shaped pattern as a stencil to trace a bear onto their paper.

2. Encourage the children to paint the bear with glue; then sprinkle with coffee grounds.
3. Glue on construction paper eyes. When the picture is dry, the children can use crayons to add other details to their pictures.

Developmental Bonus
Creative expression

Curriculum Extension
For Cooking: Bear Claws

Ages
3,4,5,6

Materials
Refrigerator biscuits, knife, cooking oil, small deep fryer, tongs, paper towels, cinnamon, sugar, bowl, spoon

Procedure
1. Take refrigerator biscuits apart and give one to each child.

2. Ask the children to flatten their biscuits and then fold them in half. Use a knife to crimp edges.

3. Place the children's biscuits, three or four at a time, in the hot oil. Leave the biscuits in just until they rise to the surface.

4. Remove the biscuits with tongs and place on paper towels.

5. Sprinkle the bear claws with a sugar and cinnamon mixture. Enjoy when cool!

Developmental Bonus
Change of state concepts

For Language: Brown Bear Book

Ages
4,5,6

Materials
Plastic sandwich bags, tagboard or posterboard cut to fit the baggies, crayons, stapler, plastic tape, *Brown Bear, Brown Bear* by Bill Martin Jr.

Procedure
1. Read *Brown Bear Brown Bear* by Bill Martin, Jr. to the children.

2. Have the children create their own Brown Bear stories by making pictures on the tagboard or posterboard.

3. Make a book to hold their stories by placing six plastic bags together and stapling across the bottom. Cover the staples with plastic tape.

4. Open the bags and place the children's stories in sequence, or allow older children to sequence their own story.

Developmental Bonus
Creative expression
Sequencing

For Math: Mountains

Ages
3,4,5

Materials
Playdough or clay

Procedure
1. Encourage the children to make playdough or clay mountains.

2. Arrange the mountains from lowest to highest or tallest to shortest.

Developmental Bonus
Size comparisons
Vocabulary development

For Science: Both Sides

Ages
3,4,5,6

Materials
Several items that look alike on both sides—purse, block, paintbrush, etc.; several items that look different on each side—clock, doll, book,etc.

Procedure
1. Show the children the items that are alike on both sides and the items that are different on each side.

2. Ask the children to group the objects into those that look alike on both sides and those that look different on each side.

3. What about objects that have four sides?

Developmental Bonus
Visual discrimination
Visual memory

Related Bibliography

Lemieux, Michele. *What's That Noise?* Morrow, 1985. Before falling asleep for the winter, Brown Bear identifies the mysterious sound he hears as his own heartbeat.

Martin, Bill, Jr. *Brown Bear, Brown Bear, What Do You See?* Henry Holt, 1983. A rhyming verse to teach color and animal names.

McCloskey, Robert. *Blueberries for Sal.* Viking, 1948. A little girl and a bear cub cross each other's paths while out picking berries with their mothers.

Murphy, Jill. *Peace at Last.* Dial, 1990. Mr. Bear can't get to sleep because every little noise disturbs him.

Rose, Michael. *We're Going on a Bear Hunt.* McElderry, 1989. Looking for a bear is fun for Dad and four kids until they find one.

Related Records and Tapes

Beall, Pamela Conn and Susan Hagen Nipp. "The Bear Went Over the Mountain" from *Wee Sing Silly Songs.* Price Stern Sloan, 1986.

Stewart, Georgiana Liccione. Walk Like the Animals. Kimbo, 1976.

Crocodile Song

She sailed away on a sunny day
On the back of a Crocodile.
"You see," said she,
"He's as tame as he can be,
As I float him down the Nile."
The Crock winked an eye
As she waved a merry bye
Wearing a happy smile.
At the end of the ride
The lady was inside,
And the smile was on the Crocodile.

Thematic Connections

Crocodiles
Zoo
Nature
Animals

Things to Talk About

1. Do you know other stories or songs about crocodiles (Peter Pan, Rock-A-Bye Crocodile, etc.)?
2. How are crocodiles and alligators different? How are they alike?

Curriculum Extension

For Art: Crocodiles

Ages
3, 4, 5, 6

Materials
Clothespins (the kind that have a spring), green spray paint, small wiggly eyes, glue

Procedure
1. Help the children spray paint the clothespins with green paint. (Clip clothespins to the top of a cardboard box for ease while spraying and drying.) *NOTE*: Always use spray paint outside or in a well-ventilated room.
2. The children glue two eyes to the top of one side of the clothespin.
3. Show the children how, when it is pinched, the clothespin now looks like a crocodile snapping.

Developmental Bonus
Creative thinking
Creative expression

Curriculum Extension

For Cooking: Crocodile Smile Snacks

Ages
3, 4, 5

Materials
Green apples, peanut butter, miniature marshmallows

Procedure
1. Cut the apples into four wedges and then cut each wedge again.

2. Give each child two slices.

3. Encourage the children to spread peanut butter on each slice, place a marshmallow on top of one slice, and then place the second slice on top to create a sandwich and a crocodile smile.

4. Yum!

Developmental Bonus

Creative thinking

For Dramatic Play: Shadow Play

Ages

3,4,5,6

Materials

Light source—overhead projector, flashlight, lamp, etc.; sheet

Procedure

1. Show the children how to make crocodiles with their hands (put thumb to tips of fingers).

2. Put your hand in front of the light and cast a shadow on the wall. Then place a sheet in front of the light and put your hand between the light and the sheet.

3. Encourage the children to try both methods of playing with shadows.

4. Create crocodile shadows and other animal shadows.

Developmental Bonus

Science concept—interruption of light

Creative expression

Curriculum Extension

For Fine Motor: Crocodile Pickup

Ages

3,4,5

Materials

Clothespin crocodiles from the art activity, 1 inch pompoms, small wiggly eyes, red felt, scissors, glue, bowl

Procedure

1. Cut the red felt into smile shapes to fit the pompoms. Glue two wiggly eyes and a red felt mouth on each pompom.

2. Encourage the children to use their crocodile clothespin to move pompom smiling faces from the table to a bowl.

Developmental Bonus

Hand-eye coordination

Fine motor development

Curriculum Extension

For Language: Crocodile Tale

Ages

4,5,6

Materials

Chart tablet paper, marker

Procedure

1. Encourage the children to make up a story about riding on the back of a crocodile.

2. Transcribe the story onto the chart tablet paper.

3. Read the completed story to the children.

Developmental Bonus

Creative thinking

Related Bibliography

Aruego, José and Ariane. *A Crocodile's Tale.* Scribner, 1972. Philippine folk story of an ungrateful crocodile who decides to eat a boy who has freed him from a trap.

Aruego, José. *Rockabye Crocodile.* Greenwillow, 1988. Two bears with different personalities babysit a crocodile and find out their behaviors affect the crocodile's behavior.

Galdone, Paul. *The Monkey and the Crocodile: A Jataka Tale from India.* Clarion, 1987. A hungry crocodile plans to have a monkey for dinner, but the monkey is far too cunning.

Jorgensen, Gail. *Crocodile Beat.* Bradbury, 1989. The jungle animals wake up a mean crocodile with their boom, chitter-chatter, roar, growl, and hissssss.

Waber, Bernard. *Lyle, Lyle, Crocodile.* Houghton Mifflin. 1965. Lyle, the crocodile, is committed to the zoo by a crocodile-hating next door neighbor.

Related Records and Tapes

Beall, Pamela Conn and Susan Hagen Nipp. "The Crocodile" from *Wee Sing Silly Songs.* Price Stern Sloan, 1986.

Sharon, Lois and Bram. "The Smile on the Crocodile" from *Singing 'n Swinging.* Elephant Records.

"Jungle Rhythms" from *A Zippity Zoo Day.* Melody House.

Fiddle-I-Fee

I had a cat and the cat pleased me,
Fed my cat under yonder tree,
Cat went fiddle-i-fee.

I had a hen and the hen pleased me,
Fed my hen under yonder tree,
Hen went chimmey chuck, chimmey
chuck,
Cat went fiddle-i-fee.

I had a dog and the dog pleased me,
Fed my dog under yonder tree,
Dog went bow-wow, bow-wow,
Hen went chimmey chuck, chimmey
chuck,
Cat went fiddle-i-fee.

Thematic Connections
Animals
Cats
Dogs

Things to Talk About
1. What do you think the different animals had to eat?
2. Can you think of other sounds the animals make?

Curriculum Extension

For Creative Movement: Animal Movements

Ages
3,4,5,6

Materials
None needed

Procedure
1. Encourage the children to walk like a dog, stretch like a cat, gallop like a horse, walk like a hen, pig, cow, etc.
2. Have an animal parade with all the children moving like animals.

Developmental Bonus
Creative expression

Curriculum Extension

For Dramatic Play: Animal Tea Party

Ages
3,4,5,6

Materials
Stuffed animals, tea cups and saucers

Procedure
1. Encourage the children to plan a pretend tea party for the animal guests.
2. Let them plan a menu, prepare the food and serve it.

Developmental Bonus
Creative expression

Curriculum Extension

For Fine Motor: Animal Shapes

Ages
3,4,5,6

Materials

Playdough, animal-shaped cookie cutters

Procedure

1. The children use the cookie cutters to make shapes from playdough.

2. Make a tree out of playdough and place the animals around the tree.

3. Encourage the older children to create three-dimensional animals with the playdough.

Developmental Bonus

Creative expression
Fine motor development

Curriculum Extension

For Language: Flannel Board Animals

Ages

3,4,5

Materials

Animal shapes (those mentioned in the song) cut from felt and flannel board

Procedure

1. Encourage the children to create animal stories on the flannel board.

2. Ask them to sequence the animals in the same order they are introduced in the song.

Developmental Bonus

Creative expression
Sequencing

Curriculum Extension

For Math: Animal Patterns

Ages

3,4,5

Materials

Animal shapes cut from felt or colored construction paper

Procedure

1. Encourage the children to create animal patterns, for example, cat, cat, dog, cat, cat, dog, etc.

2. Create patterns and ask the children to copy your patterns.

3. Copy the children's patterns.

Developmental Bonus

Patterning
Visual discrimination

Related Bibliography

Anello, Christine. *The Farmyard Cat*. Scholastic, 1987. A hungry cat creates a chain of humorous events involving several other animals in the farmyard.

Ets, Marie Hall. *Play With Me*. Puffin, 1976. A little girl tries repeatedly to get the forest animals to play with her, but they all run away. When she finally sits still, they all come near.

G'ag, Wanda. *Millions of Cats*. Coward, 1928. An old man can't pick just one—the result is millions of cats.

Keats, Ezra Jack. *Pet Show!*. Macmillan, 1972. When Archie can't find a stray cat to enter in the school pet show, he brings a germ in a jar.

Traditional. *Fiddle-I-Fee: A Farmyard Song for the Very Young*. Little, Brown, 1992. Big book story of the song.

Related Records and Tapes

Lois, Sharon and Bram. "I Know A Little Pussy" and "The Cat Came Back" from *Singing 'n Swinging*. Elephant Records, 1980.

Scelsa, Greg and Steve Millang. "Copycat" from *Kidding Around with Greg and Steve*. Youngheart Records, 1985.

Rosenshontz. *Share It*. RS Records, 1980.

One Elephant

One elephant went out to play,
Out on a spider's web one day,
He had such enormous fun,
He called for another elephant to come.

Thematic Connections
Animals
Circus
Jungle

Things to Talk About
1. How are elephants different from spiders? What would happen if an elephant really stepped on a spider web?
2. Why do you think the song uses "enormous" to describe the fun the elephant was having?

Curriculum Extension
For Art: Elephant Mask

Ages
4,5,6

Materials
Paper plates, scissors, 12 x 18 inch pink and black construction paper, glue, tongue depressor or popsicle stick

Procedure
1. With the children, cut eyes out of each paper plate.
2. Cut two large pink ears from construction paper and glue them to the plate.
3. Fold accordion style a 2 x 18 inch strip of black construction paper and glue on the plate to make an elephant nose.
4. Glue the head on a tongue depressor or popsicle stick.
5. Repeat for the rest of the children.

Developmental Bonus
Creative expression

Curriculum Extension
For Creative Movement: One Elephant

Ages
3,4,5,6

Materials
None needed

Procedure

1. Sit in a circle. Select one child. She places one arm out in front to make a trunk and walks around the circle while the group sings the song.

2. After singing, "She had such enormous fun, she called for another elephant to come," the first child chooses a second child.

3. Now the two children walk around the group. The first child continues to put one arm out front for a trunk. She also extends her other arm between her legs to hold the hand of the second child.

4. Continue with "Two elephants went out to play..." and so on.

Developmental Bonus
Coordination
Large muscle development

Curriculum Extension

For Language: Elephant Patterns

Ages
3,4,5

Materials
Elephants cut from gray felt; several felt saddles in red, blue, yellow and green; flannel board

Procedure

1. The children place the animals on the flannel board and then create patterns by placing the saddles on elephants' backs.

2. Create patterns that the children can copy or continue.

Developmental Bonus
Patterning

Curriculum Extension

For Math: Feeding the Elephant

Ages
4,5,6

Materials
Peanuts, cutout elephants

Procedure

1. Put numerals 1-10 on the elephants.

2. Encourage the children to count the appropriate number of peanuts for each elephant, 1 to 10.

3. Younger children can match one elephant to one peanut.

4. Older children can sequence the elephants numerically.

Developmental Bonus
One-to-one correspondence
Numeral recognition
Counting

Curriculum Extension

For Science: Heavy/Light

Ages
3, 4,5,6

Materials
Heavy and light classroom items, classroom scale

Procedure

1. The children hold the items and sort them into heavy and light categories.

2. Bring out the scale and let the children weigh the items.

3. Ask the children if elephants are heavy or light.

Developmental Bonus
Measurement concepts
Concept development

Related Bibliography

Caple, Kathy. *The Biggest Nose*. Houghton Mifflin, 1988. Eleanor Elephant is so embarrassed by her big nose that she ties it in a knot.

Riddle, Chris. *The Trouble With Elephants*. HarpeCollins, 1988. A young girl describes all the problems one encounters with an elephant: they run the bath water over, take all the covers, and drink your lemonade.

Robinson, Deborah. *No Elephants Allowed*. Houghton Mifflin, 1981. Justin tries to chase elephants out of his room so he can sleep.

Vipont, Elfrida. *The Elephant and the Bad Baby*. Putnam, 1986. An elephant teaches a baby to say please by taking away the things the baby wants, like his ice cream and cookies.

Westcott, Nadine Bernard. *Peanut Butter and Jelly: A Play Rhyme*. Dutton, 1987. The chant that describes how a peanut butter and jelly sandwich is made with an elephant demonstrating.

Related Records and Tapes

Sharon, Lois and Bram. *Monte Saw An Elephant*. Elephant Records.

Sharon, Lois and Bram. *One Elephant, Deux Elephants*. Elephant Records, 1978.

The Three Bears

Tune: Twinkle, Twinkle, Little Star

There were once three brown bears
Mother, Father, Baby Bear
Mother Bear's food was cold
Father Bear's food was hot
Baby's food was all gone
Someone ate it, so she cried.

There were once three brown bears
Mother, Father, Baby Bear
Mother's chair was too low
Father's chair was too high
Baby's chair was just right
But when she sat—she broke it.

There were once three brown bears
Mother, Father, Baby Bear
Mother's bed was too soft
Father's bed was too hard
Baby's bed was occupied
Someone strange was sleeping there.

"Come here quick," said Baby Bear
"Someone's sleeping in my bed."
"Who are you?" said Baby Bear
"Who are you?" said Goldilocks
"You better run," said Baby Bear
"I will," said Goldilocks.

Thematic Connections
Bears
Animals
Fairy Tales
Manners

Things to Talk About
1. How would the song be different if the bears had been home and had answered the door when Goldilocks knocked?
2. Do you think it was okay for Goldilocks to go inside the house when no one was home?

Curriculum Extension
For Art: Sponge Bears

Ages
3,4,5

Materials
Bear-shaped sponges in several sizes, brown tempera paint, paper, crayons

Procedure
1. The children make bear prints on their paper with the sponges.
2. Decorate with crayons when the paint is dry.

Developmental Bonus
Creative expression

Curriculum Extension
For Cooking: Put the Bear to Bed

Ages
3,4,5

Materials
1 1/2 slices of bread for each student, 1 piece of cheese for each student, bear cookie cutter

Procedure
1. The children use the cookie cutter to cut a bear shape from the cheese.

2. Then instruct the children to lay the bear on the whole piece of bread and cover it with the half piece.

3. Eat and enjoy.

Developmental Bonus
Whole/part relationships

Curriculum Extension
For Fine Motor: Lacing Bears

Ages
3,4,5

Materials
Large bear shapes cut from tagboard, laces, hole punch

Procedure
1. Punch holes around the perimeter of the tagboard bears.

2. Encourage the children to use the laces to lace around the bear.

Developmental Bonus
Hand-eye coordination
Fine motor coordination

Curriculum Extension
For Gross Motor: Walk-on Nursery Rhyme

Ages
3,4,5

Materials
A 15-foot-long piece of bulletin board paper, crayons

Procedure
1. Draw the following items on the bulletin board paper in this sequence: a pair of walking feet (trace shoes), a spiral arrow, a pair of walking feet, grass, a pair of walking feet, door, a pair of walking feet, bowl, a pair of walking feet, chair, a pair of walking feet, bed, a pair of walking feet going off the end of the paper.

2. The children walk down paper reciting this rhyme:

Goldilocks, Goldilocks, turn around. (turn around)

Goldilocks, Goldilocks, touch the ground. (touch ground)

Goldilocks, Goldilocks, knock on the door. (knock with hands)

Goldilocks, Goldilocks, eat some porridge. (pretend to eat porridge)

Goldilocks, Goldilocks, have a seat. (squat)

Goldilocks, Goldilocks, go to sleep. (put cheek on folded hands)

Goldilocks, Goldilocks, run, run, run. (run off paper and back to beginning)

Developmental Bonus
Following directions

Curriculum Extension
For Math: Set Search

Ages
4,5,6

Materials
Three chairs, three bowls, three spoons

Procedure
1. Talk to the children about sets of three.

2. Ask the children to go around the room making sets of three, for example, three crayons, three cups, three blocks, etc.

Developmental Bonus
Number concepts

Related Bibliography

Brett, Jan. *Goldilocks and the Three Bears*. Dodd, Mead, 1987. Goldilocks enters the home of the three bears without permission. This version is told with beautiful illustrations and bear-filled borders.

Galdone, Paul. *The Three Bears*. Clarion, 1985. Another version of the story that inspired the song.

Goldstein, Bobbye S. *Bear in Mind: A Book of Bear Poems*. Puffin, 1991. A collection of bear poems.

Turkle, Brinton. *Deep in the Forest*. Dutton, 1987. A wordless switch whereby three bears visit a forest cabin after a human mama, papa, and young girl leave the house.

Yolen, Jane. *The Three Bears Rhyme Book*. Harcourt, 1987. Several rhymes based on the presumed friendship of Goldilocks and Baby Bear.

Related Records and Tapes

Rosenshontz. *Rock 'N' Roll Teddy Bear*. Kimbo.

Stewart, Georgiana Liccione. *Walk Like the Animals*. Kimbo, 1976

"Bear Hunt" from *Circle Around*. Tickle Tune Typhoon, 1983

Totally Teddy. Melody House.

Three Little Monkeys

Three little monkeys
Jumping on the bed,
One fell off and bumped his head,
Mother called the doctor and the doctor said,
"No more monkeys jumping on the bed."

Two little monkeys
Jumping on the bed,
One fell off and bumped his head,
Mother called the doctor and the doctor said,
"No more monkeys jumping on the bed."

One little monkey
Jumping on the bed,
One fell off and bumped his head,
Mother called the doctor and the doctor said,
"Get those monkeys back to bed."

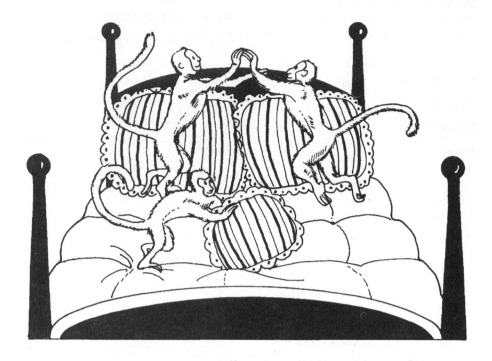

Thematic Connections
Nature
Animals
Jungle
Monkeys

Things to Talk About
1. Why do you think the monkeys kept jumping on the bed?
2. Can you think of a better place for the monkeys to jump?

Curriculum Extension
For Art: Monkey Mask

Ages
3, 4, 5, 6

Materials
Paper plates, scissors, construction paper, crayons, stapler

Procedure
1. Cut several paper plates in half and give each child a whole plate and a half plate.
2. The children design and color the whole plate to be the face of a monkey.
3. Staple the half plate onto the back of the whole plate to form a pocket for holding the mask.

Developmental Bonus
Creative expression

Curriculum Extension
For Cooking: Banana Delights

Ages
3, 4, 5, 6

Materials
Bananas, popsicle sticks, plastic knife

Procedure
1. The children peel the bananas.
2. Using a plastic knife, allow the children to cut the bananas in half.
3. Give one half to each child. Place the bananas on popsicle sticks.
4. Freeze the bananas.
5. Eat and enjoy.

Developmental Bonus
Fine motor development
Hand-eye coordination

Curriculum Extension
For Creative Movement: Monkey See, Monkey Do

Ages
3,4,5

Materials
None needed

Procedure
1. Appoint one child to be the lead monkey.
2. The leader performs a series of actions to be copied by the group.
3. Then the leader picks a new leader, and the activity can be repeated.

Developmental Bonus
Visual memory

Curriculum Extension
For Gross Motor: Pin the Tail on the Monkey

Ages
3,4,5,6

Materials
Bulletin board paper, crayons, masking tape, construction paper, scissors, scarf

Procedure
1. Draw a large monkey without a tail on the bulletin board paper and tape it on the wall.
2. Make tails out of the construction paper. Put a piece of masking tape on each tail.
3. The children wear the scarf as a blindfold and attempt to tape the tail to the monkey.

Developmental Bonus
Coordination

Curriculum Extension
For Outdoors: Swinging Monkeys

Ages
3,4,5,6

Materials
None needed

Procedure
1. The children choose partners.
2. One partner is the swinger, and the other is "it."
3. All swingers hold their partners by their arms and swing them until the teacher says, "Monkeys stop."
4. At that point, the swingers let go, the teacher yells, "Freeze," and the "its" freeze in their current positions.
5. The winner is the "it" who can hold his position the longest.

Developmental Bonus
Coordination

Related Bibliography

Christelow, Eileen. *Five Little Monkeys Jumping on the Bed*. Clarion, 1991. And one fell off and bumped his head. The rhyme that follows the song.

Galdone, Paul. *The Monkey and the Crocodile: A Jataka Tale from India*. Clarion, 1987. A cunning monkey outwits a crocodile who plans to have him for dinner.

Perkins, Al. *Hand, Hand, Fingers, Thumb*. Random House, 1969. A simple and silly story of monkeys drumming on a drum with a great repetitive line.

Rey, H. A. *Curious George*. Houghton Mifflin, 1973. A curious monkey is forever making trouble and creating havoc.

Slobodkina, Esphyr. *Caps for Sale*. HarperCollins, 1947. Monkeys steal a peddler's caps as he naps, and getting them back is a story of monkey see, monkey do.

Related Records and Tapes

Beall, Pamela Conn and Susan Hagen Nipp. "Three Little Monkeys" from *Wee Sing Children's Songs and Fingerplays*. Price Stern Sloan, 1979.

Sharon, Lois and Bram. "Five Little Monkeys" from *One Elephant, Deux Elephants*. Elephant Records, 1978.

Sharon, Lois and Bram. "Three Little Monkeys" from *Smorgasbord*. Elephant Records, 1980.

"Monkey Do" from *A Zippity Zoo Day*. Melody House.

10
▼▼▼▼▼▼▼▼▼▼▼▼▼

JUNE

Billy Boy
Down By the Bay
Kookaburra
Mister Moon
She Waded in the Water
Twinkle, Twinkle, Little Star

Billy Boy

Oh, where have you been, Billy Boy, Billy Boy?
Oh, where have you been, charming Billy?
I have been to seek a wife,
She's the joy of my life,
She's a young thing and cannot leave her mother.

Did she ask you to come in, Billy Boy, Billy Boy?
Did she ask you to come in, charming Billy?
Yes, she asked me to come in,
There's a dimple in her chin,
She's a young thing and cannot leave her mother.

Can she make a cherry pie, Billy Boy, Billy Boy?
Can she make a cherry pie, charming Billy?
She can make a cherry pie,
Quick as a cat can wink its eye,
She's a young thing and cannot leave her mother.

How old is she, Billy Boy, Billy Boy?
How old is she, charming Billy?
Three times six and four times seven,
Twenty-eight and eleven,
She's a young thing and cannot leave her mother.

Thematic Connections
Celebrations
Love

Things to Talk About
1. Why do you think someone wanted to know if she could bake a cherry pie?
2. How many candles do you think Billy's wife had on her cake?

Curriculum Extension
For Art: Making Aprons

Ages
3,4,5,6

Materials
Heavyweight napkins, crayons, stapler, ribbon, scissors

Procedure
1. The children use crayons to decorate the napkins.
2. Staple the napkins to two pieces of ribbon to form an apron.

3. The children use the aprons in the dramatic play center.

Developmental Bonus
Creative expression

Curriculum Extension
For Cooking: Fried Pies

Ages
3,4,5,6

Materials
Refrigerator biscuits, cherry pie filling, cooking oil, deep fryer, slotted spoon

Procedure
1. Give each child a biscuit.
2. Ask the children to press the biscuit flat, then place one tablespoon of pie filling on top.
3. The children then fold the biscuit in half and crimp edges together.
4. Use the slotted spoon to put the pies in the hot oil.

5. Fry for three minutes, turning over once.
6. Eat and enjoy.

Developmental Bonus
Measurement concepts
Fine motor development

Curriculum Extension
For Dramatic Play: Making Cherry Pies

Ages
3,4,5,6

Materials
Dough-colored playdough, red playdough, pie pans, rolling pin

Procedure
1. Provide materials for the children to make playdough cherry pies.
2. Use the dough-colored playdough for crust and roll red playdough into balls to make cherries.
3. The children can play pretend tea party with the pies.

Developmental Bonus
Fine motor development
Creative expression

Curriculum Extension
For Language: Alliteration

Ages
4,5,6

Materials
Chart tablet paper, crayons or markers

Procedure
1. Talk about the repetitive sounds in "Billy Boy."
2. Ask the children to think of other words they can put together that have the same beginning sounds, for example, Greta girl, Mother mine, Father fox, etc.

3. Invite children to think of alliterative words that go with their names, for example, terrific Tiffany, rosy Rich, wonderful Wally, etc.
4. Write the names on the tablet.

Developmental Bonus
Auditory discrimination

Curriculum Extension
For Science: Billy's Path

Ages
3,4,5,6

Materials
Masking tape, cookie sheet, tagboard or posterboard, scissors, glue, marker, washer, large magnet, tape

Procedure
1. Use masking tape to create a zig-zag path from one right-hand corner of the cookie sheet to a left-hand corner.
2. Cut a quarter-size circle from tagboard. Draw a face on one side of it and glue a washer to the other side.
3. Cut a second quarter-size circle from tagboard and draw a face on it. Tape this face to the end of the masking tape path on the left-hand side of the cookie sheet.
4. Encourage the children to use the large magnet to move the first face along the zigzag path to the second face.

Developmental Bonus
Coordination

Related Bibliography

Bauman, A. F. *Guess Where You're Going, Guess What You'll Do.* Houghton Mifflin, 1989. The reader is given a series of clues then asked "Where are you going? and "What will you do?"

Caseley, Judith. *Three Happy Birthdays.* Greenwillow, 1989. A description of three very different birthdays.

Kraus, Robert. *Where Are You Going, Little Mouse?* Greenwillow, 1986. A little mouse runs away because he feels unloved, but he returns at dark.

Chorao, Kay. *The Cherry Pie Baby.* Dutton, 1989. A little girl named Annie trades a cherry pie for baby Claude, then discovers that taking care of a baby isn't very easy.

Williams, Vera B. *Cherries and Cherry Pits.* Greenwillow, 1986. Four stories about people and cherries.

Related Records and Tapes

Jenkins, Ella. "No More Pie" from *Play Your Instruments and Make a Pretty Sound.* Folkways, 1968.

"Billy Boy" from *Sing-A-Long.* Peter Pan, 1987.

Down by the Bay

Down by the bay
Where the watermelons grow.
Back to my home
I dare not go.
For if I do
My mother will say,
"Did you ever see a bear combing his hair?"
Down by the bay.

Suggestions: Sing the song again using bee with a sunburned knee, moose kissing a goose, whale with a polka dot tail, etc.

Curriculum Extension

Thematic Connections
Summer
Water
Animals

Curriculum Extension

Things to Talk About
1. Make up more verses to the song.
2. How many ways can you get across the bay?

Curriculum Extension

For Art: Sun Visors

Ages
3, 4, 5, 6

Materials
Paper plates, scissors, crayons, stapler

Procedure
1. Cut the center out of a paper plate, keeping the rim in one piece.
2. Cut the center in half.
3. The children decorate one-half of the center.
4. Staple the decorated half of the center onto the rim of the plate to create a sun visor.

Developmental Bonus
Creative expression

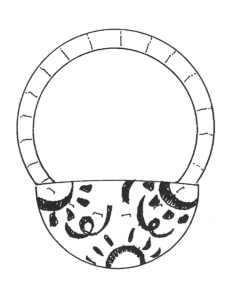

For Cooking: Watermelon Freezes

Ages
3,4,5,6

Materials
Watermelon, grape juice, water, blender, measuring cups, paper cups, popsicle sticks

Procedure
1. In a blender, mix 1 cup of seedless watermelon, 1 cup of grape juice and 1 cup of water.
2. Pour into paper cups. Stick a popsicle stick in each cup and freeze.
3. Eat and enjoy.

Developmental Bonus
Measurement concepts
Change-of-state concept

For Dramatic Play: Picnic

Ages
3,4,5

Materials
Picnic basket with dishes, tablecloth and pretend foods

Procedure
1. Encourage the children to plan and carry out a pretend picnic.

Developmental Bonus
Creative thinking

For Math: Watermelon Seed Count

Ages
4,5,6

Materials
Green, dark pink and black construction paper; scissors

Procedure
1. Make a watermelon by cutting green construction paper into slices and then overlapping with pink.
2. Cut the black construction paper into watermelon seeds.
3. Write the numerals 1 to 5 on the slices.
4. Encourage the children to count the appropriate number of seeds onto each slice of watermelon.

Developmental Bonus
Numeral recognition
Counting

For Science: Liquid Experiments

Ages
3,4,5,6

Materials
Three baby food jars, corn syrup, water, cooking oil, three marbles, glue

Procedure
1. Fill each jar with one of the clear substances. Put a marble in each jar and seal the lids with glue.
2. Let the children turn the jars upside down and see which marble falls to the bottom of the jar first.

Developmental Bonus
Observation
Concept development

Related Bibliography

McMillan, Bruce. *One Sun: A Book of Terse Verse*. Holiday House, 1990. Two-word rhyming poems about a day at the shore accompanied by full page color photographs.

Marshall, Edward. *Three By the Sea*. Dial, 1981. Lolly, spider and Sam lie on the beach and each attempts to create the perfect story.

Raffi. *Down By the Bay*. Crown, 1988. A storybook that illustrates the song with Raffi's special touch.

Robbins, Ken. *Beach Days*. Viking, 1987. Real photos and simple text depict what people do at the beach on a typical day.

Samton, Sheila White. *Beside the Bay*. Philomel, 1987. Seashore colors and creatures are introduced in simple rhyming text and bright illustrations.

Related Records and Tapes

Beall, Pamela Conn and Susan Hagen Nipp. "Down by the Bay" from *Wee Sing Silly Songs*. Price Stern Sloan, 1986.

Raffi. "Down By the Bay" from *Singable Songs for the Very Young*. Shoreline, 1988.

Kookaburra

Kookaburra sits in the old gum tree-ee.
Merry, merry king of the bush is hee-ee.
Laugh, Kookaburra, laugh, Kookaburra,
Gay your life must be.

Kookaburra, sits in the old gum tree-ee.
Eating all the gumdrops he can see-ee.
Stop, Kookaburra, stop, Kookaburra,
Leave a few for me.

Thematic Connections
Australia
Birds

Things to Talk About
1. What is a kookaburra? (Kookaburra, actually kookle-berry, is a bird that lives in the bush in Australia. The favorite nesting place for kookaburras is a tree known in Australia as a gum tree.)

2. The gumdrops in the song are special berries that grow on Australian gum trees, not gumdrops that we know as candy.

Curriculum Extension
For Fine Motor: Pass the Gumdrop

Ages
3,4,5,6

Materials
A clothespin for each child, one 4-inch gumdrop cut from posterboard

Procedure
1. Distribute a clothespin to each child. Show the children how the clothespins resemble the beak of a bird.

2. Sit in a circle. Ask the children to pass the gumdrop using the clothespins.

Developmental Bonus
Coordination
Fine motor development

Curriculum Extension
For Language: Patterning

Ages
4,5,6

Materials
Construction paper, scissors, small styrofoam beads, glue, paint, paintbrushes

Procedure
1. Make large colored gumdrops by cutting gumdrop shapes from construction paper, painting them with glue

and sprinkling with small sty-rofoam beads.

2. Encourage the children to create color patterns with gum-drops.

3. Paint the gumdrops when the glue is dry.

Developmental Bonus
Patterning

Curriculum Extension

For Math: Counting Gumdrops

Ages
4,5,6

Materials
Sealable plastic bags, candy gumdrops

Procedure
1. Draw a vertical line down the center of each plastic bag.

2. Print a numeral 1 to 5 on each bag.

3. Place the appropriate num-ber of gumdrops in each bag.

4. Encourage children to ma-nipulate the gumdrops in the bags to explore number families.

Developmental Bonus
Number concepts

Curriculum Extension

For Outdoors: Coconut Shell Relay

Ages
3,4,5,6

Materials
14 cups

Procedure
1. Explain to the children that this is an Australian game. In Australia children play the game with coconut shells.

2. Divide the class into two teams. Each team stands in a line.

3. Give the first child on each team seven cups.

4. When you say "start," the first child in line should begin passing the cups one at a time.

5. The team who finishes passing all the cups first is the winner.

Developmental Bonus
Coordination

Curiculum Extension

For Science: Australian Animals

Ages
3,4,5,6

Materials
Magazine pictures or book photos of animals indigenous to Australia (koala bear, kooka-burra, kangaroo, wombat)

Procedure
1. Fill the science center with pictures of animals that live in Australia.

2. Talk about the climate these animals live in and talk about what each animal eats.

3. Leave the pictures out so the children can examine them.

Developmental Bonus
Observation skills

Related Bibliography

Cox, David. *Bossyboots*. Crown, 1988. A small, bossy girl from old Australia named Abigail saves her fellow stagecoach passengers from dangerous desperados.

Fox, Mem. *Koala Lou*. Harcourt Brace Jovanovich, 1989. A young koala trying to get her mother's attention enters a gum tree race and plans to win. The kookaburra starts the race and a lesson on competition is woven into this story about a mother's love.

Payne, Emmy. *Katy No Pocket*. Houghton Mifflin, 1973. A kangaroo worries about having no pocket for her baby, but her friends help her find a solution.

Schlein, Miriam. *Big Talk*. Bradbury Press, 1990. Little Kangaroo keeps boasting of all he can be but is still very reassured by his mother's confirmation.

Vaughan, Marcia K. *Wombat Stew*. Silver Burdett. 1984. An outback Australian dingo attempts to make wombat stew but is tricked into setting the wombat free. This book is filled with Australian animals.

Related Records and Tapes

Beall, Pamela Conn and Susan Hagen Nipp. "Kookaburra" from *Wee Sing Sing-Alongs*. Price Stern Sloan, 1990.

Mister Moon

O Mister Moon, Moon,
Bright and shiny Moon,
Won't you please
Shine down on me.

O Mister Moon, Moon,
Bright and shiny Moon,
Won't you please
Set me fancy free.

I'd like to linger
But I've got to run,
Mama's callin'
"Baby, get your homework done!"

O Mister Moon, Moon,
Bright and shiny Moon,
Won't you please
Shine down on,
Talk about your shine on,
Please shine down on me.

Thematic Connections

Moon
Nature

Things to Talk About

1. Have you ever thought the moon was following you?
2. Where does the moon go at night?

Curriculum Extension

For Art: Night Pictures

Ages

3,4,5,6

Materials

12 x 18-inch pieces of black or blue construction paper, silver and white tempera paint, paint-brushes

Procedure

1. Encourage the children to create a night picture using the light colors of tempera paints on the dark construction paper.
2. Splatters will make nice stars.

Developmental Bonus

Creative expression

Curriculum Extension

For Cooking: Moon Candy

Ages

3,4,5,6

Materials

Evaporated milk, margarine, confectioners sugar, mixing bowl and spoon, green food coloring, sifter, measuring cups

Procedure

1. Mix 1/3 cup of evaporated milk, 1/2 cup margarine and 2 1/2 cups of sifted confectioner's sugar in a bowl.
2. Add just a touch of green food coloring to create a pale green.
3. Form into round patterns with the children.
4. Eat and enjoy!

Developmental Bonus

Measurement

For Gross Motor: Moon Toss

Ages
3,4,5,6

Materials
Three pingpong balls, one circular piece of white felt (15 inches in diameter), felt pen, Velcro, glue

Procedure
1. Draw a face on the moon (white felt circle) using a felt pen.
2. Glue Velcro to the pingpong balls.
3. Invite the children to throw the balls at the "man in the moon" and attempt to hit him in the nose. (The ball will stick to the felt.)

Developmental Bonus
Hand-eye coordination

For Language: Mr. Moon

Ages
3,4,5,6

Materials
White paper plates, crayons, pen, tongue depressor or popsicle stick, stapler

Procedure
1. Give each child a paper plate. Discuss the similar shape of the plate and a full moon.
2. Ask the children what they like best about the moon.
3. Encourage the children to illustrate their thoughts on their paper plate moons.
4. Invite the children to dictate descriptions of their pictures and transcribe them onto the backs of the plates.
5. Staple the plates onto a tongue depressor, and let children use their puppet moons when they sing "Mister Moon."

Developmental Bonus
Creative expression

For Math: Moon Sequence

Ages
4,5,6

Materials
Three pieces of white construction paper, scissors

Procedure
1. Cut three moons (circles) from white construction paper.
2. Cut one moon in half and discard one of the halves.
3. Cut another moon to create 3/4 and 1/4 sections.
4. The children place the moons in size order from 1/4 to 1/2 to 3/4 to full.

Developmental Bonus
Seriation
Concept development

Related Bibliography

Asch, Frank. *Happy Birthday Moon.* Simon & Schuster, 1988. Bear is convinced the moon is talking to him but it's really his own echo.

Asch, Frank. *Moongame.* Simon & Schuster, 1987. Bear plays hide and seek with the moon.

Carle, Eric. *Papa, Please Get the Moon for Me.* Picture Book Studio, 1991. When Monica asks for the moon, her father takes along a ladder and gets it.

Dayrell, Elphinstone. *Why the Sun and Moon Live in the Sky.* Houghton Mifflin, 1990. An African folktale that explains the phenomenon of the sky.

McDermott, Gerald. *Anansi the Spider: A Tale from the Ashanti.* Henry Holt, 1972. West African story from Ghana about Anansi's six talented sons and how the moon came to be.

Related Records and Tapes

Scelsa, Greg and Steve Millang. "Nocturne" from *We All Live Together*, Vol. 3, Youngheart, 1979.

"By the Light of the Silvery Moon" from *Sing-A-Long.* Peter Pan, 1987.

She Waded in the Water

Tune: "Battle Hymn of the Republic"

She waded in the water,
And she got her feet all wet,
She waded in the water,
And she got her feet all wet,
But she didn't get her (clap, clap) wet,
(clap) yet. (clap)

Chorus:
Glory, glory, hallelujah!
Glory, glory, hallelujah!
Glory, glory, hallelujah!
But she didn't get her (clap, clap) wet,
(clap) yet. (clap)

She waded in the water,
And she got her ankles wet,
She waded in the water,
And she got her ankles wet,
But she didn't get her (clap, clap) wet,
(clap) yet. (clap)

(Chorus)
She waded in the water,
And she got her knees all wet,
She waded in the water,
And she got her knees all wet,
But she didn't get her (clap, clap) wet,
(clap) yet. (clap)

(Chorus)

She waded in the water,
And she got her thighs all wet,
She waded in the water,
And she got her thighs all wet,
But she didn't get her (clap, clap) wet,
(clap) yet. (clap)

(Chorus)

She waded in the water,
And she finally got it wet,
She waded in the water,
And she finally got it wet,
She finally got her bathing suit wet!

Thematic Connections
Summer
Beach
Water

Things to Talk About
1. Name some places where we can wade in the water.
2. What other parts of the body didn't get wet if the bathing suit wasn't wet?

Curriculum Extension

For Art: Squirt Bottle Art

Ages
3,4,5,6

Materials
Squirt bottles, tempera paint, butcher paper, tape

Procedure
1. Fill the squirt bottles with tempera paint.
2. Tape a piece of butcher paper on a fence or side of the building.

3. Let the children squirt tempera paint onto the butcher paper.

Developmental Bonus
Creative expression
Fine motor development

Curriculum Extension
For Dramatic Play: Washing Clothes

Ages
3,4,5,6

Materials
Doll clothes, washtub, soap, clothespins, clothesline

Procedure
1. Bring all the material outdoors and encourage the children to wash doll clothes from the dramatic play center.
2. Hang clothes to dry.

Developmental Bonus
Concept development

Curriculum Extension
For Gross Motor: Balloon Toss

Ages
3,4,5,6

Materials
Balloons, water, laundry basket or box

Procedure
1. Go outside with the children. Fill the balloons with water and tie.
2. Toss the balloons into laundry basket or box.
3. Be sure to pick up the balloon pieces since it can be dangerous if children pick them up and put them in their mouths.

Developmental Bonus
Coordination

Curriculum Extension
For Math: Wading Pool

Ages
3,4,5,6

Materials
Wading pool, measuring cups, measuring spoons, pots, funnels

Procedure
1. Fill the wading pool with water and let the children experiment pouring water into various pans.
2. They can count the number of cups of water that can be poured into various containers.

Developmental Bonus
Measurement concepts
Counting

Curriculum Extension
For Science: Bubbles, Bubbles, Bubbles

Ages
3,4,5,6

Materials
Straws, scissors, dishwashing soap, water, glycerine, measuring cup and spoon, bowl

Procedure
1. Cut four vertical 1-inch slits in one end of the plastic straws.
2. Mix 1/2 cup of dishwashing soap, 1/2 cup of water and 1 tablespoon of glycerine in a bowl.
3. Encourage the children to blow bubbles.
4. Fill the playground with bubbles by gently blowing or fanning.

Developmental Bonus
Air concepts

Related Bibliography

Hughes, Shirley. *Alfie's Feet.* Lothrop, 1983. Alfie loves to splash through puddles, so his mom buys him a pair of new boots.

Hughes, Shirley. *An Evening at Alfie's.* Lothrop, 1985. A pipe bursts in the ceiling, making puddles all over the floor.

Munsch, Robert. *Mud Puddle.* Annick, 1982. Each time a little girl puts on clean clothes, a mud puddle attacks her.

Palmer, Helen. *A Fish Out of Water.* Random House, 1961. An overfed fish outgrows his fish bowl and continues to need a bigger and bigger place to live.

Samton, Sheila White. *Beside the Bay.* Philomel, 1987. Rhyme is used to introduce seashore colors and creatures one at a time during a walk along the shore.

Related Records and Tapes

Beall, Pamela Conn and Susan Hagen Nipp. "She Waded in the Water" from *Wee Sing Silly Songs.* Price Stern Sloan, 1986.

Twinkle, Twinkle, Little Star

Twinkle, twinkle little star,
How I wonder what you are.
Up above the world so high,
Like a diamond in the sky.
Twinkle, twinkle little star,
How I wonder what you are.

Thematic Connections
Nature
Up, Down and All Around

Things to Talk About
1. Why do the stars stay in the sky? What keeps them from falling?
2. Why do we see stars some nights but not others?
3. The person who wrote the song compared the star to a diamond. Can you think of other things a star might look like?

Curriculum Extension
For Art: Star Designs

Ages
3, 4,5

Materials
Drawing paper, crayons, star templates cut from cardboard

Procedure
1. Provide the children with the star shapes cut from cardboard.

2. Encourage the children to use the star shapes as templates. As they trace around them, have them move the shapes around and even trace on top of already traced stars.
3. Changing colors of crayons used will add an interesting dimension.

Developmental Bonus
Creative expression

Curriculum Extension
For Gross Motor: Which Shapes Roll?

Ages
4,5,6

Materials
Cardboard stars, circles and squares

Procedure
1. Cut cardboard stars, circles and squares.

2. Encourage the children to experiment with the shapes, figuring out which ones roll and which ones will not roll.

Developmental Bonus
Critical thinking

Curriculum Extension

For Language: Star Wishes

Ages
4,5,6

Materials
Paper stars, pencil

Procedure
1. Ask the children to think about a wish they would make on a star.
2. The children dictate their wishes and record them on paper stars.
3. Use for bulletin board decorations.

Developmental Bonus
Creative expression
Creative thinking

Curriculum Extension

For Math: Sorting

Ages
3,4, 5

Materials
Construction paper, scissors

Procedure
1. Cut stars of different sizes and colors.
2. The children sort the stars by color and by size.

Developmental Bonus
Visual discrimination

Curriculum Extension

For Science: Constellations

Ages
5,6

Materials
Pictures or photographs of stars in the sky from magazines or reference books, black or blue construction paper, gummed stars

Procedure
1. Show the children pictures or photographs of stars. Describe how some groups of stars look like certain objects, for example, Big Dipper, Little Dipper, etc.
2. Encourage the children to arrange the gummed stars on a piece of paper to form objects of their choice.
3. Older children can copy star constellations.

Developmental Bonus
Concept development
Creative expression

Related Bibliography

Berger, Barbara Helen. *Grandfather Twilight*. Philomel, 1984. A peaceful bedtime story. Grandfather Twilight spreads dusk, shadows, and brings the moon to night.

Dayrell, Elphinstone. *Why the Sun and Moon Live in the Sky*. Houghton-Mifflin, 1990. An African folktale explaining why the moon and the sun are in the sky.

Hines, Anna Grossnickle. *Sky All Around*. Clarion, 1989. A young girl and her father hike to a nearby hilltop where they watch the sun set and the stars appear.

Meigs, Mildred Plew. *Moon Song*. Morrow, 1990. A reprint of the 1923 version. The man in the moon watches over the night sky.

Related Records and Tapes

Beall, Pamela Conn and Susan Hagen Nipp. "Twinkle, Twinkle, Little Star" from *Wee Sing Children's Songs and Fingerplays*. Price Stern Sloan, 1979.

Moore, Thomas. *Opera Singer*, ("Twinkle, Twinkle, Little Star") from *Singing, Moving and Learning*. Thomas Moore Records.

Sharon, Lois and Bram. "Starlight" from *One Elephant, Deux Elephants*. Elephant, 1978.

"Twinkle, Twinkle, Little Star" from Sing-A-Long. Peter Pan, 1987.

JULY

Yankeee Doodle
The Grand Old Duke of York
A-Hunting We Will Go
The Ants Go Marching
Do Your Ears Hang Low?
Humpty Dumpty

Yankee Doodle

Father and I went down to camp
Along with Captain Gooding,
And there we saw the men and boys
As thick as hasty puddin'.

Chorus:
Yankee Doodle keep it up,
Yankee Doodle Dandy,
Mind the music and the step,
And with the girls be handy.

And there was Captain Washington
Upon a strappin' stallion,
And all the men and boys around,
I guess there was a million.

(Chorus)

Yankee Doodle went to town
Ridin' on a pony,
Stuck a feather in his cap
And called it macaroni.

(Chorus)

Thematic Connections
Holidays
Fourth of July
Patriotism

Things to Talk About
1. Yankee Doodle went to town on a pony. How do you get to town?
2. What does "thick as hasty puddin'" mean?

Curriculum Extension
For Art: Hand Print Flags

Ages
3,4,5,6

Materials
Red, white and blue tempera paint; large easel paper; three pie tins

Procedure
1. Put one color of tempera paint in each of the pie tins.
2. Allow the children to select a color.
3. The children use their hand prints to make a flag on the easel paper. Those who choose blue make a hand print in the upper left corner of the paper.
4. Those who choose red and white make hand print stripes.

Developmental Bonus
Concept development
Creative expression

Curriculum Extension
For Cooking: Red, White and Blue Salad

Ages
3,4,5,6

Materials
Strawberries, marshmallows, blueberries, whipped topping, mixing bowl and spoon, bowls and spoons

Procedure
1. With the children, wash the strawberries and blueberries. Mix them up in a bowl.

2. Add marshmallows, and stir in whipped topping.

3. Eat and enjoy!

Developmental Bonus

Concept development

Curriculum Extension

For Creative Movement: Patriotic Parade

Ages

3,4,5,6

Materials

Paper towel tubes; red, white and blue crepe paper streamers; tape; recording of march music

Procedure

1. The children tape 18-inch strips of red, white and blue crepe paper to a paper towel tube.

2. Play a patriotic march record and let the children march and wave their patriotic batons.

Developmental Bonus

Large muscle development

Curriculum Extension

For Fine Motor: Macaroni Sort

Ages

4,5,6

Materials

Jars, macaroni, alcohol, tablespoon, red and blue food coloring, paper towels, three small bowls, tweezers

Procedure

1. Dye macaroni by placing a cup of dry macaroni in a jar with two tablespoons of alcohol and enough red food coloring to create a rich color.

2. Shake the macaroni and dump on paper towels to dry. Repeat this process with the blue food coloring. Use undyed macaroni for white.

3. Mix the red, blue and white macaroni together.

4. Invite the children to use tweezers to sort the three colors of macaroni into bowls or onto separate pieces of paper towel.

Developmental Bonus

Fine motor development
Classification

Curriculum Extension

For Language: Fireworks Stories

Ages

3,4,5,6

Materials

Several colors of tempera paint, straws, scissors, paper, pencils, teaspoon

Procedure

1. Cut drinking straw in half and provide a half-straw for each child.

2. Spoon a teaspoon of liquid tempera onto the paper and encourage the children to blow through the straw to move the paint in streaks across the paper.

3. The result should look like fireworks.

4. Encourage the children to describe their pictures, then transcribe their description onto their artwork.

Developmental Bonus

Written communication

Related Bibliography

Bangs, Edward. *Yankee Doodle.* Macmillan, 1989. A richly illustrated story using the song as a theme.

Brown, Marcia. *Stone Soup.* Macmillan, 1979. A folktale about how three soldiers outwit some selfish villagers and everyone profits.

Kherdian, David and Nonny Hogrogian. *The Cat's Midsummer Jamboree.* philomel, 1990. A roaming mandolin-playing cat encounters a number of other musical animals on his travels, and the result is a jamboree in a tree.

Spier, Peter. *Crash! Bang! Boom!*Doubleday, 1990. A colorful parade with marching and all the sound effects.

Van Rynbach, Iris. *The Soup Stone.* Greenwillow, 1988. Revolutionary war soldier outsmarts a village of selfish people and everyone profits.

Related Records and Tapes

Weissman, Jackie. "Yankee Doodle" from *Miss Jackie and Her Friends Sing About Peanut Butter, Tarzan and Roosters.* Miss Jackie, 1981.

"Yankee Doodle" from *Sing-A-Long.* Peter Pan, 1987.

The Grand Old Duke of York

Tune: "Farmer in the Dell"

The grand old Duke of York
He had ten thousand men,
He marched them up to the top of the hill,
And he marched them down again.
And when they're up, they're up,
And when they're down, they're down,
But when they're half way up,
They're neither up nor down.

Directions: The children sit when they begin the song, stand on the word "up," then squat on the word "down." On "half way up," they stoop down. They stand on the last line of the song, then jump high and clap their hands over their heads.

Thematic Connections
Patriotism

Things to Talk About
1. Do you think the Duke's men were more tired going up the hill or down the hill?
2. How many is ten thousand? (Show ten fingers, open and close them 10 times). Explain to the children that 10,000 is a lot of men. It is 10 times and 10 times again what you have just shown them. The idea is to convey that 10,000 is a lot, not to teach number concepts.

Curriculum Extension
For Art: Paper Hats

Ages
3, 4, 5

Materials
16 x 20-inch sheets of newspaper; red, white and blue paint; sponges; meat trays

Procedure
1. Fold paper in half, short end to short end.
2. Fold the top corners down and over to the center.
3. Fold the bottom of the hat up as shown.
4. The children dip sponges into the paint and decorate their hats with paint.

Developmental Bonus
Creative expression

For Creative Movement: Marching

Ages
3,4,5

Materials
March music

Procedure
1. Encourage the children to march to the music.
2. If hills are available outdoors, march up and down the hill.

Developmental Bonus
Coordination
Large muscle development

For Math: Half

Ages
3,4,5

Materials
Construction paper, scissors

Procedure
1. Cut construction paper into circles, squares, rectangles and triangles.
2. The children fold the shapes in half and then cut them with scissors.
3. Then they can put the shapes back together.

Developmental Bonus
Concept development
Fine motor development

For Outdoors: Up/Down Moves

Ages
3,4,5

Materials
Twenty index cards, marking pen

Procedure
1. Draw one arrow on each index card, so that the arrows on ten cards point up and the arrows on the other ten point down.
2. Shuffle the cards.
3. Use the cards like flash cards and have children stand up or sit down as directed by the cards.

Developmental Bonus
Visual discrimination
Large muscle development

For Science: Up and Down Machines

Ages
3,4,5,6

Materials
Pulley, basket, rope, hook

Procedure
1. Attach a pulley to the ceiling with a hook. Run a rope through the pulley.
2. Tie the basket to one end of the rope and anchor the other end of the rope by tying it to a table or chair.
3. The children use the pulley to raise and lower the basket.
4. Try putting blocks in the basket. Talk about how the pulley helps make work easier.

Developmental Bonus
Concept development

Related Bibliography

Anno, Mitsumasa. *Upside-Downers: More Pictures to Stretch the Imagination*. Putnam, 1988.   Great illustrations and rhymes about up and down.

Brown, Marcia. *Stone Soup*. Macmillan, 1979. A folktale about how three soldiers outwit some selfish villagers and everyone profits.

Hughes, Shirley. *Up and Up*. Lothrop, 1986. A little girl imagines she can fly, and after several attempts, she does.

Spier, Peter. *Crash! Bang! Boom!*Doubleday, 1990. A colorful parade with marching and all the sound effects.

West, Colin. *"Pardon?" Said the Giraffe*. HarperCollins, 1986. A lively frog wonders what it's like to see the world from a giraffe's point of view "way up there."

Related Records and Tapes

Palmer, Hap. *Mod Marches*. Activity Records, 1965.

Moore, Thomas. "I Am Special March" from *I Am Special*. Thomas Moore Records.

A-Hunting We Will Go

Oh a-hunting we will go,
A-hunting we will go,
We'll catch a little fox,
And put him in a box,
And then we'll let him go.

Thematic Connections
Animals
Foxes

Things to Talk About
1. What other things might we put in a box? What can we do with a fox?
2. What would a fox put us in if he caught us?

Curriculum Extension
For Art: Special Box

Ages
3,4,5, 6

Materials
One shoe box for each child, scissors, wallpaper scraps, construction paper, tempera paint, ribbons, buttons, glitter, glue, leaves, etc.

Procedure
1. Allow the children to decorate their special box using the paints and other materials available.
2. Ask them what they will keep in their boxes.

Developmental Bonus
Creative expression

Curriculum Extension
For Gross Motor: Box Toss

Ages
3,4,5,6

Materials
Beanbags, box

Procedure
1. Encourage the children to toss beanbags into a box.
2. Younger children can stand close to the box and older children farther away.

Developmental Bonus
Large muscle development
Hand-eye coordination

For Language: Word Substitution

Ages
4,5,6

Materials
Chart tablet paper, crayons or markers

Procedure
1. Ask the children to think of words to substitute for fox and box, for example, "We'll catch a fish and put it in a dish and then..."
2. Try bear/chair, snake/lake, etc.
3. Write the words on the chart tablet.

Developmental Bonus
Auditory discrimination

For Math: Boxes and Boxes

Ages
3,4,5,6

Materials
Boxes, ranging in size from a match box to an appliance box

Procedure
1. The children arrange the boxes from smallest to largest and from largest to smallest.
2. Try fitting one box into another.
3. Guess how many of the smaller boxes will fit into the largest. Let the children try it and see if they were right.

Developmental Bonus
Sequencing

For Outdoors: Fox Hunt

Ages
3,4,5,6

Materials
Picture of a fox

Procedure
1. Hide the picture of a fox outside.
2. Make up a series of clues that lead to the fox.
3. The children listen to the clues while on this "fox hunt."

Developmental Bonus
Critical thinking

Related Bibliography

Browne, Anthony. *Bear Hunt.* Atheneum, 1979. A bear foils two hunters when he draws escape routes with his trusty pencil.

Dr. Seuss. *Thidwick, the Big-Hearted Moose.* Random House, 1948. While looking for nice tender moose moss munch, Thidwick doesn't mind giving a bug a ride until the bug invites all his free-loading friends to come aboard.

Gomi, Taro. *The Big Book of Boxes.* Chronicle Books, 1991. Easy to follow directions and patterns can be transferred into beautiful boxes in minutes.

Jeffers, Susan. *The Three Jovial Huntsmen.* Aladdin, 1989. Three incompetent huntsmen make their way through a shadowy forest, and the calm and serenely confident animals elude the blundering strangers.

Rosen, Michael. *We're Going On a Bear Hunt.* McElderry Books, 1989. Looking for a bear is fun for Dad and four kids until one is found.

Related Records and Tapes

Beall, Pamela Conn and Susan Hagen Nipp. "A Hunting We Will Go" from *Wee Sing Nursery Rhymes and Lullabies.* Price Stern Sloan, 1985.

Sharon, Lois and Bram."Bear Hunt" from *Circle Around.* Tickle Tune Typhoon, 1983.

The Ants Go Marching

The ants go marching one by one,
Hurrah, hurrah.
The ants go marching one by one,
Hurrah, hurrah.
The ants go marching one by one,
The little one stops to suck his thumb,
And they all go marching down
Into ground to get out of the rain,
BOOM! BOOM! BOOM!

Two...tie his shoe...
Three...climb a tree...
Four...shut the door...
Five...take a dive...
Six...pick up sticks...
Seven...pray to heaven...
Eight...shut the gate...
Nine...check the time...
Ten...say "THE END"

Thematic Connections
Ants
Insects

Things to Talk About
1. Where do the ants go when it rains?
2. Describe the ants you've seen. Have you ever seen ants moving in a straight line? What happens when you disturb an ant hill?

Curriculum Extension
For Art: Thumb Print Ants

Ages
3,4,5

Materials
Ink pad, markers, paper

Procedure
1. Show the children how to create an ant by making three connected thumb prints and then to use a marker to add details—six legs, antennas, etc.

Developmental Bonus
Creative expression

Curriculum Extension
For Cooking: Ants on a Log

Ages
3,4,5,6

Materials
Celery, peanut butter, raisins

Procedure
1. The children spread peanut butter on celery to create a log.
2. Place raisins on the peanut butter to look like ants.
3. Yum!

Developmental Bonus
Creative expression
Symbolic representation

For Language: Rhyming Words Match

Ages
4,5,6

Materials
Pictures of items that rhyme, index cards with the numbers 1-10 written on them

Procedure
1. Talk about the rhyming words in the song.
2. Ask the children to match pictures of items that rhyme.
3. If pictures can be found of items mentioned in the song, for example, shoe, gate, door, have children match pictures to the correct numeral card.

Developmental Bonus
Auditory discrimination
Numeral recognition

For Outdoors: Nature's Cleanup Crew

Ages
3,4,5

Materials
Chicken bones

Procedure
1. Place chicken bones with a little bit of meat remaining on the ground outside and watch.
2. Ants will come and, in a very short time, will strip the bones clean.

Developmental Bonus
Concept development

For Science: Ant Watch

Ages
3,4,5,6

Materials
Large jar, shovel, pictures of ant life underground

Procedure
1. Place the pictures of ant life in the science area of the classroom.
2. Pick up an ant hill with a shovel and place it in a jar. Try to capture the queen who will be deep in the hole.
3. Place the jar in the classroom for observation.
4. Feed the ants pieces of bread or other table scraps.
5. Place the ants back outside when the class is finished studying them.

Developmental Bonus
Concept development
Observation

Related Bibliography

Dorros, Arthur. *Ant Cities*. Crowell, 1987. Wonderful illustrations show how ants build their nests and run their empires.

Myrick, Mildred. *Ants Are Fun*. Harper, 1968. A close up look at ants—how they work and how they increase their population.

Parker, Nancy Winslow and Joan Richards Wright. *Bugs*. William Morrow, 1987. An unusual collection of rhymes and scientific information about bugs.

Peet, Bill. *The Ant and the Elephant*. Houghton Mifflin, 1980. After an ant rescues an elephant, the elephant returns the favor.

Sage, James. *The Little Band*. Margaret K. McElderry Books, 1991. A little band marches through town delighting everyone with its beautiful music.

Related Records and Tapes

Beall, Pamela Conn and Susan Hagen Nipp. "The Ants Go Marching" from *Wee Sing Silly Songs*. Price Stern Sloan, 1986.

Moore, Thomas. "When the Kids Go Marching In" from *The Family*. Thomas Moore Records.

Palmer, Hap. "Ants" from *Pretend*. Educational Activities.

Palmer, Hap. *Mod Marchers*. Activity Records, 1965.

Do Your Ears Hang Low?

Tune: "Turkey in the Straw"

Do your ears hang low?
Do they wobble to and fro?
Can you tie 'em in a knot?
Can you tie 'em in a bow?
Can you throw 'em o'er your shoulder
Like a continental soldier?
Do your ears hang low?

Motions:

ears hang low—place back of hands on ears, fingers down

wobble to and fro—sway fingers

tie 'em in a knot—tie large knot in air

tie 'em in a bow—draw bow in air with both hands

throw o'er shoulders—throw both hands over left shoulder

Continental soldier—salute

ears hang low—place back of hands on ears, fingers down

Thematic Connections

Me, Myself and I
Patriotism

Things to Talk About

1. What does it mean to ask "do your ears hang low"?
2. Can you think of some animals that have long ears?

Curriculum Extension

For Art: Big Ears

Ages
3, 4, 5, 6

Materials
Construction paper, posterboard, markers, scissors

Procedure
1. Use posterboard to cut patterns for several pairs of odd-shaped long ears.
2. Make the patterns so that the large ears can hook over the top of a child's ear.
3. The children select a pattern and trace a pair of ears.
4. The children cut out their ears and hook them over their ears.

Developmental Bonus
Creative expression
Fine motor development
Hand-eye coordination

Curriculum Extension

For Creative Movement: Marching

Ages
3, 4, 5, 6

Materials
Ears from the art activity, recording of march music

Procedure
1. Play the music and let the children march around the room or playground wearing their ears.

Developmental Bonus
Rhythm
Large muscle development

For Fine Motor: Tying

Ages
4,5,6

Materials
Manilla folder, marker, stapler, yarn or ribbon, optional—hole punch

Procedure
1. Draw a shoe shape on each side of an open manilla folder.
2. Staple yarn or ribbon to the shoes and let the children practice tying a bow.
3. For older children, punch hole to lace the yarn or ribbon before tying it in a bow.

Developmental Bonus
Hand-eye coordination
Concept development

For Science: Low/High

Ages
3,4,5,6

Materials
Eight identical containers (glasses or bottles), water, ruler, spoon

Procedure
1. Fill the containers (glasses or bottles) with water in one inch increments, for example, glass number one has 1 inch of water, glass number two has 2 inches of water, glass number three has 3 inches of water, etc.
2. The children use the spoon to tap the containers and see if the resulting sound is high or low.
3. Invite the children to experiment with various water levels.

Developmental Bonus
Concept development
Auditory discrimination

For Social Studies: Long Ears

Ages
3,4,5

Materials
Pictures of animals including an elephant, dog (a cocker would be great), cat, rabbit, mule, horse, etc.

Procedure
1. The children separate the animal pictures into the categories of those animals that have long ears and those that have short ears.

Developmental Bonus
Concept development

Related Bibliography

Aardema, Verna. *Why Mosquitoes Buzz in People's Ears: A West African Tale.. Dial, 1975.* A West African cumulative tale about the events in nature that lead to the mosquito buzzing in people's ears.

Brown, Marcia. *Stone Soup.* Macmillan, 1979. A folktale about how three soldiers outwit some selfish villagers and everyone profits.

Herford, Oliver. *The Most Timid in the Land: A Bunny Romance.* Chronicle Books, 1992. A traditional fairy tale set in an imaginary medieval bunny kingdom with knights that are bunnies and a very non-traditional princess.

Kraus, Robert. *Daddy Long Ears.* Simon and Schuster, 1989. Daddy Long Ears serves as both mother and father to 32 bunnies and discovers an Easter tradition in the process.

Van Rynbach, Iris. *The Soup Stone.* Greenwillow, 1988. Revolutionary war soldier outsmarts a village of selfish people and everyone profits.

Related Records and Tapes

Beall, Pamela Conn and Susan Hagen Nipp. "Do Your Ears Hang Low?" from *Wee Sing Silly Songs.* Price Stern Sloan, 1986.

Moore, Thomas. "High/Low" and "I Am Special March" from *I Am Special.* Thomas Moore Records.

Moore, Thomas. "When the Kids Go Marching" from *The Family.* Thomas Moore Records.

Palmer, Hap. *Mod Marches.* Activity Records, 1965.

Sharon, Lois and Bram. "Do Your Ears Hang Low" from *Stay Tuned.* A&M, 1987.

Humpty Dumpty

Humpty Dumpty sat on a wall,
Humpty Dumpty had a great fall;
All the King's horses and all the King's men
Couldn't put Humpty together again.

Thematic Connections
Nursery Rhymes

Things to Talk About
1. What do you think made Humpty Dumpty fall off the wall?
2. What do you think the king's men used to try to hold Humpty Dumpty together? Super glue? Tape?

Curriculum Extension
For Art: Dress Me Dumpties

Ages
3, 4,5,6

Materials
Tagboard or posterboard, scissors, black construction paper, tissue paper, wallpaper, glue

Procedure
1. Cut egg shapes (ovals) from tagboard.
2. Cut black construction paper into strips. Ask the children to fold these strips accordion style.
3. Allow the children to glue the folded construction paper pieces onto the egg shapes for arms and legs.
4. Invite the children to use tissue paper and wallpaper to decorate or dress their Humpty Dumpty.

Developmental Bonus
Creative expression

Curriculum Extension
For Cooking: Deviled Dumpties

Ages
3,4,5,6

Materials
Hard-boiled eggs, knives, masher, salad dressing, pickle, onion, bowl and mixing spoon

Procedure
1. Let the children shell eggs, cut pickles and dice onions.
2. The children cut the eggs in half and remove yolks.

3. The children can mix the yolks, 1 tablespoon diced onion, 2 tablespoons of diced pickles and 2 tablespoons salad dressing in a bowl. (This is enough for 24 eggs.)

4. Spoon the egg mixture back into egg halves.

5. Enjoy! Yum!

Developmental Bonus
Measurement concepts
Fine motor development

Curriculum Extension
For Fine Motor: Humpty Dumpty Puzzles

Ages
3,4,5

Materials
Tagboard, crayons, scissors

Procedure
1. Cut tagboard into egg shapes and decorate. Then cut into puzzle pieces.

2. Invite children to put puzzles together.

3. Make complicated puzzles with older children and simple ones with younger children.

Developmental Bonus
Hand-eye coordination

Curriculum Extension
For Math: Egg Halves Match

Ages
4,5,6

Materials
Plastic eggs, permanent marker, dot stickers

Procedure
1. Use the marker to put numerals on one half of each plastic egg and the appropriate number of dots on the corresponding half.

2. Open all the eggs and mix them up.

3. Encourage the children to put the eggs together matching dots to corresponding numerals.

Developmental Bonus
Numeral recognition
Counting

Curriculum Extension
For Science: Egg in a Bottle

Ages
4,5,6

Materials
Jar, hard-boiled egg (shelled), paper, matches

Procedure
1. Place a hard-boiled egg in the opening of the jar (the egg should rest in the opening but not fall inside).

2. Call the children's attention to the fact that the egg won't go in the jar.

3. Take the egg out. Put paper in the jar and light it with a match.

4. Place the egg in the opening of the jar again.

5. The heat will burn up oxygen and draw the egg inside the jar.

6. Ask the children how they think the experiment works.

Developmental Bonus
Concept development

Related Bibliography

Briggs, Raymond. *The Mother Goose Treasury*. Dial, 1986. Vivid colors and comic illustrations are used to relate a number of nursery rhymes, British style.

De Angeli, Marguerite. *Marguerite De Angeli's Book of Nursery and Mother Goose Rhymes*. Doubleday, 1979. The rhymes are illustrated with a delicate and old-fashioned charm.

Dr. Seuss. *Green Eggs and Ham*. Random House, 1960. Sam I Am tries every trick to get his friend to try his green eggs and ham.

Dr. Seuss. *Horton Hatches the Egg*. Random House, 1940. Horton, a faithful elephant, helps a lazy bird who takes a long vacation and leaves Horton responsible for sitting on her eggs.

San Souci, Robert D. *The Talking Eggs*. Dial, 1989. A good sister is rewarded for her kindness to an old woman, and a bad sister is punished for her nasty ways.

Related Records and Tapes

Beall, Pamela Conn and Susan Hagen Nipp. "Humpty Dumpty" from *Wee Sing Nursery Rhymes and Lullabies*. Price Stern Sloan, 1985.

Sharon, Lois and Bram. "Humpty Dumpty" from *Mainly Mother Goose*, Elephant, 1984.

12

▼▼▼▼▼▼▼▼▼▼▼▼▼

AUGUST

Where Is Thumbkin?

Where is thumbkin?
Where is thumbkin?
Here I am, Here I am;
How are you today, sir?
Very well, I thank you,
Run away, Run away.

Where is pointer?
Where is pointer?
Here I am, Here I am;
How are you today, sir?
Very well, I thank you,
Run away, Run away.

Where is middle finger?

Where is ring finger?

Where is pinky?

Thematic Connections

Me, Myself and I
Play
Family

Things to Talk About

1. Can you think of other words to greet Thumbkin than "How are you this morning?"
2. Are there other names for the fingers than those used in the song?

Curriculum Extension

For Art: Tactile Finger Painting

Ages
3,4,5

Materials
Finger paint, textured wallpaper

Procedure
1. Provide each child with a sheet of wallpaper and finger paint.
2. Let the children create designs on their paper.

3. Ask the children to describe how their paper feels.

Developmental Bonus
Tactile expression
Creative expression

Curriculum Extension

For Creative Movement: Guitars

Ages
3,4,5

Materials
Small boxes, rubber bands

Procedure
1. Take the lid off of a box.
2. Put 6 or 8 rubber bands around the box.
3. Repeat with other boxes.
4. The children use their fingers to strum the rubber bands. Call attention to the connection between the sound the rubber band makes and the tightness of the rubber band.

Developmental Bonus
Auditory discrimination
Concept development

Curriculum Extension
For Fine Motor: Tactile Playdough

Ages
3,4,5,6

Materials
Peanut butter, nonfat dry milk, confectioners sugar, corn syrup, granola, measuring cups, mixing bowl and spoon

Procedure
1. With the children, mix 1 cup peanut butter, 1 1/4 cup confectioners sugar, 1 cup corn syrup and 1 1/4 cup nonfat dry milk to make a dough.
2. Add 1 cup of granola to the dough.
3. Allow children to play with the playdough and when they've finished, they can eat it.

Developmental Bonus
Tactile expression

Curriculum Extension
For Math: Patterns

Ages
3,4,5,6

Materials
Forty clothespins; red, yellow, blue and green spray paint; paper plates

Procedure
1. Spray-paint the clothespins (10 of each color). NOTE: Be sure to use the spray paint outside or in a well-ventilated room.
2. Give the children paper plates and clothespins. Ask them to create color patterns. Remind the children that using a clothespin requires using "thumbkin" and "pointer."
3. Encourage the children to create a circular pattern.

Developmental Bonus
Patterning
Fine motor development

Curriculum Extension
For Science: Feely Box

Ages
3,4,5,6

Materials
Empty oatmeal box or coffee can; sock; tape; scissors; assorted items for feeling—block, spool, sponge, sandpaper

Procedure
1. Remove the lid from the oatmeal box or coffee can.
2. Tape the top of the sock around the opening of the oatmeal box or coffee can.
3. Cut the toe of the sock off.
4. Place assorted items inside the box or can.
5. Invite children to stick their hand through the sock and into the box or can to touch the various items. The children attempt to identify the items by touch only.

Developmental Bonus
Tactile experience

Related Bibliography

Allen, Laura Jean. *Where is Freddy?*. HarperCollins, 1986. Detective Tweedy, a mouse, is on the case and follows the clues to find Freddy in a very unusual place.

Anderson, Hans Christian. *Thumbelina*. Dial, 1979. A little girl the size of your thumb is lost in a forest and almost trapped into marrying a mole but is saved by a tiny prince.

Brown, Marc. *Hand Rhymes*. Dutton, 1985. A collection of fingerplays and singing games for young children.

Martin, Bill, Jr.and John Archambault. *Here Are My Hands*. Henry Holt, 1988. A rhyming verse about use of the hands and other body parts.

Whitney, Alma Marshak. *Just Awful*. Addison-Wesley,1971. A little boy cuts his finger and is afraid to go to the school nurse for fear of what she might do. What she does is a pleasant surprise.

Related Records and Tapes

Beall, Pamela Conn and Susan Hagen Nipp. "Where is Thumbkin?" from *Wee Sing Children's Songs and Fingerplays*. Price Stern Sloan, 1979.

Sharon, Lois and Bram. "Where is Thumbkin?" from *One, Two, Three, Four, Live!*. Elephant, 1982.

"Count My Fingers" from *Songs About Me*. Kimbo.

"This Old Man" from *Sing-A-Long*. Peter Pan, 1987.

Apples and Bananas

*I like to eat, eat, eat
Apples and bananas.*

*I like to eat, eat, eat,
Apples and bananas.*

*I like to ite, ite, ite,
Ipples and bininis.*

*I like to ite, ite, ite,
Ipples and bininis.*

*I like to ote, ote, ote,
Opples and bononos.*

*I like to ote, ote, ote,
Opples and bononos.*

*I like to ute, ute, ute,
Upples and bununus.*

*I like to ute, ute, ute,
Upples and bununus.*

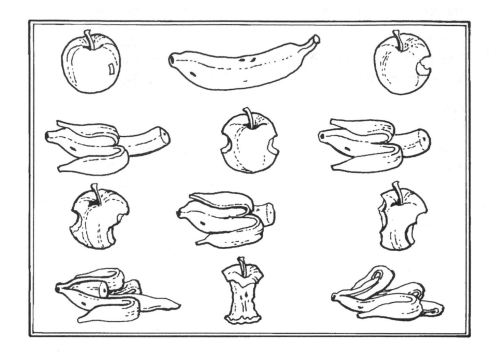

Thematic Connections
Farm
Nutrition
Fruits

Things to Talk About
1. What if the song was about vegetables? Can you think of two vegetables we could sing about?
2. Could we sing this song using names of friends?

Curriculum Extension
For Art: Apple Prints

Ages
3, 4, 5

Materials
Drawing paper, tempera paint, apple halves, optional—crayons or pencils

Procedure
1. The children dab the apple halves in the paint and make a print on their paper.
2. Designs can be enhanced by using crayons or pencils.

Developmental Bonus
Creative Expressions

Curriculum Extension
For Cooking: Apple and Banana Salad

Ages
3,4,5

Materials
Apples, bananas, cutting boards, kitchen knives, mixing bowl and spoon, bowls, spoons, coconut, optional—fruit juice, mayonnaise or salad dressing

Procedure
1. With the children, slice the bananas and cup up the apples using kitchen knives. (Save the seeds to use in the fine motor activity.)
2. Mix in a bowl with enough juice or salad dressing to moisten.
3. Serve in bowls. Eat and enjoy.

Developmental Bonus
Fine motor development

Curriculum Extension
For Fine Motor: Apple Seed Transfer

Ages
4,5,6

Materials
Apple seeds, tweezers, jar lids, meat tray

Procedure
1. This activity takes a lot of concentration!
2. Place several apple seeds in a meat tray.
3. The children use the tweezers to pick up seeds and transfer them to a jar lid.

Developmental Bonus
Fine motor development

Curriculum Extension
For Math: Dividing Apples

Ages
4,5,6

Materials
Apples, knife, cutting board

Procedure
1. Show the children one apple and ask how it could be eaten by two children.
2. Some children will say share, and some will say cut in half.
3. Cut the apple in half. Now, say you want to have enough for four children. Ask the children how we can share it four ways.
4. Help the children understand the concepts of cutting in half, dividing fairly and fraction vocabulary—half, fourth.
5. Cut the apples so the whole class can share them.

Developmental Bonus
Fraction concepts

Curriculum Extension
For Science: Dried Apples

Ages
4,5,6

Materials
Apples, kitchen knives, cutting boards, lemon juice, cookie sheet, net or cheesecloth, cinnamon, and sugar

Procedure
1. With the children, peel apples, then quarter and slice them into very thin slices.
2. Lay the slices on a cookie sheet and sprinkle with lemon juice.
3. Cover the slices with cheesecloth and place out in the sun to dry. (Be sure to bring the slices in at night and place in a cabinet.)
4. This process will take two to three days.
5. Explain to children that Native Americans and early pioneers used this process to preserve their food.

Developmental Bonus
Concept development

Related Bibliography

Barton, Byron. *Applebet Story*. Viking, 1973. An alphabet sequence story beginning with apples.

Gibbons, Gail. *The Seasons of Arnolds's Apple Tree*. Harcourt Brace Jovanovich, 1984. Arnold learns about seasons as he watches his apple tree through the year.

Martin, Bill, Jr. and John Archambault. *Chicka Chicka Boom Boom*. Simon and Schuster, 1989. The whole alphabet goes up the coconut tree, and when the tree is too full, they all fall down.

Pearson, Tracy Campbell. *A, Apple Pie*. Dial, 1986. An apple pie travels down a table of 26 rambunctious children in a delightful re-working of a traditional verse.

Scheer, Julian. *Rain Makes Applesauce*. Holiday, 1964. A nonsensical story that only makes sense when you look at the illustrations — rain is making applesauce.

Related Records and Tapes

Sharon, Lois and Bram. "Apple Pickers Red" from *One, Two, Three, Four, Live!* Elephant, 1982.

Roll Over

Ten in the bed,
And the little one said,
"Roll over! Roll over!"
So they all rolled over,
And one fell out.

Nine in the bed,...
Eight in the bed,...
Seven in the bed,...
Six in the bed,...
Five in the bed,...
Four in the bed,...
Three in the bed,...
Two in the bed,...

One in the bed,
And the little one said,
"Alone at last!" (spoken)

Thematic Connections

Family
Numbers

Things to Talk About

1. Have you ever shared a bed with several people? What was it like?
2. What was the "little one" trying to do? Was the "little one" smart?

Curriculum Extension

For Art: Roller Painting

Ages

3,4,5

Materials

Small paint rollers, cake pan, bulletin board or butcher paper, tempera paint

Procedure

1. Place a large piece of bulletin board or butcher paper on the floor.
2. Pour tempera paint into the cake pan.
3. The children paint on the bulletin board paper with rollers.

Developmental Bonus

Concept development
Creative expression

Curriculum Extension

For Cooking: Peanut Butter Rollers

Ages

3,4,5,6

Materials

Peanut butter, honey, powdered milk, measuring cups, mixing bowl and spoon, granola cereal, wax paper

Procedure

1. With the children, mix 1 cup honey, 2 cups powdered milk and 2 cups of peanut butter in a bowl.
2. Sprinkle granola on sheets of wax paper. Encourage the children to knead mixture,

then make snake shapes to roll in granola.

3. Eat and enjoy!

Developmental Bonus
Measurement concepts
Fine motor development

Curriculum Extension
For Dramatic Play: Roll Over

Ages
3,4,5,6

Materials
Butcher paper

Procedure
1. Brainstorm ways to roll over.

2. Ask the children to demonstrate as many ways as possible to roll over.

3. Act out the song using butcher paper for the bed.

Developmental Bonus
Large muscle development
Creative thinking

Curriculum Extension
For Math: Dice Rolling Tally

Ages
4,5,6

Materials
12 x 18-inch sheet of paper, dice, crayons

Procedure
1. Write the numerals 1 to 6 at the top of the paper and draw columns under each numeral.

2. Invite the children to roll a die and tally the number of times the die lands on each number. Put a mark under the number rolled.

3. What number is rolled most often? What number is rolled the least?

Developmental Bonus
Counting
Numeral recognition

Curriculum Extension
For Science: Roll Over Races

Ages
4,5,6

Materials
Three coffee cans with lids, four large washers, super glue, sand, two 4-foot lengths of 1 x 4-inch boards

Procedure
1. Glue four washers in a straight line down the inside of one of the coffee cans. Glue on the lid.

2. Fill a second coffee can with sand and glue on the lid. Leave the third can empty.

3. Place the two boards on a slope (making an incline plane).

4. Encourage the children to race the cans by rolling two at a time down the slopes, then race the winner against the remaining can.

5. Encourage the children to race the cans on the floor.

6. Talk about why the cans roll at different paces.

Developmental Bonus
Motion concepts

Related Bibliography

Bang, Molly. *Ten, Nine, Eight*. Greenwillow, 1983. Bedtime turns into playtime with a rhyming game as a father puts his daughter to sleep.

Keller, Holly. *Ten Sleepy Sheep*. Greenwillow, 1983. Lewis can't fall asleep, so his parents tell him to count sheep.

Gerstein, Mordicai. *Roll Over!*. Crown, 1988. A yawning tyke heads for bed only to find it occupied by ten guests. The little one says "roll over" and out rolls a pig, an alligator, and eight other animals.

Waber, Bernard. *Ira Sleeps Over*. Houghton Mifflin, 1972. Ira spends the night away from home for the first time and worries about taking his teddy bear with him.

Ziefert, Harriet. *I Won't Go to Bed!* Little, Brown, 1987. Harry won't go to bed, so his father leaves him downstairs where everything grows scarier until Harry falls asleep on the floor.

Related Records and Tapes

Beall, Pamela Conn and Susan Hagen Nipp. "Ten in A Bed" from *Wee Sing Silly Songs*. Price Stern Sloan, 1986.

"Roly Poly" from *Have a Ball*. Kimbo.

There Was an Old Lady

There was an old lady who swallowed a fly,
I don't know why she swallowed a fly,
Perhaps she'll die.

There was an old lady who swallowed a spider,
That wriggled and wriggled and tickled inside her;
She swallowed the spider to catch the fly,
I don't know why she swallowed the fly,
Perhaps she'll die.

There was an old lady who swallowed a bird,
Now, ain't it absurd to swallow a bird;
She swallowed the bird to catch the spider,
She swallowed the spider to catch the fly,
etc.

There was an old lady who swallowed a cat,
Now fancy that, to swallow a cat, etc.

There was an old lady who swallowed a dog,
Oh, what a hog to swallow a dog, etc.

There was an old lady who swallowed a cow,
I don't know how she swallowed a cow, etc.

There was an old lady who swallowed a horse,
(Spoken) She died, of course!

Thematic Connections
Insects
Animals

Things to Talk About
1. Discuss the cause and effect relationship in the song, for example, "She swallowed the spider to catch the fly, she swallowed the bird to catch the spider," etc.
2. Did the old lady make good decisions?
3. How would the song be different if the old lady swallowed the horse first?

Curriculum Extension
For Art: Wiggly Spiders

Ages
4,5,6

Materials
Four pipe cleaners and 18 inches of elastic thread for each child, scissors

Procedure
1. Cut the pipe cleaners in half.
2. Put four pipe cleaners together and twist in the middle.
3. Move each of the resulting "legs" into a spider leg shape.
4. Attach an 18-inch piece of elastic thread to the middle to create a wiggly spider.

Developmental Bonus
Hand-eye coordination
Creative expression

Curriculum Extension
For Creative Movement: Dancing Spiders

Ages
3,4,5,6

Materials
Spiders from art activity, music

Procedure
1. Encourage the children to have their spider puppets dance to the music.

2. Sing the song while making the spiders "dance."

Developmental Bonus
Coordination
Large muscle development

Curriculum Extension
For Language: Old Lady Puppet

Ages
5,6

Materials
Scissors, 6 x 12-inch paper bags, plastic acetate or vinyl, tape, posterboard, stapler, paper plate, crayons, cotton balls, construction paper, index cards

Procedure
1. To make a see-through old lady with the children, cut a 6 x 6-inch square out of the front or back of the paper bag. Tape a 7 x 7-inch piece of acetate inside the bag to cover the 6-inch square opening.
2. Decorate a paper plate as a face. Add cotton balls for hair and staple on the bottom flap of the bag (the head of the "old lady").
3. Cut legs and arms from posterboard and staple on the bag in the correct places.
4. Cut hands and shoes from construction paper and attach with a stapler or tape.
5. Place a second grocery sack the opposite way inside the first sack and staple together at the bottom.
6. Cut a slit through the sides of the two bags, large enough to fit a hand.
7. Cut index cards in two and draw things the old lady ate on them.

8. Sing the song, feeding the old lady as you sing.
9. Retrieve cards from the side slit after you have finished.

Developmental Bonus
Sequencing

Curriculum Extension
For Math: Sequencing

Ages
3,4,5

Materials
Pictures of each item the old lady swallowed or small plastic animals/insects representing each animal swallowed

Procedure
1. Ask children to sequence the animals or animal pictures from smallest to largest.
2. Ask them if this is the order in which the old lady swallowed the animals.

Developmental Bonus
Sequencing
Size relationship

Curriculum Extension
For Science: Classification

Ages
4,5,6

Materials
Pictures of plastic animals from the song, plus some additional insects and animals

Procedure
1. Ask the children to classify the pictures or plastic animals into categories of animals and insects.

Developmental Bonus
Classification

Related Bibliography

Carle, Eric. *The Very Hungry Caterpillar*. Putnam, 1981. A newborn caterpillar eats through a variety of foods before becoming a butterfly.

Kent, Jack. *The Fat Cat: A Danish Folktale*. Parent's Magazine Press, 1971. A Danish tale of a greedy cat who eats everyone in his path.

Galdone, Paul. *The Greedy Old Fat Man: An American Folktale*. Clarion, 1983. An old man consumes 100 biscuits, a barrel of milk, then a boy, girl, dog, fox, and some rabbits before being stopped by a squirrel.

Prelutsky, Jack. *The Terrible Tiger*. Macmillan, 1989. A tiger swallows a baker, a grocer, and worse.

Westcott, Nadine Bernard. *I Know An Old Lady Who Swallowed a Fly*. Little, Brown, 1981. An illustrated book of the traditional song.

Related Records and Tapes

Peter, Paul and Mary. "I'm Being Swallowed by a Boa Constrictor" from *Peter, Paul and Mary*. Warner, 1962.

"There Was An Old Lady" from *Sing-A-Long*. Peter Pan. 1987.

This Old Man

This old man, he played one,
He played nick-nack on my thumb;
With a nick-nack paddy whack,
Give a dog a bone,
This old man (point to self)
Came rolling home (roll hands over each
other).

Two...on my shoe (tap shoe)
Three...on my knee (tap knee)
Four...on my door (knock forehead)
Five...on my hive (wiggle fingers for flying
bees)
Six...on my sticks (tap index fingers)
Seven...up in heaven (point skyward)
Eight...on my gate (knock on imaginary
gate)
Nine...on my spine (tap backbone)
Ten...nick-nack once again (clap hands)

Thematic Connections
Numbers

Things to Talk About
1. How would the song be different if the old man was using the alphabet instead of numbers?
2. Think of other rhyming words to go with each number.

Curriculum Extension

For Art: Number Rubbings

Ages
3,4,5,6

Materials
Tagboard or posterboard, marker, scissors, drawing paper, crayons, stapler

Procedure
1. Cut block numerals 1-9 out of posterboard.
2. The children place the numerals under drawing paper and rub with crayons to create designs.

3. Sequence numerals or just create a mixed design.
4. Invite children to make number books. They can make a rubbing and then illustrate the appropriate number of objects for that numeral. Staple the pages together to make a book.

Developmental Bonus
Creative expression
Numeral concepts

Curriculum Extension

For Gross Motor: Roly Poly Races

Ages
3,4,5

Materials
Masking tape

Procedure
1. Place two strips of masking tape on the floor 10 feet apart.
2. Encourage the children to have rolling races.

3. Two children start at the same time. See who can roll over the finish line first.

Developmental Bonus
Coordination

Curriculum Extension

For Language: Rhyme Time

Ages
4,5,6

Materials
Index cards, markers, simply-drawn pictures or magazine photos

Procedure
1. Write numerals 1-10 on the index cards.
2. Invite children to match numerals with items that rhyme.

Developmental Bonus
Auditory discrimination

Curriculum Extension

For Math: Number Worm

Ages
4,5,6

Materials
Construction paper, scissors, crayons

Procedure
1. Cut ten construction paper circles about 3 inches in diameter.
2. Write the numerals 1-9 on the circles.
3. Draw a face on the remaining circle.
4. The children start with the head and then sequence the circles 1-9 to create a worm.

Developmental Bonus
Number sequence

Curriculum Extension

For Outdoors: Dog and Bone

Ages
3,4,5

Materials
A bone cut from construction paper or a real dog bone

Procedure
1. Sit outside in a circle.
2. One child is appointed "it."
3. "It" walks around the outside of the circle and places the bone behind one of the other children.
4. This second child picks up the bone and chases "it" around the circle attempting to tag "it" before "it" can get back around the circle to the second child's place.
5. If the second child tags "it," "it" goes to the "dog house" (the middle of the circle).
6. If the second child fails to tag "it," the second child becomes the new "it."

Developmental Bonus
Large muscle development

Related Bibliography

Aylesworth, Jim. *One Crow: A Counting Rhyme*. Lippincott, 1988. Farm animals are used to illustrate numbers one to ten first with a summer slant and then with a winter slant.

Crews, Donald. *Ten Black Dots*. Greenwillow, 1986. A counting rhyme from one to ten that shows a number of items made from simple black dots.

Koontz, Robin Michael. *This Old Man*. Putnam, 1989. A modern interpretation of the song. Ten little sweat-suited men are the focus of the book.

Leedy, Loreen. *A Number of Dragons*. Holiday House, 1985. A rhyming 10 to 1 and back again dragon-counting book.

Sendak, Maurice. *One Was Johnny: A Counting Book*. HarperCollins, 1962. A number of intruders destroy Johnny's peace until he issues an ultimatum.

Related Records and Tapes

Beall, Pamela Conn and Susan Hagen Nipp. "This Old Man" from *Wee Sing Nursery Rhymes and Lullabies*. Price Stern Sloan.

Scelsa, Greg and Steve Millang. "One, Two, Buckle My Shoe" from *We All Live Together*, Vol. 3. Youngheart Records, 1979.

"This Old Man" from *Sing-A-Long*. Peter Pan, 1987.

Three Little Kittens

Three little kittens, they lost their mittens,
And they began to cry,
"Oh, mother dear, we sadly fear
Our mittens we have lost."
"What! Lost your mittens? You naughty kittens!
Then you shall have no pie."
Meow, meow, meow, meow.

Three little kittens, they found their mittens
And they began to cry,
"Oh, mother dear, see here, see here,
Our mittens we have found."
"What! Found your mittens, you darling kittens,
Then you shall have some pie."
Meow, meow, meow, meow.

The three little kittens put on their mittens,
And soon ate up the pie;
"Oh, mother dear, we greatly fear
Our mittens we have soiled."
"What! Soiled your mittens, you naughty kittens!"
Then they began to sigh.
Meow, meow, meow, meow.

The three little kittens washed their mittens,
And hung them up to dry;
"Oh, mother dear, look here, look here,
Our mittens we have washed."
"What! Washed your mittens, you darling kittens,
But I smell a rat close by."
Hush! Hush! Hush! Hush!

Thematic Connections
Cats
Mittens
Animals
Nursery Rhymes

Things to Talk About
1. How are mittens different from gloves?
2. What time of year do you think the kittens wore their mittens?

Curriculum Extension
For Art: Paper Bag Kittens

Ages
3,4,5,6

Materials
Paper bags, construction paper, scissors, glue

Procedure
1. Cut out eyes, ears, nose and whiskers from construction paper. (Younger children may need some help.)

2. Glue the cat features on the bags.
3. Demonstrate how to make the puppets "talk."

Developmental Bonus
Creative expression

For Creative Movement: Be Like a Cat

Ages
3,4,5

Materials
Record with a variety of music

Procedure
1. Demonstrate how to stalk, slink and run like a cat.
2. Show the children how a cat might sleep.
3. Let the children imitate a cat.
4. Play the music and move like a cat to the music.

Developmental Bonus
Creative expression
Large muscle development

For Fine Motor: Pretend Pies

Ages
3,4,5

Materials
Playdough; small pie tins; styrofoam chips, dried macaroni, beans, rice

Procedure
1. Invite children to make playdough pies.
2. Use styrofoam chips, macaroni, beans, etc., to create a filling.

Developmental Bonus
Creative expression
Fine motor development

For Language: Mitten Match

Ages
3,4,5

Materials
Pairs of mittens

Procedure
1. Mix up the mittens, then ask the children to divide the mittens into pairs.
2. The mittens can be sorted by color, by size or by design.

Developmental Bonus
Visual discrimination

For Math: Mitten Sizes

Ages
3,4,5

Materials
Several construction paper mittens in a variety of sizes

Procedure
1. Ask the children to match mittens by size.
2. Encourage the children to arrange mittens from smallest to largest.

Developmental Bonus
Size concepts
Visual discrimination
Sequencing

Related Bibliography

Brett, Jan. *The Mitten: A Ukrainian Folktale*. Putnam, 1990. A lost mitten becomes a home for an assortment of forest animals until it finally becomes overcrowded.

Cauley, Lorinda Bryan. *The Three Little Kittens*. Putnam, 1982. The story of mittens lost, found, soiled, and cleaned.

G'ag, Wanda. *Millions of Cats*. Coward, 1928. Classic tale of an old man who can't pick one, so he ends up with millions.

McMillan, Bruce. *Kitten Can: A Concept Book*. Lothrop, 1984. Photographs of a kitten's ability to stare, squeeze, stretch, scratch, and more.

Slobodkin, Florence and Louis. *Too Many Mittens*. Vanguard, 1958. Twins lose one red mitten and after a search end up with many mittens.

Related Records and Tapes

Beall, Pamela Conn and Susan Hagen Nipp. "Three Little Kittens" from *Wee Sing Nursery Rhymes and Lullabies*. Price Stern Sloan, 1985.

JUST FOR TODDLERS

SEPTEMBER
Good Morning to You

If You're Happy and You Know It

OCTOBER
Little Boy Blue

Old MacDonald Had a Farm

NOVEMBER
I'm a Little Teapot

Jack and Jill

DECEMBER
Jingle Bells

We Wish You a Merry Christmas

JANUARY
The Muffin Man

Rock-a-Bye, Baby

FEBRUARY
The Bus Song

London Bridge

MARCH
Mary Had a Little Lamb

Three Little Kittens

APRIL
Eensy Weensy Spider

Little Miss Muffet

MAY
Baa, Baa, Black Sheep

The Mulberry Bush

JUNE
Six White Ducks

Twinkle, Twinkle, Little Star

JULY
Humpty Dumpty

Row, Row, Row, Your Boat

AUGUST
Ring Around a Rosy

Where Is Thumbkin?

Good Morning to You

Good morning to you,
Good morning to you,
We're all in our places
With bright, shining faces,
Good morning to you.

Thematic Connections
Me, Myself and I

Things to Talk About
1. Show your shining faces. Show an un-shining face.
2. What do you say when you wake up in the morning?

Curriculum Extension
For Art: Seating Mats

Materials
12 x 18-inch construction paper, crayons, laminating film or clear contact paper

Procedure
1. Ask the children to decorate a piece of construction paper.
2. Write the children's names on their mats and laminate.
3. The children sit on their mats during circle time.

Developmental Bonus
Creative expression

Curriculum Extension
For Cooking: Good Morning Cheese Faces

Materials
One slice of cheese for each child, kitchen knife, bottle caps, moon-shape cookie cutters

Procedure
1. With the children, cut the cheese into circles to make faces.
2. Let children use bottle caps to cut out eyes in the face and a moon-shape cookie cutter to make a smiling mouth.
3. Eat and enjoy.

Developmental Bonus
Fine motor development

Curriculum Extension
For Dramatic Play: Happy Faces

Materials
Paper plates, crayons, scissors, tongue depressors, stapler

Procedure
1. Ask the children to use the crayons to decorate the plates with happy faces.
2. Cut out eyes and staple the plate onto a tongue depressor.
3. Let the children play with happy face masks.

Developmental Bonus
Creative expression

Curriculum Extension
For Language: Good Morning

Materials
Towels or cloths

Procedure
1. The children cover their heads with the towels or cloths.
2. Teach them to come out from under the towel when they hear "good morning."
3. Say, "good night, hello, good-bye, good morning" so the children learn to wait for "good morning" before taking the towels off.

Developmental Bonus
Auditory discrimination

Curriculum Extension
For Math: Patterns

Materials
None needed

Procedure
1. Seat children in a girl, boy, girl, boy pattern.
2. Ask the children to verb alize the pattern.
3. Try other patterns.

Developmental Bonus
Patterning

Related Bibliography

Dryden, Emma. *Good Morning, Good Night.* Random House, 1990. Romp through morning routines with six furry animals in one book. Turn the book over and get ready for bed.

Ginsburg, Mirra. *Good Morning, Chick.* Greenwillow, 1980. The barnyard wakes up in this simple, beautifully illustrated book.

Tafuri, Nancy. *Early Morning in the Barn.* Greenwillow, 1983. The rooster wakes them up and each animal responds by saying good morning in its own way.

Tafuri, Nancy. *Rabbit's Morning.* Greenwillow, 1985. A shimmering sun wakes rabbit and he starts his day's journey.

Ormerod, Jan. *Sunshine.* Lothrop, 1981. This wordless picture book chronicles the start of a little girl's day.

Related Records and Tapes

Beall, Pamela Conn and Susan Hagen Nipp. "Good Morning" from *Wee Sing Children's Songs and Fingerplays.* Price Stern Sloan, 1979.

Scelsa, Greg and Steve Millang. "Say Hello" from *Kidding Around with Greg and Steve.* Youngheart Records, 1985.

Scelsa, Greg and Steve Millang. "Good Morning" from *We All Live Together*, Vol. 2. Youngheart Records, 1978.

Moore, Thomas. "Good Morning" from *Songs for the Whole Day.* Thomas Moore Records.

Hammett, Carol and Elaine Bueffel. "Top of the Morning" from *It's Toddler Time.* Kimbo.

If You're Happy and You Know It

If you're happy and you know it,
Clap your hands. (clap, clap).
If you're happy and you know it,
Clap your hands. (clap, clap).
If you're happy and you know it,
Then your life will surely show it.
If you're happy and you know it,
Clap your hands. (clap, clap).

If you're happy and you know it,
Stomp your feet (stomp, stomp)...

If you're happy and you know it,
Shout "Hooray!" (shout "Hooray!")...

Thematic Connections
Me, Myself and I
Feelings

Things to Talk About
1. Ask the children what makes them happy.
2. Ask the children what makes them sad.

Curriculum Extension
For Art: Hand Prints

Materials
Finger paint, drawing paper

Procedure
1. Allow the children to finger paint on the table top.
2. Before the children clean their hands, ask them to make hand prints on drawing paper.

Developmental Bonus
Creative expression

Curriculum Extension
For Cooking: Happy Face Snack

Materials
Round crackers, peanut butter, kitchen knives, raisins

Procedure
1. Help the children spread peanut butter on the crackers.
2. Invite the children to decorate the "faces" with raisins.

Developmental Bonus
Coordination

Curriculum Extension
For Dramatic Play: Faces

Materials
Paper plates, marking pens, tongue depressors, staplers

Procedure
1. Draw a different face on each paper plate—some happy, some sad, some angry.

2. Attach the plates to the tongue depressors.

3. Allow the children to play creatively with the plates.

Developmental Bonus
Creative expression

Curriculum Extension

For Gross Motor: Happy and Sad

Materials
Happy and sad face puppets from the dramatic play activity

Procedure
1. Sit in a circle.

2. When the happy face is held up, ask the children to clap their hands.

3. When the sad face is shown, ask the children to stomp their feet.

Developmental Bonus
Visual discrimination
Large muscle development
Coordination

Curriculum Extension

For Language: Face Match Up

Materials
Paper plates, marking pens, scissors

Procedure
1. Draw faces on paper plates.

2. Cut each plate in half using a simple zigzag puzzle pattern. Vary the zigzag pattern for each puzzle.

3. The children put the puzzles back together.

Developmental Bonus
Visual discrimination

Related Bibliography

Aliki. *Feelings*. Greenwillow, 1984. A catalog of emotions—love, hate, fear, frustration and more.

Holzenthaler, Jean. *My Hands Can*. Dutton, 1978. Simple text describes the many things children can do with their hands.

Hennessy, B. G. *A, B, C, D, Tummy, Toes, Hands, Knees*. Puffin Books, 1991. A mother and child together explore the toddler's unfolding world.

Martin, Bill, Jr. and John Archambault. *Here Are My Hands*. Henry Holt, 1987. A rhyming verse about how we use our hands and other body parts.

Waltenberg, Jane. *Mrs. Mustard's Baby Faces*. Chronicle Press, 1992. A collection of happy baby faces!

Related Records and Tapes

Beall, Pamela Conn and Susan Hagen Nipp. "If You're Happy" from *Wee Sing Children's Songs and Fingerplays*. Price Stern Sloan, 1979.

Little Boy Blue

Little Boy Blue,
Come blow your horn,
The sheep's in the meadow,
The cow's in the corn,
Where is the boy
Who looks after the sheep?
He's under the haystack,
Fast asleep.

Thematic Connections
Nursery Rhymes
Farm

Things to Talk About
1. Have you ever blown a horn?
2. Explain to the children that Little Boy Blue's job was to watch the sheep.

Curriculum Extension
For Art: Blue, Blue, Blue

Materials
Easel paper, blue tempera paint, variety of paintbrushes, smocks

Procedure
1. Set up the paper and paints.
2. The children paint blue pictures with the paint.

Developmental Bonus
Creative expression
Concept development

Curriculum Extension
For Dramatic Play: Little Boy Blue Horns

Materials
Toilet paper tubes

Procedure
1. Provide each child with a toilet paper tube to use as a horn.
2. Show the children how to "toot" their horns.
3. Make certain the children do not put their horns up to another child's ear.

Developmental Bonus
Creative expression

Curriculum Extension
For Gross Motor: Farm Animals

Materials
Plastic farm animals, small boxes, blocks

Procedure

1. Place farm animals and small boxes on the floor.
2. The boxes can be used as barns.
3. Make fenced areas with blocks.
4. The children play with the animals, putting them in the "barns" and inside the fences.

Developmental Bonus

Creative play

For Language: In and Out

Materials

Boxes

Procedure

1. Put several boxes on the floor.
2. Demonstrate in the box and out of the box by first placing a toy in the box and then taking it out of the box. If one box is big enough, let the children get in and out of the box. Talk about the words in the song that say "the sheep's in the meadow, the cow's in the barn."
3. Play in the box and out of the box by simply calling out one of the phrases and then the other.

Developmental Bonus

Concept development
Vocabulary development

Curriculum Extension

For Science: Blue Waters

Materials

Water, plastic tub, blue food coloring, cups, funnels, strainers, basters

Procedure

1. Fill a tub with water and add a few drops of blue food coloring.
2. Encourage the children to pour water through the funnels and strainers and to use the basters and other containers.

Developmental Bonus

Coordination

Related Bibliography

Galdone, Paul. *Little Bo-Peep*. Clarion, 1986. The Mother Goose rhyme is updated in this version of a pretty blue-eyed girl and her twelve wayward sheep.

Henley, Claire. *Farm Day*. Dial, 1991. After the rooster's cock-a-doodle-do starts the day, all the other farm animals join in.

Hoban, Tana. *Is It Red? Is It Yellow? Is It Blue?* Greenwillow, 1978. A wordless book of photographs teaches the concepts of colors.

Mother Goose. *Tomie dePaola's Favorite Nursery Tales*. Putnam, 1986. Over 200 nursery rhymes, including "Little Boy Blue," accompanied by dePaola's large cheery paintings.

Mother Goose. *Complete Mother Goose*. Children's Classics, 1987. Beautiful illustrations of some of the favorite Mother Goose rhymes.

Related Records and Tapes

Beall, Pamela Conn and Susan Hagen Nipp. "Little Boy Blue" from *Wee Sing Nursery Rhymes and Lullabies*. Price Stern Sloan, 1985.

Sharon, Lois and Bram. "Little Boy Blue" from *Mainly Mother Goose*. Elephant, 1984.

"In the Barnyard" from *Put Your Finger in the Air*. Kimbo.

Old MacDonald Had a Farm

Old MacDonald had a farm,
E—I—E—I—O;
And on his farm he had a cow,
E—I—E—I—O;
With a moo-moo here and a moo-moo there,
Here a moo, there a moo, everywhere a moo-moo,
Old MacDonald had a farm,
E—I—E—I—O.

Continue with other animals:
Pig...oink-oink....
Duck...quack-quack....
Horse...neigh-neigh....
Donkey...hee-haw....
Chickens...chick-chick..., etc.

Thematic Connections
Farm
Animals

Things to Talk About
1. Which one of Old MacDonald's animals is the largest? Which is the smallest?
2. Name animals Old MacDonald doesn't have on his farm.

Curriculum Extension
For Art: Animal Prints

Materials
Cookie cutters (animal shapes), tempera paint, pie pans, drawing paper

Procedure
1. Mix tempera paint, keeping it thick.
2. Pour into pie pans.
3. The children dip the cookie cutters in the paint and press gently onto their paper to create animal shapes.

Developmental Bonus
Creative expression

Curriculum Extension
For Dramatic Play: Farm Animal Puppets

Materials
Paper plates, construction paper, scissors, glue, tongue depressors

Procedure
1. Make several animal puppets from paper plates. Be sure to cut out the eyes. Toddlers like to be able to see.
2. Attach the plate faces onto tongue depressors.
3. Encourage the children to play creatively with the puppets.

Developmental Bonus
Creative expression

For Gross Motor: Put The Snout On The Pig

Materials
Tagboard or posterboard, scissors, markers, thumbtack

Procedure
1. Cut a 15-inch diameter circle from posterboard.
2. Draw pig's ears (inverted triangles) on the top of the pig's head.
3. Color the face pink if you have not used pink posterboard.
4. Cut a snout—a 4-inch diameter circle from the remaining posterboard.
5. Draw two circles for nostrils.
6 Invite the children to pin the snout on the pig, using tape to hold it in place.
7. Older children might like a blindfold, but younger ones can just close their eyes. Getting the snout in position is challenging enough.

Developmental Bonus
Coordination

For Math: Who's The Biggest?

Materials
Picture of farm animals (coloring books are a good source), cardboard, scissors

Procedure
1. Cut out three or four farm animals. Laminate on cardboard to make them more sturdy.
2. Ask the children to place the animals in a line from the smallest to the largest, for example, duck, dog, goat, horse.

Developmental Bonus
Sequencing

For Science: Making Butter

Materials
Whipping cream, baby food jars, crackers, kitchen knives

Procedure
1. Put three or four tablespoons of room temperature whipping cream in each baby food jar.
2. Encourage the children to shake the jars until the cream turns to butter.
3. Pour off leftover liquid.
4. Serve the butter on crackers.

Developmental Bonus
Change of state concept
Large muscle development

Related Bibliography

Brown, Margaret Wise. *Big Red Barn*. HarperCollins, 1956. The story of a farm filled with animals but no people.

Chochola, Frantisek. *On the Farm*. Floris Books, 1987. Lively pictures of events in farm life.

Henley, Claire. *Farm Day*. Dial, 1991. A rooster's crow starts the day on the farm, and each animal is shown doing its thing.

Jones, Carol. *Old MacDonald Had A Farm*. Houghton, 1989. The story and illustrations of the traditional song.

Shapiro, Arnold. L. *Who Says That?* Dutton, 1991. A bright book full of animals and sounds.

Related Records and Tapes

Beall, Pamela Conn and Susan Hagen Nipp. "Old MacDonald Had a Farm" from *Wee Sing Children's Songs and Fingerplays*. Price Stern Sloan, 1979.

Jenkins, Ella. "I Like the Way That They Stack the Hay" from *This-A-Way, That-A-Way*. Folkways, 1973.

Jenkins, Ella. "Did You Feed My Cow" from *You'll Sing a Song, and I'll Sing a Song*. Folkways, 1989.

Weissman, Jackie. "Old MacDonald Had a Whzz" from *Miss Jackie and Her Friends Sing About Peanut Butter, Tarzan and Roosters*. Miss Jackie, 1981.

Rosenshontz. "The Garden Song" from *Rosenshontz Tickles You*. RS Records, 1980.

"In the Barnyard" from *Put Your Finger in the Air*. Kimbo.

I'm a Little Teapot

I'm a little teapot,
Short and stout,
Here is my handle,
Here is my spout.
When I get all steamed up,
Hear me shout,
Just tip me over and pour me out.

Thematic Connections

Home
Family
Friends

Things to Talk About

1. What would you like to eat at a tea party? If we had a pretend tea party, what would we serve?

2. Show a teapot and how it pours. Let the children sample the juice or water you pour.

Curriculum Connections
For Art: Tea Paint

Materials

Tea bags, hot water, teapot, paintbrushes, paper

Procedures

1. Show children a tea bag. Tear it open and show them the leaves.

2. Brew some tea. Make it strong.

3. Allow the children to paint with the undiluted tea.

Developmental Bonus

Creative expression

Curriculum Extension
For Dramatic Play: Tea Party

Materials

Tea cups and saucers, teapots, table and chairs

Procedure

1. Sit with the children and have a pretend tea party.

2. Suggest foods to "eat."

Developmental Bonus

Concept development

Curriculum Extension
For Language: Tall/Short

Materials

Pairs of items that are tall and short—tall teapot, short teapot; tall flower, short flower; tall glass, short glass; tall paper towel tube, short toilet paper tube, etc.

Procedure

1. Encourage the children to group the items into tall and short categories.

Developmental Bonus

Concept development

<u>Curriculum Extension</u>

For Math: Tea Cup Match

Materials

Tea cups and saucers

Procedure

1. Ask the children to match the cups with the correct saucers.

Developmental Bonus

One-to-one correspondence

<u>Curriculum Extension</u>

For Water Play: Pouring

Materials

Teapots with different-sized spouts, cups, tub, water

Procedure

1. Allow the children to explore pouring water into cups from teapots with different-sized spouts.

Developmental Bonus

Hand-eye coordination

Related Bibliography

Hutchins, Pat. *The Door Bell Rang*. William Morrow, 1986. Will there be enough cookies for everyone? Wait, I hear the doorbell ringing!

Kelley, True. *Let's Eat!*. Dutton, 1989. This book explores children's fascination with food. Children of all ages romp across the pages nibbling, sipping, and munching a variety of foods.

Kennedy, Jimmy. *The Teddy Bears' Picnic*. Simon & Schuster, 1991. All the teddy bears have their picnic in the woods on a special day.

Nister, Ernest. *Special Days*. Philomel, 1989. A miniature pull-tab book follows young children as they build castles, play on a tree swing, enjoy tea parties, and share special days.

Pienkowski, Jan. *Little Monsters: Eggs for Tea*. Doubleday, 1990. Five litle monsters share six eggs—poached, fried, scrambled and boiled.

Related Records and Tapes

Beall, Pamela Conn and Susan Hagen Nipp. "I'm a Little Teapot" from *Wee Sing Children's Songs and Fingerplays*. Price Stern Sloan, 1979.

Jack and Jill

Jack and Jill went up the hill,
To fetch a pail of water;
Jack fell down and broke his crown,
And Jim came tumbling after.

Up Jack got and home did trot,
As fast as he could caper,
Went to bed and bound his head
With vinegar and brown paper.

Thematic Connections
Nursery Rhymes

Things to Talk About
1. What made Jack fall down?
2. Why were Jack and Jill going up the hill? What do you think Jack and Jill were going to do with the water?

Curriculum Extension
For Art: Sprinkle Art

Materials
Water, art paper, paintbrushes, salt shakers, dry tempera paint

Procedure
1. Fill the salt shakers with dry tempera paint.
2. Encourage the children to paint water on their papers.
3. After they have covered their papers with water, allow them to shake dry tempera on their papers.
4. The children will enjoy watching the paints run.

Developmental Bonus
Creative expression

Curriculum Extension
For Fine Motor: Pick-Ups

Materials
Pails, construction paper, scissors

Procedure
1. Cut flower shapes from construction paper.
2. Put the flowers on the floor.
3. The children pick up the flowers and put them in their pails.

Developmental Bonus
Hand-eye coordination

Curriculum Extension
For Gross Motor: Tumbling

Materials
Carpeted area or tumbling mat

Procedure

1. Talk about Jack and Jill tumbling down the hill.
2. Show the children how to roll and do somersaults.
3. Encourage the children to tumble and roll on mats.

Developmental Bonus

Large muscle development

Curriculum Extension

For Outdoors: Water Painting

Materials

Pails, water, paintbrushes

Procedure

1. Bring the pails, water and paintbrushes outside.
2. Encourage the children to paint with water on the sidewalks, fences or building.
3. If it is too cold outdoors, try painting water on a piece of paper. Place the paper in a sunny window and watch what happens.

Developmental Bonus

Coordination

Curriculum Extension

For Water Play: Filling Pails

Materials

Tub or water table, water, pails, cups

Procedure

1. Fill a tub or water table with water.
2. Invite the children to pour water from cups to pails.

Developmental Bonus

Hand-eye coordination

Related Bibliography

Ginsburg, Mirra. *The Sun's Asleep Behind the Hill.* Greenwillow, 1982. This book conveys the gathering stillness and sunset as families, children, animals and even the trees come to rest.

Mother Goose. *The Random House Book of Mother Goose: A Treasury of 306 Timeless Nursery Rhymes.* Random House, 1986. Over 300 nursery rhymes including "Little Boy Blue."

Shaw, Nancy. *Sheep in a Jeep.* Houghton, 1986. Silly sheep travel in a jeep, push it up a hill, and get stuck in the mud.

Voake, Charlotte. *Over the Moon: A Book of Nursery Rhymes.* Candlewick, 1992. This version of Mother Goose rhymes is beautifully illustrated and includes a double page spread of Jack and Jill.

Watson, Wendy. *Wendy Watson's Mother Goose.* Lothrop, 1989. Two hundred of the traditional Mother Goose rhymes, some old favorites, and some less familiar—all richly illustrated.

Related Records and Tapes

Beall, Pamela Conn and Susan Hagen Nipp. "Jack and Jill" from *Wee Sing Children's Songs and Fingerplays.* Price Stern Sloan, 1979.

Beall, Pamela Conn and Susan Hagen Nipp. "Jack and Jill" from *Wee Sing Nursery Rhymes and Lullabies.* Price Stern Sloan, 1985.

Sharon, Lois and Bram. "Jack and Jill" from *Mainly Mother Goose.* Elephant, 1984.

Jingle Bells

*Dashing through the snow
In a one horse open sleigh
O'er the fields we go
Laughing all the way*

*Bells on bobtails ring
Making spirits bright
What fun it is to ride and sing
A sleighing song tonight.*

*Jingle bells, jingle bells,
Jingle all the way.
O what fun it is to ride
In a one horse open sleigh.*

*Jingle bells, jingle bells,
Jingle all the way.
O what fun it is to ride
In a one horse open sleigh.*

Thematic Connections

Christmas
Sounds

Things to Talk About

1. Name different kinds of bells, for example, phone, doorbell, Christmas bells, church bells, etc.
2. Have you ever seen snow? What does it look like? What does it feel like?

Curriculum Extension

For Art: Sponge Painting

Materials

Sponges, scissors, tempera paint, drawing paper, meat trays

Procedure

1. Cut sponges into bell shapes.
2. Pour tempera paint into meat trays.

3. Encourage the children to use the sponges to make prints on their paper.

Developmental Bonus

Creative expression

Curriculum Extension

For Creative Movement: Shakes

Materials

Bells, small boxes with lids, tape

Procedure

1. Place several bells in each box and tape shut.
2. Allow the children to shake bells as they sing "Jingle Bells."

Developmental Bonus

Coordination
Rhythm

Curriculum Extension

For Fine Motor: Sweeping Bells

Materials

Bells, pastry brushes, buckets

Procedure

1. Place the bells and pastry brushes on a table, and the buckets on the floor around the table.
2. Invite the children to use the pastry brushes to sweep the bells off the table into the buckets.

Developmental Bonus
Hand-eye coordination

Curriculum Extension

For Gross Motor: Sleighs

Materials
Shallow boxes, rope, scissors

Procedure

1. Cut the rope into 3-foot long pieces.
2. Attach one end of a length of rope to one end of each box to create a box with a pulling rope.
3. Allow the children to put dolls and stuffed animals in the sleighs (boxes) and pull them around the room.

Developmental Bonus
Large muscle development

Curriculum Extension

For Outdoors: Snow

Materials
Shaving cream

Procedure

1. Spray shaving cream on the sidewalk or on an outside table. *NOTE:* If it is too cold outside, do this activity indoors.

2. Encourage the children to play in the shaving cream, making designs and sculptures.
3. Ask the children if they think the shaving cream looks like snow? Feels like snow?

Developmental Bonus
Fine motor development

Related Bibliography

Briggs, Raymond. *The Snowman Storybook.* Random House, 1990. A retelling of Frosty with the same story line.

Day, Alexandra. *Carl's Christmas.* Farrar Straus Giroux, 1990. A wonderful Christmas adventure with Carl.

Pearson, Tracy Campbell. *We Wish You a Merry Christmas.* Dial, 1983. Eight bundled-up little carolers proceed through the snow singing their song until they reach the home of an elderly couple who invite them in. Of course, they demand figgy pudding.

Moreheads, Ruth J. *Christmas Is Coming With Ruth J. Morehead's Holly Babes: A Book of Poems and Songs.* Random House, 1990. A book of poems and songs for very young children.

Traditional. *Jingle Bells.* Aladdin, 1990. Beautiful illustrations accompany the traditional lyrics.

Related Records and Tapes

Palmer, Hap. *Holidays and Rhythms.* Educational Activities, 1971.

Raffi. *Raffi's Christmas Album.* Shoreline, 1983.

We Wish You a Merry Christmas

We wish you a merry Christmas,
We wish you a merry Christmas,
We wish you a merry Christmas,
And a Happy New Year.

Now bring us some figgy pudding,
Now bring us some figgy pudding,
Now bring us some figgy pudding,
And a cup of good cheer.

We won't go until we get some,
We won't go until we get some,
We won't go until we get some,
So bring it out here.

We wish you a merry Christmas,
We wish you a merry Christmas,
We wish you a merry Christmas,
And a Happy New Year.

Thematic Connections
Holidays
Christmas

Things to Talk About
1. Talk about how Christmas cards are used to send greetings and how the phrase "Merry Christmas" is used.
2. List as many things as you can think of that relate to Christmas.

Curriculum Extension
For Art: Christmas Tree Lights

Materials
Green construction paper; scissors; glue; red, yellow and blue tempera paint; cotton swabs

Procedure
1. Cut a Christmas tree shape from the green construction paper for each child.
2. Color a couple of tablespoons of glue with each color of tempera—red, yellow and blue.
3. Encourage the children to dip the cotton swabs in the colored glue and make dots on the trees.

Developmental Bonus
Creative expression

Curriculum Extension
For Fine Motor: Pudding Painting

Materials
Instant pudding, milk, baby food jars, waxed paper

Procedure
1. Mix the pudding and pour into several baby food jars.
2. Encourage the children to shake the jars until the pudding is thick.
3. Empty the pudding on wax paper and allow the children to use it as finger paint.

4. Be sure each child has a sheet of wax paper with an individual portion of pudding because lots of finger-licking will be going on.

Developmental Bonus
Small and large muscle development

Curriculum Extension
For Gross Motor: Red and Green Hop

Materials
Laminated pieces of red and green construction paper (five of each color)

Procedure
1. Place the papers on the floor in a red/green pattern.
2. Encourage the children to hop from paper to paper.
3. See if they can hop on just the green papers. Try just the red papers.

Developmental Bonus
Large muscle development
Coordination

Curriculum Extension
For Math: Ornaments

Materials
Green and red construction paper, scissors

Procedure
1. Cut construction paper into round tree ornaments.
2. Encourage the children to sort the ornaments into the categories of red and green.

Developmental Bonus
Visual discrimination

Curriculum Extension
For Social Studies: Tree of Hands

Materials
Green and red construction paper, scissors, pencil

Procedure
1. Trace each child's hand several times.
2. Cut out each hand.
3. Create a tree on the bulletin board by making overlapping rows of hands (fingers down) and decreasing the number of hands in each row. End with one hand at the top and cover with a red construction paper star.

Developmental Bonus
Creative expression

Related Bibliography

dePaola, Tomie. *Baby's First Christmas*. Putnam, 1988. This board book for toddlers features simple text about all the symbols of Christmas.

Hill, Eric. *Spot's First Christmas*. Putnam, 1983. A lovable puppy named Spot goes through the antics of all small children at Christmas, wrapping gifts, decorating the tree, peeking at presents, and waking up early.

Ingle, Annie. *The Smallest Elf*. Random House, 1990. Elwyn is Santa's smallest elf, but he is the only one who can lift a small boy's depressed spirit.

Moore, Clement. *The Night Before Christmas*. Putman, 1987. A version of the traditional poem with a bear family in the key roles.

Pearson, Tracy Campbell. *We Wish You a Merry Christmas*. Dial, 1983. Eight bundled-up little carolers proceed through the snow singing their song until they reach the home of an elderly couple who invite them in. Of course, they demand figgy pudding.

Related Records and Tapes

Beall, Pamela Conn and Susan Hagen Nipp. "We Wish You a Merry Christmas" from *Wee Sing Children's Songs and Fingerplays*. Price Stern Sloan, 1979.

Palmer, Hap. *Holiday Songs and Rhythms*. Activity Records, 1971.

Raffi. *Raffi's Christmas Album*. Shoreline, 1983.

Richman, Trudie. *I Love a Holiday*. Melody House.

The Muffin Man

Oh, do you know the muffin man,
The muffin man, the muffin man?
Oh, do you know the muffin man,
Who lives in Drury Lane?

Oh, yes we know the muffin man,
The muffin man, the muffin man,
Oh, yes we know the muffin man,
Who lives in Drury Lane.

Thematic Connections
Food/Nutrition
Community Helpers
Cooking

Things to Talk About
1. The muffin man bakes all kinds of muffins. He could be called a baker. Have you ever visited a bakery?
2. Show several types of muffins. Muffins are like cupcakes. Let the children sample the muffins.

Curriculum Extension
For Cooking: Muffins

Materials
Whole wheat flour, sifter, sugar, baking powder, salt, rolled oats, egg, milk, salad oil, measuring cups and spoons, mixing bowl and spoon, muffin tin, oven

Procedure
1. With the children, sift 1 cup whole wheat flour into the bowl.
2. Add 1/4 cup sugar and 3 teaspoons baking powder.
3. Then add 1/2 teaspoon salt, 1 cup oats, 1 slightly beaten egg, 1 cup milk and 3 teaspoons salad oil.
4. Fill each cup of a 12-cup greased muffin pan 2/3 full.
5. Bake at 425 degrees about 15 minutes.
6 Serve and eat. (Increase the recipe for larger classes.)

Developmental Bonus
Measurement concepts

Curriculum Extension
For Dramatic Play: Baker Hats

Materials
White construction paper, scissors, large durable white dinner napkins, stapler

Procedure
1. Cut 2-inch strips of white paper large enough to fit as a band around each child's head. Staple.

2. Open a napkin and staple each of the four corners inside the headband to create a poofed effect.

3. Encourage children to wear their hats for pretend play.

Developmental Bonus
Creative expression

Curriculum Extension

For Fine Motor: Bakery Delights

Materials
Playdough, rolling pin, cookie cutters, cookie sheet

Procedure
1. Encourage the children to use the cookie cutters to make playdough cookies.

2. Place the cookies on the cookie sheet and pretend to bake.

Developmental Bonus
Creative expression
Fine motor development

Curriculum Extension

For Math: Muffin Tin Sort

Materials
Red, yellow, blue and green construction paper; scissors; 12-cup muffin tin; laminating film or clear contact paper

Procedure
1. Cut three circles each of red, yellow, blue and green construction paper to fit in the bottom of the muffin holders.

2. Cut the remainder of the paper into 1-inch squares and laminate.

3. The children sort the paper squares by color into the corresponding muffin holders.

Developmental Bonus
Visual discrimination

Curriculum Extension

For Outdoors: Mud Pies

Materials
Pie tins, mud, leaves, acorns, shells, rocks, sticks

Procedure
1. If necessary, wet the dirt to create mud. If an area of the playground is not available, use potting soil and place in a tub. If the ground is frozen, bring the dirt inside. Bringing something to an unusual place is often enough to spark the children's interest.

2. Encourage the children to make pies from mud and decorate with leaves, sticks, acorns, shells, rocks, etc.

Developmental Bonus
Creative expression
Fine motor development

Related Bibliography

Barkan, Joanne. *Whiskerville Bake Shop.* Putnam, 1990. Two little mice learn what goes on in a bakery.

Fujikawa, Gyo. *See What I Can Be!* Putnam and Gossett, 1990. A great concept book to open little minds to be all they can become.

Galdone, Paul. *The Gingerbread Boy.* Clarion, 1975. The gingerbread boy eludes the grasp of a host of hungry characters until he encounters a clever fox.

Numeroff, Laura Joffe. *If You Give a Moose a Muffin.* HarperCollins, 1991. A cause and effect book that starts with giving a moose a muffin and ends with giving a moose a muffin.

Pryor, Ainslie. *The Baby Blue Cat and the Whole Batch of Cookies.* Puffin, 1991. Baby Blue Cat eats a whole batch of cookies that mother has fixed for all the kittens to eat after playtime, and he has to find a way to confess.

Related Records and Tapes

Scelsa, Greg and Steve Millang. "Muffin Man" from *We All Live Together*, Vol. 2. Youngheart Records. 1978

Moore, Thomas. "Make Myself Some Cookies" from *I Am Special.* Thomas Moore Records.

Rock-a-Bye, Baby

Rock-a-bye, baby,
On the tree top.
When the wind blows,
The cradle will rock.
When the bough breaks,
The cradle will fall,
And down will come baby,
Cradle and all.

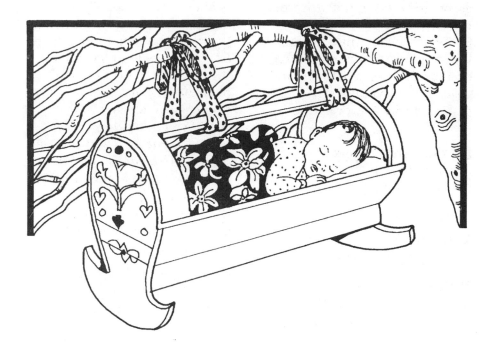

Thematic Connections
Me, Myself and I
Family
Babies

Things to Talk About
1. How do you go to sleep at night? Do you get rocked?
2. Discuss other ways people get to sleep, for example, reading a book, taking a warm bath, watching TV, thinking of nice things, etc.

Curriculum Extension
For Art: Baby Designs

Materials
Tagboard or posterboard; scissors; drawing paper; tempera paint; empty spray bottles; simple patterns of baby items—baby bottle, rattle, stroller, etc.

Procedure
1. Use patterns to cut several baby item shapes from posterboard.
2. Mix tempera to a thick consistency. Fill the spray bottles with paint.
3. Place the baby pattern cutouts on drawing paper.
4. Encourage the children to spray paint from the bottle onto their paper.
5. Pick up the cutouts to expose baby designs.

Developmental Bonus
Creative expression
Content development

Curriculum Extension
For Cooking: Put the Baby to Bed

Materials
One and one-half slices of bread per child, cheese slices, gingerbread boy/girl cookie cutter, optional—toaster oven

Procedure
1. Give each child one and one-half pieces of bread.

2. Help the children cut a gingerbread boy or girl shape from the cheese.

3. Show the children how to lay the gingerbread man shape on the whole slice of bread and cover with the half slice.

4. Toast and eat, or eat untoasted.

Developmental Bonus
Coordination
Creative thinking

Curriculum Extension

For Dramatic Play: Bathe the Baby

Materials
Dolls, tub, towels, empty powder bottles, rocking chair, doll bed

Procedure
1. Show the children how to give a baby a bath, rock it and put it to bed.

2. Encourage the children to give the baby (dolls) a bath, rock them to sleep and put them to bed.

Developmental Bonus
Creative expression

Curriculum Extension

For Language: Baby Books

Materials
Sealable plastic bags, stapler, plastic or cloth colored tape, posterboard or tagboard, scissors

Procedure
1. Staple sealable plastic bags together at the bottom of the bags. Use enough bags to represent one half of the total class members. Use colored tape to cover the staples and to provide a spine for the baggie book.

2. Cut the posterboard or tagboard to fit inside each bag.

3. Send a note home, asking the children to bring a baby picture of themselves to school.

4. On the cover of the book, write "You must have been a beautiful baby." Insert the children's photos in the baggie book and place in the language arts center.

5. Children can find themselves in the book and also look for friends.

Developmental Bonus
Visual discrimination
Concept development

Curriculum Extension

For Science: Mother/Baby Match

Materials
Pictures of mother and baby animals

Procedure
1. Encourage the children to match the pictures of baby animals correctly with their mothers.

Developmental Bonus
Visual discrimination
Concept development

Related Bibliography

Aragon, Jane Chelsea. *Lullaby*. Chronicle Books, 1989. A mother's lullaby carries over farms and towns, meadows and woods, and back again to mother and baby.

Bang, Molly. *Ten, Nine, Eight*. Greenwillow, 1983. Bedtime turns to fun and rhymes as a father puts his daughter to bed.

Fujikawa, Gyo. *Good Night, Sleep Tight! Shhh*. Random House, 1990. A little boy vows that when he grows up, he will play all the time and never sleep.

Ormerod, Jan. *Sleeping*. Lothrop, 1985. Dad and baby go through the ritual of going to bed.

Rice, Eve. *Goodnight, Goodnight*. Greenwillow, 1980. A bedtime story that includes fluorescent white against white-flecked black.

Related Records and Tapes

Beall, Pamela Conn and Susan Hagen Nipp. "Rock-A-Bye, Baby" from *Wee Sing Nursery Rhymes and Lullabies*. Price Stern Sloan, 1985.

The Bus Song

The people in the bus go up and down,
Up and down, up and down.
The people in the bus go up and down,
All around the town.

The wiper on the bus goes "Swish, swish,
swish, ...

The brake on the bus goes "Roomp,
roomp, roomp, ...

The money in the bus goes "Clink, clink,
clink, ...

The wheels on the bus go round and
round, ...

The baby on the bus goes "Wah, wah,
wah," ....

Thematic Connections
Transportation
Community Helpers

Things to Talk About
1. Have you ever ridden on a bus? What was it like?
2. Let's name all the different ways we get from one place to another, for example, walk, run, ride in a car, ride in a stroller, buses, trains, planes, etc.

Curriculum Extension
For Art: Spool Painting

Materials
Yellow construction paper, scissors, tempera paint, meat trays, spools

Procedure
1. Cut construction paper into simple bus shapes.
2. Mix tempera paint and put into meat trays.

3. Encourage the children to use the spools to make wheel shapes all over their buses.

Developmental Bonus
Creative expression
Hand-eye coordination

Curriculum Extension
For Fine Motor: Car Rolling Tracks

Materials
Meat trays, tempera paint, drawing paper, small cars

Procedure
1. Mix tempera paint and place in meat trays.
2. Encourage the children to run cars through paint and then across their paper.

Developmental Bonus
Coordination
Creative expression

For Gross Motor: Buses

Materials
Boxes (large enough for children to fit into), construction paper, scissors, glue

Procedure
1. Cut out construction paper wheels and glue onto the boxes.
2. Place the boxes on the floor.
3. Encourage the children to pretend the boxes are buses.

Developmental Bonus
Creative expression

For Language: Things That Go

Materials
A variety of pictures, some land transportation items (cars, trucks, trains, buses) and some not (animals, furniture, people)

Procedure
1. Go through the pictures with the children and talk about the things that take us places.
2. Invite children to sort through the pictures and find all the means of transportation (things that take us places).

Developmental Bonus
Classification

For Outdoors: Sand Play

Materials
Cars, trucks, buses, mister

Procedure
1. Dampen the sand just a little with the mister.
2. Encourage the children to make tracks in the sand with the vehicles.

Developmental Bonus
Movement concepts

Related Bibliography

Crews, Donald. *School Bus*. Penguin, 1984. Follow the daily journey of a school bus.

Gomi, Taro. *Bus Stops*. Chronicle Books, 1988. A bus makes several stops along its way.

Kovalski, Maryann. *The Wheels on the Bus*. Little, Brown, 1987. While Grandma and kids wait for the bus, they sing "The Wheels on the Bus" and get so involved they miss the bus.

Raffi. *Wheels on the Bus*. McKay, 1990, 1988. A cheerfully illustrated version of the song.

Rockwell, Anne. *Things That Go*. Dutton, 1986. This book covers a variety of familiar vehicles and other movable objects of interest to young children.

Related Records and Tapes

Weissman, Jacki. "Wheels on the Bus" from *Miss Jackie and Her Friends Sing About Peanut Butter, Tarzan and Roosters*. Miss Jackie.

Hammett, Carol Totsky and Elaine Bueffel. "Wheels on the Bus" from *Toddlers on Parade*. Kimbo, 1985.

London Bridge

London Bridge is falling down,
Falling down, falling down,
London Bridge is falling down,
My fair lady.

Build it up with iron bars,
Iron bars, iron bars,
Build it up with iron bars,
My fair lady.

Iron bars will bend and break....

Build it up with pins and needles....

Pins and needles will rust and bend....

Build it up with gravel and stone....

Gravel and stone will wash away....

Thematic Connections
Nursery rhymes
Bridges

Things to Talk About
1. Explain to the children that bridges help us get across water or gullies or any place where our cars couldn't go.
2. There are lots of different kinds of bridges. (Show pictures of examples.)

Curriculum Extension
For Dramatic Play: Building Bridges

Materials
Blocks

Procedure
1. Provide the children with blocks and space for building with them.
2. Help the children build a bridge.

Developmental Bonus
Gross motor development

Curriculum Extension
For Fine Motor: Lock and Key

Materials
Locks, keys

Procedure
1. Make several locks and keys available to the children.
2. Encourage the children to match the keys to the locks.
3. How can the locks be used in the classroom? Try the ideas.

Developmental Bonus
Hand-eye coordination
Fine motor development

Curriculum Extension
For Gross Motor: Walking the Bridge

Materials
Masking tape, beanbag

Procedure

1. Place two or three 6-foot strips of masking tape on the floor.
2. Encourage the children to walk the masking tape line (bridge).
3. Challenge the children to cross the "bridge" with a bean-bag on their heads.

Developmental bonus
Coordination

Curriculum Extension

For Language: Key Match

Materials
Keys, tagboard or posterboard, marker

Procedure

1. Place the keys on the posterboard and trace around each one. Color the keys if you like.
2. Ask the children to match the keys to the shapes on the posterboard.

Developmental Bonus
Visual discrimination

Curriculum Extension

For Science: Falling Down

Materials
Tissue, feather, jar lid, block, leaves, baskets

Procedure

1. Talk about things that fall down, for example, rain, children, snow, leaves, etc.
2. Let the children drop various items into the baskets and observe which falls fast and which falls slowly.

Developmental Bonus
Observation
Concept development

Related Bibliography

Galdone, Paul. *The Three Billy Goats Gruff.* Houghton, 1981. A well-illustrated version of the traditional story of three goats and a mean troll.

Hellard, Susan. *Billy Goats Gruff.* Putnam, 1986. A hilarious version of the story of a mean troll who lives under the bridge where three billy goats are trying to cross.

Hutchins, Pat. *Changes, Changes.* Macmillan, 1987. A wordless book that illustrates wooden dolls building and rebuilding with wooden blocks.

Pragoff, Fiona. *Opposites.* Doubleday, 1989. Various toys help demonstrate opposites such as high-low, empty-full, and up-down.

Spier, Peter. *London Bridge is Falling Down.* Doubleday, 1985. The song comes to life when accompanied by the outstanding illustrations in this book.

Related Records and Tapes

Jenkins, Ella. "If You Go to London Town" from *Hopping Around from Place to Place.* Educational Activities, 1983.

Scelsa, Greg and Steve Millang. "Across the Bridge" from *We All Live Together*, Vol. 4. Youngheart Records, 1980.

"London Bridge" from *Sing-A-Long.* Peter Pan, 1987.

Mary Had a Little Lamb

Mary had a little lamb,
Little lamb, little lamb,
Mary had a little lamb,
Its fleece was white as snow.

And everywhere that Mary went,
Mary went, Mary went,
And everywhere that Mary went,
The lamb was sure to go.

It followed her to school one day,
School one day, school one day,
It followed her to school one day,
Which was against the rule.

It made the children laugh and play,
Laugh and play, laugh and play,
It made the children laugh and play,
To see a lamb at school.

Thematic Connections
Farm
Nursery rhymes
Animals

Things to Talk About
1. How little was Mary's lamb?
2. Do you think Mary's lamb was soft? What does "fleece as white as snow" mean?

Curriculum Extension
For Art: Mary's Lamb

Materials
Paper, markers, glue, paintbrushes, cotton balls

Procedure
1. Draw a lamb on a sheet of paper for each child.
2. Paint glue on the lamb.
3. The toddlers place cotton balls on the lamb.

Developmental Bonus
Creative expression

Curriculum Extension
For Creative Movement: Walk Like a Lamb

Materials
Recording of "Mary Had a Little Lamb"

Procedure
1. Play the music and ask the children to crawl on all fours to imitate Mary's lamb.
2. Act out the story in the song.

Developmental Bonus
Concept development
Large muscle development

Curriculum Extension
For Fine Motor: Lamb Cookies

Materials
Playdough, rolling pin, lamb cookie cutters

Procedure

1. With the children, roll out the playdough.

2. Encourage the children to cut out lamb shapes with the cookie cutters.

Developmental Bonus

Visual discrimination

Curriculum Extension

For Math: Big and Little Lambs

Materials

Two sizes of cutout lambs—big and little, two boxes or baskets

Procedure

1. Help the children sort the lambs according to size.

Developmental Bonus

Concept developmental
Visual discrimination

Curriculum Extension

For Science: Hard and Soft

Materials

A variety of items that are hard (golf ball, spool, crayon, block) and soft (cotton ball, sponge, tissue, sock); small boxes or baskets

Procedure

1. Place all the items on the table.

2. Help the children sort hard into one basket and the soft items into another.

Developmental Bonus

Tactile discrimination
Concept development

Related Bibliography

Barrett, Judi. *Animals Should Definitely Not Act Like People*. Aladdin, 1988. A humorous explanation of how funny it would be if animals acted like people.

Barrett, Judi. *Animals Should Definitely Not Wear Clothing*. Aladdin, 1988. A funny cause and effect story of what would happen if animals wore clothes.

Beskow, Elsa. *Pelle's New Suit*. HarperCollins, 1929. Swedish story of a little boy's acquisition of new clothes from sheep to wool.

Hale, Sarah J. *Mary Had a Little Lamb*. Holiday, 1984. The nursery rhyme and related illustrations.

Archambault, John. *Counting Sheep*. Henry Holt, 1989. A little boy who can't sleep counts sheep.

Related Records and Tapes

Beall, Pamela Conn and Susan Hagen Nipp. "Mary Had a Little Lamb" from *Wee Sing Nursery Rhymes and Lullabies*. Price Stern Sloan, 1985.

Buck, Dennis. "Mary Had A Little Lamb" from *Singable Nursery Rhymes*. Kimbo, 1986.

Three Little Kittens

Three little kittens, they lost their mittens,
And they began to cry,
"Oh, Mother dear, see here, see here,
Our mittens we have lost!"
"What, lost your mittens? You naughty kittens!
Then you shall have no pie."
"Meow! Meow! Meow! Meow!"

Three little kittens, they found their mittens,
And they began to cry,
"Oh, Mother dear, see here, see here,
Our mittens we have found!"
"What, found your mittens? You darling kittens!
Then you shall have some pie."
"Meow! Meow! Meow! Meow!"

Three little kittens, put on their mittens,
And soon ate up the pie.
"Oh, Mother dear, we greatly fear,
Our mittens we have soiled."
"What, soiled your mittens? You naughty kittens!
And they began to sigh,
"Meow! Meow! Meow! Meow!"

Three little kittens, they washed their mittens,
And hung them up to dry.
"Oh, Mother dear, see here, see here,
Our mittens we have washed!"
"What, washed your mittens? You darling kittens!
But I smell a mouse close by!
"Hush! Hush! Hush! Hush!"

Thematic Connections
Nursery Rhymes
Animals

Things to Talk About
1. Have you ever lost anything? What was it? Did you find it?
2. What do you think would have happened if the kittens didn't find their mittens?

Curriculum Extension
For Art: Marvelous Mittens

Materials
Construction paper, scissors, sequins, beads, confetti, tissue paper, glue

Procedure
1. Cut mittens from construction paper.
2. Invite the children to decorate a pair of mittens using sequins, beads, confetti, tissue paper, wallpaper scraps, or any other scrap materials.

Developmental Bonus
Creative expression

Curriculum Extension
For Creative Movement: Move Like a Cat

Materials
None needed

Procedure
1. Demonstrate different ways cats move and behave—slink, stretch, arch, paw, sleep.
2. Ask the children to copy your movements.

Developmental Bonus
Coordination
Creative expression

Curriculum Extension
For Fine Motor: Playdough Pies

Materials
Playdough, pie tins

Procedure
1. Provide the children with playdough and pie tins.

2. Encourage them to make pies.

Developmental Bonus
Creative expression

For Language: Mitten Match

Materials
Red, yellow, blue, green, purple and orange construction paper; scissors

Procedure
1. Cut out a pair of mittens from each color of construction paper.
2. Encourage the children to put mitten pairs together.

Developmental Bonus
Visual discrimination

Curriculum Extension
For Math: Big and Little Mittens

Materials
Construction paper, scissors, stapler

Procedure
1. Cut several pairs of mittens from construction paper in two different sizes (one small, one much larger).
2. Staple the pairs together.
3. Encourage the children to sort the mittens into large and small pairs.

Developmental Bonus
Visual discrimination

Related Bibliography

Cauley, Lorinda Bryan. *The Three Little Kittens*. Putnam, 1982. The traditional tale of mittens lost and found.

Galdone, Paul. *Three Little Kittens*. Clarion, 1988. Three careless little kittens lose their mittens and find them just in time to avoid being in trouble.

McMillian, Bruce. *Kitten Can...* Lothrop, 1984. An engaging calico kitten can do a lot of things. This book is filled with action words.

Polushkin, Maria. *Here's That Kitten!*. Bradbury Press, 1990. A little kitten runs through the house in an attempt to escape the weekly house cleaning.

Tufts, Mary L. *The Wee Kitten Who Sucked Her Thumb*. Platt and Munk, 1988. An amazing parade of animal mothers who offer comical solutions to a little kitten's common childhood "problem."

Related Records and Tapes

Beall, Pamela Conn and Susan Hagen Nipp. "Three Little Kittens" from *Wee Sing Nursery Rhymes and Lullabies*. Price Stern Sloan, 1985.

Jenkins, Ella. "No More Pie" from *Play Your Instruments and Make a Pretty Sound*. Folkways, 1968.

Eensy Weensy Spider

The eensy weensy spider
Climbed up the water spout.
Down came the rain
And washed the spider out.

Out came the sun
And dried up all the rain,
And the eensy weensy spider
Climbed up the spout again.

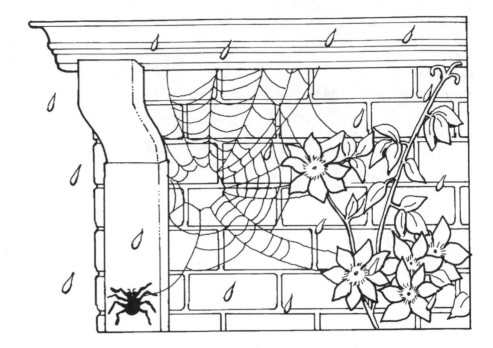

Thematic Connections
Nature
Insects
Living Things

Things to Talk About
1. Where was the spider going?
2. What happened when the rain started?

Curriculum Extension
For Art: Squirt Spider

Materials
Squirt bottles, tempera paint, drawing paper

Procedure
1. Fill squirt bottles with tempera paint.
2. The children squirt the paint onto bulletin board paper or easel paper. (You may want to do this outside.)
3. The resulting spots on the paper will look like spiders.

Developmental Bonus
Creative expression
Small muscle development

Curriculum Extension
For Gross Motor: Pretend Spiders

Materials
None needed

Procedure
1. Ask the children to pretend to be spiders while singing the song.
2. As they pretend to climb the water spout, they will have to stretch their arms and legs.

Developmental Bonus
Large muscle development

Curriculum Extension
For Language: Directions

Materials
Teacher-made spider (pipe cleaners make a good spider), box

Procedure

1. Ask the children to demonstrate positional words by placing the spider **on** the box, **under** the box, **out** of the box, **in** the box, etc.
2. Ask the children where they think spiders live.

Developmental Bonus

Vocabulary development
Concept development

Curriculum Extension

For Outdoors: Invisible Paint

Materials

Bucket, water, paintbrushes

Procedure

1. Let children paint the fence or building outside with water.
2. Talk about how the water disappears when the sun dries it.

Developmental Bonus

Large muscle development
Coordination

Curriculum Extension

For Science: Water Play

Materials

Tub, water, funnels, basters, cups, etc.

Procedure

1. Fill a tub or water table with water.
2. Allow the children to play with the water.
3. Be sure to provide funnels, basters and cups so the children learn about the properties of water.

Developmental Bonus

Hand-eye coordination

Related Bibliography

Carle, Eric. *The Very Busy Spider*. Putnam, 1989. A spider spins a web in a barnyard despite interruptions from barnyard animals.

Graham, Margaret B.. *Be Nice to Spiders*. HarpeCollins, 1967. A collection of good things spiders do for mankind.

Heuninck, Ronald. *Rain or Shine*. Floris Books, 1989. A board book filled with lively pictures of playing in rain and sunshine.

Piper, Watty. *The Little Engine That Could*. Platt and Munk, 1984. The story of a little engine with the same try, try-again attitude as the "Eensy Weensy Spider."

Traditional. *Itsy Bitsy Spider*. DLM, 1991. The lesson behind the song (try, try again) applied to the lives of children.

Related Records and Tapes

Beall, Pamela Conn and Susan Hagen Nipp. "Eentsy Weentsy Spider" from *Wee Sing Children's Songs and Fingerplays*. Price Stern Sloan, 1979.

Hammett, Carol Totsky and Bueffel. "Itsy Bitsy Spider" from *It's Toddler Time*. Kimbo.

Moore, Thomas. "Spiders" from *Singing, Learning and Moving*. Thomas Moore Records.

Richard, Little. "Itsy Bitsy Spider" from *For the Children*.

Little Miss Muffet

Little Miss Muffet
Sat on a tuffet,
Eating her curds and whey;
Along came a spider,
And sat down beside her,
And frightened Miss Muffet away.

Thematic Connections
Spiders
Insects
Nursery Rhymes

Things to Talk About
1. What do you think the spider might have said to frighten Miss Muffet?
2. Describe curds and whey and tuffet.

Curriculum Extension
For Art: Spider's Webs

Materials
Golf ball, white tempera paint, black construction paper, spoon, shallow box

Procedure
1. Place black construction paper in the bottom of a shallow box.
2. Dip a golf ball in white tempera paint and then place it in the box.
3. Ask a toddler to rock the box, rolling the ball back and forth creating a spider web effect.

Developmental Bonus
Creative expression
Coordination

Curriculum Extension
For Cooking: Curds and Whey

Materials
Two cups milk, 1 tablespoon vinegar, salt, crackers, saucepan, hot plate, mixing spoon, spoons and bowls

Procedure
1. Heat 2 cups milk and 1 tablespoon vinegar.
2. Stir to separate curds and whey.
3. Salt to taste and chill.
4. Serve with crackers.

Developmental Bonus
Concept development

For Fine Motor: Spider Dance

Materials
Recorded music

Procedure
1. Ask the children to use one hand as a spider and let it dance to several types of music.
2. Play different kinds of music.
3. While the music is playing, talk about spiders crawling up something, running around, spinning a web.
4. What would it be like to walk on a web?

Developmental Bonus
Fine motor development
Concept development

For Language: Role Playing

Materials
Stool, bowl and spoon

Procedure
1. Let the children take turns acting out the story of "Little Miss Muffet." One child can be Miss Muffet and another the spider.
2. Encourage the child who is the spider to say something to frighten Miss Muffet.
3. Brainstorm ideas of what the spider might have said to frighten Miss Muffet.

Developmental Bonus
Vocabulary development
Concept development

For Science: Close-up Spiders

Materials
Pictures of spiders and spider webs, spider in a jar if possible, spider web preserved on black paper if possible

Procedure
1. Place the pictures of spiders and spider webs in the science area so the children can spend time looking at the pictures.
2. Provide a magnifying glass for close-up inspection of the spider and web.
3. Talk to the children about the parts of a spider.

Developmental Bonus
Observation

Related Bibliography

Carle, Eric. *The Very Busy Spider*. Putnam, 1984. A spider spins a web in a barnyard despite interruptions from barnyard animals.

Graham, Margaret B. *Be Nice to Spiders*. HarperCollins, 1967. A collection of good things spiders do for mankind.

Heuninck, Ronald. *Rain or Shine*. Floris Books, 1989. A board book filled with lively pictures of playing in rain and sunshine.

McNulty, Faith. *The Lady and the Spider*. HarperCollins, 1986. A spider lives happily in a vegetable until one day when a lady picks the lettuce where he lives.

Traditional. *Itsy Bitsy Spider*. DLM, 1991. The lesson behind the song (try, try again) applied to the lives of children.

Related Records and Tapes

Beall, Pamela Conn and Susan Hagen Nipp. "Little Miss Muffet" from *Wee Sing Children's Songs and Fingerplays*. Price Stern Sloan, 1979.

Moore, Thomas. "Itsy Bitsy Spider" from *Singing, Learning and Moving*. Thomas Moore Records.

Moore, Thomas. "Spiders" from *Songs for the Whole Day*. Thomas Moore Records.

Baa, Baa, Black Sheep

Baa, baa, black sheep,
Have you any wool?
Yes, sir, yes, sir,
Three bags full.
One for my master,
One for my dame,
And one for the little boy
Who lives in the lane.

Thematic Connections
Animals
Sheep
Nursery Rhymes

Things to Talk About
1. Mittens, sweaters and coats are made from wool. Wool comes from sheep.
2. Most sheep are white, but every once in a while one is born black. Black sheep are unusual and rare.

Curriculum Extension
For Art: Black, Black, Black

Materials
Black tempera paint, easel paper, paintbrushes, easel

Procedure
1. Set up the easel with paper and black paint.
2. Encourage the children to paint with the black paint.

Developmental Bonus
Concept development
Creative expression

Curriculum Extension
For Fine Motor: Filling Bags

Materials
Lunch bags, styrofoam peanuts

Procedure
1. Place the styrofoam pieces and bags on the table.
2. Ask the children to fill a bag with the styrofoam pieces.
3. Talk about the bags being empty and full.

Developmental Bonus
Concept development
Fine motor development

For Math: One, Two, Three

Materials
Black construction paper, scissors, sheep pattern, three lunch bags, newspaper, string

Procedure
1. Cut three sheep from construction paper.
2. Fill three bags with wadded newspaper and tie each at the top with string.
3. Ask the children to match each sheep to a bag.
4. Model the activity, saying, "One bag for each sheep and one sheep for each bag."

Developmental Bonus
One-to-one correspondence

For Sand Play: Bags Full

Materials
Lunch bags, containers, shovels, sand, cups, scoops

Procedure
1. Encourage the children to fill the lunch bags with sand.
2. Fill other containers with sand.
3. Talk about being empty and full.

Developmental Bonus
Concept development

For Science: Fabric Match

Materials
Pieces of wool, nylon, net, silk and cotton; scissors

Procedure
1. Be sure each piece of fabric is a distinct color or pattern.
2. Cut two 2-inch squares from each fabric.
3. Mix up the squares.
4. Invite the children to match similar textures, then match colors and patterns.

Developmental Bonus
Tactile discrimination

Related Bibliography

Galdone, Paul. *Little Bo Peep*. Clarion, 1986. The Mother Goose rhyme is updated in this version of a pretty blue-eyed girl and her twelve wayward sheep.

Keller, Holly. *Ten Sleepy Sheep*. Greenwillow, 1983. Lewis can't sleep so he counts sheep until he has a room full.

Mother Goose. *Baa, Baa, Black Sheep*. Lodestar, 1991. Exuberant art work brings new life to the traditional nursery rhyme.

Pragoff, Fiona. *Opposites*. Doubleday, 1989. Various toys help demonstrate opposites such as high-low, empty-full, and up-down.

Willebeek le Mair, Henriette. *Our Old Nursery Rhymes*. Philomel, 1989. Thirty nursery rhymes, including "Baa, Baa, Black Sheep," are nicely illustrated in this book that was first printed in 1913.

Related Records and Tapes

Beall, Pamela Conn and Susan Hagen Nipp. "Baa, Baa, Black Sheep" from *Wee Sing Nursery Rhymes and Lullabies*. Price Stern Sloan, 1985.

"Baa, Baa, Black Sheep" from *Sing-A-Long*. Peter Pan, 1987.

The Mulberry Bush

Here we go round the mulberry bush,
The mulberry bush, the mulberry bush,
Here we go round the mulberry bush,
So early in the morning.

This is the way we wash our clothes...
So early Monday morning.

This is the way we iron our clothes...
So early Tuesday morning.

This is the way we mend our clothes...
So early Wednesday morning.

This is the way we scrub the floor...
So early Thursday morning.

This is the way we sweep the house...
So early Friday morning.

This is the way we bake our bread...
So early Saturday morning.

This is the way we go to church...
So early Sunday morning.

Thematic Connections
Home
Days of the Week

Things to Talk About
1. A mulberry bush is a small tree that grows berries.
2. What did you do when you got up this morning?

Curriculum Extension
For Art: Leaf Collages

Materials
Leaves, paper, glue

Procedure
1. Place the leaves, paper and glue on the table.
2. Encourage the children to glue leaves onto their paper to create a collage.

Developmental Bonus
Creative expression

Curriculum Extension
For Gross Motor: Bubbles, Bubbles

Materials
Liquid detergent, water, glycerine (available at drug stores), measuring cup and spoons, large jar, blowers

Procedure
1. Make a bubble mixture by mixing 1/2 cup liquid dishwashing soap, 1/2 cup water and 1 teaspoon glycerine in a large jar.
2. Blow bubbles.
3. Let the children chase and catch them.

Developmental Bonus
Hand-eye coordination
Large muscle development

For Language: Sock Match

Materials
Laundry basket, several pairs of socks

Procedure
1. Empty the basket of unmatched socks onto a table.
2. Encourage the children to match socks, roll pairs together and place in the basket.

Developmental Bonus
Visual discrimination

For Math: Patterning

Materials
Two pieces of differently-patterned wallpaper, scissors, yarn

Procedure
1. Cut shirt shapes from the wallpaper.
2. Cut a three-foot piece of yarn.
3. Place the yarn on the table like a clothesline.
4. Show children how to make a pattern with the wallpaper shirts.
5. Encourage children to place the clothes (shirts) on the line (yarn), alternating the patterns.

Developmental Bonus
Patterning

For Outdoors: Washing Clothes

Materials
Tub, water, soap, doll clothes, clothespins, clothesline

Procedure
1. Let the children wash doll clothes, rinse them and hang them on a line to dry.
2. This is a messy activity. Dress the children accordingly; they will get wet.

Developmental Bonus
Concept development

Related Bibliography

Carle, Eric. *The Very Hungry Caterpillar*. Putnam, 1981. A hungry caterpillar eats a variety of food from Monday through Sunday before becoming a butterfly.

Dickens, Lucy. *My Sister and Me Outside*. Penguin, 1991. This board book conveys the special bond of sister and brother as they enjoy the pleasures of outside.

Domanska, Janina. *Busy Monday Morning*. Greenwillow, 1985. A Polish folk song about the days of the week.

Hooper, Meredith. *Seven Eggs*. HarperCollins, 1989. Seven eggs hatch, one each day of the week, with a different baby inside. On Monday, it is a baby penguin, on Tuesday a baby crocodile, and so on until Sunday has a surprise for all.

Noble, Trinka Hakes. *The Day Jimmy's Boa Ate the Wash*. Dial, 1984. When Jimmy's unusual pet accompanies the class, an ordinary field trip to the farm turns into a hilarious, slapstick romp.

Related Records and Tapes

Beall, Pamela Conn and Susan Hagen Nipp. "The Mulberry Bush" from *Wee Sing Children's Songs and Fingerplays*. Price Stern Sloan.

Scelsa, Greg and Steve Millang. "Rock Around the Mulberry Bush" from *We All Live Together*, Vol. 3. Youngheart Records, 1979.

"All Around the Mulberry Bush" from *Sing-A-Long*. Peter Pan, 1989.

Six White Ducks

Six white ducks that I once knew
Fat ducks, skinny ducks, fair ones, too.
But the one little duck with a feather on his back
He ruled the others with a quack, quack, quack!
Quack, quack, quack, quack, quack, quack.
He ruled the others with a quack, quack, quack!

Down to the river they would go
Wibble, wobble, wibble, wobble, all in a row.
But the one little duck with a feather on his back
He ruled the others with a quack, quack, quack!
Quack, quack, quack, quack, quack, quack.
He ruled the others with a quack, quack, quack.

Home from the river they would come,
Wibble, wobble, wibble, wobble, ho-hum-hum!
But the one little duck with a feather on his back
He led the others with a quack, quack, quack
Quack, quack, quack, quack, quack, quack.
He led the others with a quack, quack, quack.

Thematic Connections

Animals
Numbers

Things to Talk About

1. Ducks like to live in the water. They eat corn, seeds, bread and bugs.
2. Have you ever fed the ducks? Where? What did you feed them?

Curriculum Extension
For Art: Feather Painting

Materials
Feathers, tempera paint, drawing paper

Procedure
1. Show the children how to dip the feather in the paint and brush it gently on the paper.
2. Allow the children to paint using a feather as a brush.

Developmental Bonus
Creative expression

Curriculum Extension
For Fine Motor: White, White

Materials
Shaving cream

Procedure
1. Spray shaving cream on a table and allow children to play in the cream, creating patterns and hills.
2. Talk about how some ducks are white like the shaving cream.

Developmental Bonus
Fine motor development

Curriculum Extension
Gross Motor: Follow the Leader

Materials
Feather, sheet, table

Procedure
1. Place the sheet over a table to create a tunnel.

228

2. Choose one child to be the leader. Let that child carry the feather.

3. Encourage children to follow the child with the feather around the room and through the tunnel.

4. Talk about how ducks like to walk in a line following a leader.

Developmental Bonus
Large muscle development

Curriculum Extension

For Math: Fat and Skinny

Materials
Poker chips, coffee cans with lids, super glue

Procedure
1. Glue five poker chips together to make a fat chip (make several fat chips).

2. Cut two slots in the top of each coffee can—one fat (big enough for fat chips to slip through) and one thin.

3. Let the children push the chips through the appropriate slots.

Developmental Bonus
Visual discrimination
Concept development

Curriculum Extension

For Outdoors: Ducks Afloat

Materials
Rubber ducks, tub, water, small net

Procedure
1. If it is a nice, warm day set a tub or the water table outside.

2. Fill with water.

3. Encourage the children to play creatively with the ducks in the water.

4. See if the children can catch the ducks in the net.

Developmental Bonus
Dramatic play

Related Bibliography

Cartlidge, Michelle. *Duck in the Pond*. Dutton, 1991. All the happenings in a duck's life are explored in this simple text book.

Gerstein, Mordical. *Follow Me!* Morrow, 1983. A confused and hungry group of ducks try to make it home for dinner.

Roy, Ron. *Three Ducks Went Wandering*. Seabury, 1979. Three little ducks encounter lots of surprises when they venture outside the barnyard.

Tafuri, Nancy. *Have You Seen My Duckling?* Greenwillow, 1984. A mother duck searches for her missing baby.

Wellington, Monica. *All My Little Ducklings*. Dutton, 1989. A parade of downy ducklings wiggle and waggle across the pages of this great book with a song-like text.

Related Records and Tapes

Beall, Pamela Conn and Susan Hagen Nipp. "Six Little Ducks" from *Wee Sing Nursery Rhymes and Lullabies*. Price Stern Sloan, 1985.

Raffi. "Six White Ducks" from *More Singable Songs*. Shoreline, 1988.

Twinkle, Twinkle, Little Star

Twinkle, twinkle, little star,
How I wonder what you are.
Up above the world so high,
Like a diamond in the sky.
Twinkle, twinkle little star,
How I wonder what you are.

When the blazing sun is gone,
When he nothing shines upon,
Then you show your little light,
Twinkle, twinkle, all the night.
Twinkle, twinkle, little star,
How I wonder what you are.

Thematic Connections

Nature
Up, Down and All Around

Things to Talk About

1. Where are the stars?
2. Do we see stars in the day-time?

Curriculum Extension

For Art: Crayon Resist

Materials
Drawing paper, crayons, sponge, tempera or watercolor paints

Procedure
1. Draw stars with a crayon on a piece of easel paper. (Make one for each child.)
2. Allow the children to use a sponge to wash over the paper with tempera or watercolor paints.
3. The children will be delighted when the stars come shining through.

Developmental Bonus
Creative expression

Curriculum Extension

For Cooking: Stars

Materials
Gelatin, hot water, cookie sheet, star-shaped cookie cutters

Procedure
1. Make the gelatin with the children.
2. Spread in a cookie sheet to cool.
3. When cool, encourage the children to use a star-shaped cookie cutter to make stars.

Developmental Bonus
Concept development

Curriculum Extension

Gross Motor: Star Steps

Materials
Cardboard, scissors

Procedure

1. Cut out large cardboard stars.

2. Place on the floor for children to step on, step over, hop onto, hop over, line up on, etc.

Developmental Bonus

Large muscle development

Curriculum Extension

For Math: New Words for Size

Materials

None needed

Procedure

1. Change the words in the song to reflect different-sized stars (big star, tiny star, giant star, teeny star).

2. Sing the song with a big voice when using "big" star, a quiet voice when singing about a "tiny" star, etc.

Developmental Bonus

Language development

Curriculum Extension

For Science: Where Am I Found?

Materials

Magazine pictures

Procedure

1. Provide toddlers with pictures of things found in the sky and things found on the ground.

2. Let them classify the pictures.

Developmental Bonus

Visual discrimination
Concept development

Related Bibliography

Aragon, Jane Chelsea. *Lullaby.* Chronicle Books, 1989. A mother's lullaby carries out into the night over towns, farms, meadows, and woods and back again.

Brown, Margaret Wise. *Goodnight Moon.* HarperCollins, 1947. A small rabbit says goodnight to everything in his room.

Murphy, Jill. *What Next, Baby Bear!* Dial, 1984. The stars are out, the sky is clear, and the night is right for a trip to the moon.

Oxenbury, Helen. *Goodnight, Good Morning.* Penguin, 1982. These delightful pictures tell the story of bedtime, nighttime and morning.

Zolotow, Charlotte. *The Summer Night.* HarperCollins, 1974. A little girl and her father share the evening just before bedtime.

Related Records and Tapes

Beall, Pamela Conn and Susan Hagen Nipp. "The Mulberry Bush" from *Wee Sing Children's Songs and Fingerplays.* Price Stern Sloan, 1979.

Hegner, Priscilla and Rose Grasselli. "Twinkly Little Star" from *Touch, Teach and Hug a Toddler.* Kimbo, 1985.

Moore, Thomas. *Opera Singer ("Twinkle, Twinkle Little Star")* from *Singing, Moving, and Learning.* Thomas Moore.

Humpty Dumpty

Humpty Dumpty sat on a wall,
Humpty Dumpty had a great fall;
All the King's horses and all the King's men
Couldn't put Humpty together again.

Thematic Connections
Nursery Rhymes

Things to Talk About
1. Humpty Dumpty was an egg-shaped person. Do you think Humpty was a boy or a girl? Why?
2. What do you think might have made Humpty fall?

Curriculum Extension
For Art: Colorful Eggs

Materials
Easel paper, scissors, tempera paints, easels, paintbrushes

Procedure
1. Cut easel paper into egg shapes.
2. Let the children paint on the egg-shaped paper.

Developmental Bonus
Creative expression

Curriculum Extension
For Cooking: Egg Shakes

Materials
Blender, frozen orange juice, egg, ice, pitcher, cups

Procedure
1. Keep the egg at the proper temperature and be sure that it is free of bacteria.
2. With the toddlers, mix the orange juice in the pitcher.
3. Pour the orange juice in a blender and add one raw egg and several ice cubes.
4. Blend.
5. Pour a cup for each child.

Developmental Bonus
Measurement concepts

For Creative Movement: Egg Shakers

Materials

Large plastic eggs for each child, dried corn, glue, recorded music

Procedure

1. Put a tablespoon of dried corn in each egg and glue closed.
2. Play music.
3. Let the children shake their egg shakers to music.

Developmental Bonus

Creative expression
Rhythm

For Fine Motor: Big Egg Puzzles

Materials

Tagboard or posterboard, scissors, crayons or markers

Procedure

1. Cut an oval (egg shape) from the posterboard.
2. Decorate it to look like Humpty Dumpty.
3. Cut Humpty Dumpty into simple puzzle pieces.
4. Allow children to put Humpty together again.

Developmental Bonus

Visual discrimination
Hand-eye coordination

For Gross Motor: Egg Toss

Materials

White lunch bag, markers, newspaper, string, box, beanbags

Procedure

1. Draw a face on a white paper bag, stuff with newspaper and tie the top.
2. Sit Humpty Dumpty (bag) on a box. (Decorate like a wall if desired.)
3. The children throw beanbags and knock Humpty Dumpty off the wall.

Developmental Bonus

Hand-eye coordination
Large muscle development

Related Bibliography

Ginsburg, Mirra. *Good Morning, Chick.* Greenwillow, 1980. Bright, simple illustrations depict a baby chick emerging from its shell and exploring the new world.

Hooper, Meredith. *Seven Eggs.* HarperCollins, 1989. Seven eggs hatch, one each day of the week, with a different baby inside. On Monday, it is a baby penguin, on Tuesday a baby crocodile, and so on until Sunday has a surprise for all.

Mother Goose. *Mother Goose: A Collection of Classic Nursery Rhymes.* Holt, 1984. Mother Goose, including "Humpty Dumpty."

Mother Goose. *The Random House Book of Mother Goose.* Random House, 1986. A collection of 306 Mother Goose rhymes nicely illustrated.

Pienkowski, Jan. *Little Monsters: Eggs for Tea.* Doubleday, 1990. Five little monsters share six eggs—scrambled, boiled, fried and poached.

Related Records and Tapes

Beall, Pamela Conn and Susan Hagen Nipp. "Humpty Dumpty" from *Wee Sing Nursery Rhymes and Lullabies.* Price Stern Sloan.

Moore, Thomas. "Humpty Dumpty" from *I Am Special.* Thomas Moore Records.

Row, Row, Row Your Boat

Row, row, row your boat
Gently down the stream.
Merrily, merrily, merrily, merrily
Life is but a dream.

Thematic Connections
Transportation
Boats
Nursery Rhymes

Things to Talk About
1. The song says, "Gently down the stream." What is meant by gently?
2. Can you think of some things we handle gently, for example, butterflies, eggs, glass, etc.?

Curriculum Extension
For Art: Walnut Boats

Materials
Walnuts, nutcracker, playdough, construction paper, scissors, toothpicks, tape

Procedure
1. Crack walnuts in half and remove meat.
2. Help the children place playdough in the center of a walnut half.
3. Cut a triangle (flag) from construction paper and tape to the toothpick.
4. Let the children place their flag in the playdough.

Developmental Bonus
Creative expression

Curriculum Extension
For Cooking: Banana Boats

Materials
Bananas, cottage cheese, spoons, cherries, bowls and spoons

Procedure
1. Peel bananas and split in half.
2. The toddlers spoon cottage cheese on top of the banana half and place a cherry on top.
3. Eat and enjoy.

Developmental Bonus
Hand-eye coordination

For Fine Motor: Fishing

Materials

Fish cut from construction paper, round cardboard tube from a hanger, string, magnet, paper clips

Procedure

1. Make a fishing pole using a cardboard tube from a hanger.
2. Tie a magnet to the string and attach the string to the pole.
3. Place a paper clip on the nose of each fish.
4. Encourage children to catch fish by touching the fish's nose with the magnet.

Developmental Bonus

Hand-eye coordination

For Gross Motor: Pretend Boats

Materials

Several cardboard boxes, paper towel tubes

Procedure

1. Suggest that the toddlers get in the boxes and pretend they are in boats. (It won't take much suggesting.)
2. Show them how to row using the paper towel tubes as oars.

Developmental Bonus

Large muscle development

Water Table: Boat Float

Materials

Water, tub, several small boats, boats from art activity

Procedure

1. Move this activity outdoors if it is a warm day.
2. Allow the children to float the boats.
3. Demonstrate how wind on the sails moves the boats (blow on sails, fan sails, etc.).

Developmental Bonus

Concept development

Related Bibliography

Allen, Pamela. *Who Sank the Boat?* Putnam, 1990. A cow, a donkey, a sheep, a pig, and a mouse decide to go out rowing in a boat that's too small.

Burningham, John. *Mr. Gumpy's Outing.* Henry Holt, 1990. Although Mr. Gumpy cautions his many boat passengers to behave, they ignore his warning and the boat turns over.

Graham, Thomas. *Mr. Bear's Boat.* Dutton, 1988. A bear builds a boat and sets sail straight into trouble.

Lear, Edward. *The Owl and the Pussycat.* Clarion, 1989. The story of two sweethearts who set sail in a pea-green boat.

Long, Earlene. *Gone Fishing.* Houghton Mifflin, 1984. A boy and his father get up early and go fishing.

Related Records and Tapes

Beall, Pamela Conn and Susan Hagen Nipp. "Row, Row, Row Your Boat" from *Wee Sing Sing-Alongs*. Price Stern Sloan, 1990.

Bert and Ernie. "Row, Row, Row Your Boat" from *Bert and Ernie Sing Along*. Sesame Street, 1975.

Sharon, Lois and Bram. "The Wind" from *One Elephant, Deux Elephants*. Elephant, 1978.

Ring Around a Rosy

Ring around a rosy,
A pocket full of posy,
Ashes, ashes,
All fall down.

Thematic Connections
Shapes
Flowers

Things to Talk About
1. "Ring around" means to make a circle around. A circle is round with no sides.
2. What kinds of things fall down? (rain, leaves, children)

Curriculum Extension

For Creative Movement: Circles and Circles

Materials
Masking tape, beanbags

Procedure
1. Make two or three tape circles (six feet in diameter) on the floor.
2. Invite the toddlers to walk around the circle, trying to stay on the tape.
3. Encourage them to walk the circle with a beanbag on their heads.

Developmental Bonus
Balance
Concept development

Curriculum Extension

For Dramatic Play: Bracelets

Materials
Cardboard rings from inside masking tape, colored tissue paper, scissors, glue

Procedure
1. Cut tissue paper into small squares 2 x 2 inches.
2. The children crinkle the tissue paper squares and glue them onto cardboard rings.
3. Encourage the children to use the rings as bracelets for creative play.
4. Talk about the ring (round) shape of bracelets.

Developmental Bonus
Creative expression

For Language: Ring Around the Flowers

Materials

Paper plates, scissors, pictures of flowers and other assorted items

Procedure

1. Cut center out from the paper plates to make rings.
2. Place pictures of flowers and other items on the table.
3. The children place the paper plate rings around all the flowers.
4. Then ask the children to put a paper plate ring around all the animals, etc.

Developmental Bonus

Visual discrimination

For Outdoors: Hula Hoops

Materials

Hula hoops, beanbags

Procedure

1. Talk about the ring shape of the hula hoop.
2. Encourage the children to roll hoops.
3. The children can also toss beanbags into the hoops.

Developmental Bonus

Hand-eye coordination
Concept development

For Science: Rosy Reflections

Materials

Pink cellophane, scissors, tape

Procedure

1. Cut several shapes—flower, square, circle—from the cellophane.
2. Tape the shapes on the window.
3. Show the children the rose-colored reflections that will appear when the sun shines through the cellophane.

Developmental Bonus

Observation

Related Bibliography

Artell, Mike. *I See Circles*. DLM, 1990. A rhyming verse about circle shapes everywhere.

Freeman, Don. *A Pocket for Corduroy*. Viking, 1978. Lisa loses her bear in the laundromat overnight when he wanders off while searching for a pocket.

Lobel, Arnold. *The Rose in My Garden*. Greenwillow, 1984. A cumulative text describes a garden's solitude being overturned by a field mouse, a cat, and a bee.

Miranda, Anne. *Baby Walk*. Dutton, 1988. A baby reacts to all he hears including "all fall down" in "Ring Around a Rosey."

Oxenbury, Helen. *All Fall Down*. Macmillan, 1987. All about falls from "Ring Around the Rosy" to accidents.

Related Records and Tapes

Beall, Pamela Conn and Susan Hagen Nipp. "Ring Around the Rosy" from *Wee Sing Children's Songs and Fingerplays*. Price Stern Sloan, 1979.

Where Is Thumbkin?

Where is thumbkin,
Where is thumbkin?
Here I am, here I am.
How are you this morning?
Very well, I thank you,
Run away, run away.

Where is pointer....
Where is middle finger....
Where is ring finger....
Where is pinkie....
Where's the whole family....

Thematic Connections

Me, Myself and I
Family

Things to Talk About

1. Talk about how we use our fingers, for example, for eating, for coloring.

2. Discuss how we use our hands and fingers to communicate, for example, okay, pointing, thumbs up, saying "hi," etc.

Curriculum Extension

For Art: Fingerprints

Materials

Drawing paper, finger paints

Procedure

1. Allow the children to play with finger paints on a table top.

2. Before cleaning up, help the children make finger paint designs on drawing paper.

Developmental Bonus

Creative expression

Curriculum Extension

For Cooking: Thumb Print Cookies

Materials

Frozen sugar cookie dough, sugar, red food coloring, cookie tray, oven

Procedure

1. Color sugar with red food coloring.

2. Give each child a small amount of dough to roll, flatten and place on the cookie sheet.

3. Tell the children to stick their thumbs in the colored sugar and press a thumb print in the middle of their cookie.

4. Bake and serve.

Developmental Bonus

Fine motor development

For Fine Motor: Playdough Creations

Material

Playdough, pipe cleaners, styrofoam pieces

Procedure

1. With the children, knead the playdough.
2. Show them how to make holes in the playdough with their fingers.
3. Invite them to make playdough creations with pipe cleaners, styrofoam pieces, etc.

Developmental Bonus

Fine motor development
Creative expressions

For Language: Ring Around the Middle

Materials

Paper plates (8-inch size); sets of items—three blocks, three crayons, three cups, three spools, etc.

Procedure

1. Cut out the centers from the paper plates.
2. Arrange a set of items in a line on a table.
3. Talk to children about the arrangement—items that are first, middle and last.
4. Ask the children to put a ring around the item in the middle.
5. Add another set of items and repeat until all the sets are on the table.

Developmental Bonus

Concept development

For Outdoors: Hide and Seek

Materials

None needed

Procedure

1. Encourage the toddlers to hide, then find them.
2. Reverse roles. You hide, they find you.

Developmental Bonus

Critical thinking

Related Bibliography

Brown, Marc. *Hand Rhymes*. Dutton, 1985. Fingerplays and singing games with accompanying directions and illustrations.

Brown, Margaret Wise. *The Runaway Bunny*. HarperCollins, 1977. A story of a bunny's imaginary game of hide-and-seek and the lovingly steadfast mother who finds him every time.

Oxenbury, Helen. *I Touch*. Random House, 1990. A toddler enjoys the sensation of touching everything from worms to cat's fur.

Peppe, Rodney. *Thumbprint Circus*. Delacorte, 1989. Thumbkin, the little clown, is the star of the circus. All the illustrations are made from thumbprints and simple lines.

Related Records and Tapes

Beall, Pamela Conn and Susan Hagen Nipp. "Where is Thumbkin?" from *Wee Sing Children's Songs and Fingerplays*. Price Stern Sloan, 1979.

Sharon, Lois and Bram. "Where is Thumbkin?" from *One, Two, Three, Four, Live!*. Elephant Records., 1982.

Sharon, Lois and Bram. "Where is Thumbkin?" from *In the Schoolyard*. Elephant Records, 1981.

Parents are a great source for collecting recyclable items. Use these suggestions, add your own and send them home to parents in the form of a request. You'll be surprised at the results, and the children in your classroom will be able to create "terrific treasures" from these throw-away items.

Aluminum foil
Appliance boxes
Beads
Belts
Blocks
Boards
Boots
Bottles (glass and plastic)
Bracelets
Braiding
Buttons
Calendars
Cardboard
Cardboard tubes
Carpet squares
Cellophane
Checkbooks
Cigar boxes
Coats
Computer print-out paper
Confetti
Cord
Corrugated paper
Costume jewelry
Dowels
Dresses
Earrings
Egg cartons
Film containers
Gloves
Gourds
Hairpins
Hat boxes
Hats
Jackets
Jars (all sizes)
Jugs
Keys
Laces
Linoleum
Magazines
Marbles
Metal
Mittens
Necklaces

Neckties
Newspapers
Nightgowns
Nuts
Packing bills
Pans
Pants
Panty hose containers
Paper bags
Petticoats
Photographs
Pinecones
Pipe cleaners
Plastic berry boxes
Purses
Recyclables
Ribbon
Rickrack
Rings
Rocks
Roll-on deodorant bottles
Rug yarn
Sand
Sandpaper
Scarves
Seashells
Seeds
Shirts
Shoe boxes
Shoes
Skirts
Socks
Sponges
Spools
Stamps/stickers
Stationery boxes
Sticks
Styrofoam trays
Sweaters
Tape
Telephone wire
Tin cans (all sizes)
Tongue depressors
Velcro
Wallets

Wallpaper
Wire screen
Wooden clothespins
Wrapping paper
Yarn

INDEX OF BOOKS

INDEX OF TERMS

The GIANT Encyclopedia
of Theme Activities For Children 2 to 5
Over 600 Favorite Activities
Created by Teachers for Teachers

A nationwide contest with thousands of entries produced this large book. There are 48 themes filled with more than 600 teacher-developed activities that work. From the alphabet and art to winter and zoo there are themes for every season and every day of the year.

All activities are clearly described and ready to use with a minimum of preparation. This is an ideal resource for a busy teacher. The book has a special strengthened binding which allows it to lie flat on a table. 512 pages.

ISBN 0-87659-166-7   **Gryphon House**
19216   **Paperback**

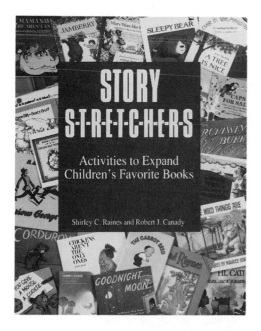

Story S-t-r-e-t-c-h-e-r-s®:
Activities to Expand Children's
Favorite Books (Pre-K and K)

Shirley C. Raines and Robert J. Canady

It's original. It's fun. It's 450 terrific teaching ideas that are based upon the latest research on how young children become good readers. It connects 90 of the best children's books to every learning center science, nature, math, art, music, movement, cooking, circle time.

Each book is "stretched" five ways with lively learning activities that heighten reading readiness and sharpen comprehension skills, too. And it's so easy to use! 256 pages.

ISBN 0-87659-119-5   **Gryphon House**
10011   **Paperback**

MORE Story S-t-r-e-t-c-h-e-r-s®: More Activities to Expand Children's Favorite Books

Shirley C. Raines and Robert J. Canady

The same lively learning as the first **Story S-t-r-e-t-c-h-e-r-s®,** The same organization with 18 completely integrated units.

What's different? **MORE Story S-t-r-e-t-c-h-e-r-s®** gives you 450 all-new teaching ideas using 90 more of the most popular children's books. With **MORE Story S-t-r-e-t-c-h-c-r-s®** you'll continue to instill a love of learning and a fondness for good books. 256 pages.

ISBN 0-87659-153-5
10020

Gryphon House
Paperback

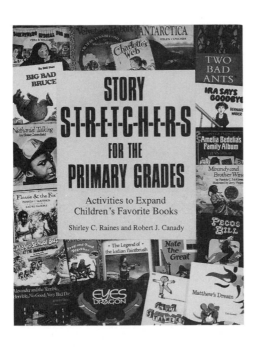

Story S-t-r-e-t-c-h-e-r® for the Primary Grades 1-3

Shirley C. Raines and Robert J.Canady

Written for grades one to three, this **Story S-t-r-e-t-c-h-e-r-s®** is total whole language — it fosters vital skills in listening, reading, speaking and writing. Using popular children's books, you'll teach science, nature, math, art, social studies, drama, writing every curriculum area! 256 pages.

- 5 titles in each unit
- 18 thematic units, completely integrated
- 450 fresh new teaching ideas — based on 90 teacher-recommended books
- Classroom-tested, developmentally sound — full of learning discoveries that children love!

ISBN 0-87659-157-8
10026

Gryphon House
Paperback

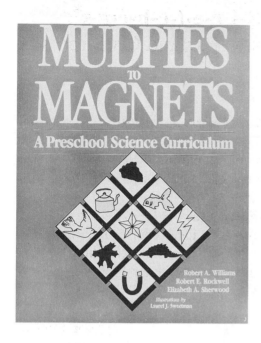

Mudpies to Magnets
A Preschool Science Curriculum

*Robert A. Williams, Robert E. Rockwell, and
Elizabeth A. Sherwood, Illustrated by
Laurel Sweetman*

   These 112 science experiments cover a wide range of topics, include the repetition that is needed for mastery and occur in a sequence that provides for growth and development. From "Pill Bug Palaces" to "Let's Get Soaked," the experiments here will delight and amaze children. 154 pages.

ISBN 0-87659-112-8   **Gryphon House**
10005   **Paperback**

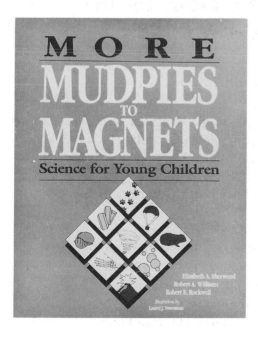

More Mudpies to Magnets
Science for Young Children

*Elizabeth A. Sherwood, Robert A. Williams,
Robert E. Rockwell*

   The hands-on activities will delight the imagination of young children. The science skills developed by projects in this book include classification, measurement, time and space relationships, communication, prediction, inference and numbers. 205 pages.

ISBN 0-87659-150-0   **Gryphon House**
10015   **Paperback**

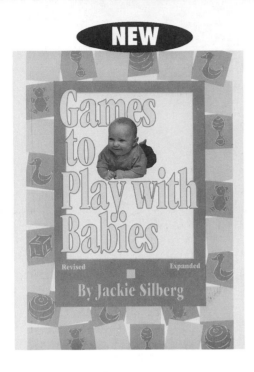

Games to Play with Babies
Revised and Expanded

Jackie Silberg

Here are 250 fun-filled games to help babies (from birth to twelve months) explore their world and learn critical developmental skills. Language, coordination and problem-solving are some of the areas covered. But the important value is fun. Both adult and baby will have hours of enjoyable time together. This book works for both parents and caregivers. 286 pages.

ISBN 0-87659-162-4   **Gryphon House**
11144   **Paperback**

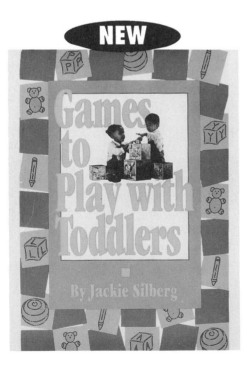

Games to Play with Toddlers

Jackie Silberg

Toddlers (twelve to twenty-four months) love to explore. The games in this practical book will help one to two year olds learn language and expand their creativity, observation and coordination skills. They will get practice in problem-solving, following directions and more. Another book for both caregivers and parents. 285 pages.

ISBN 0-87659-163-2   **Gryphon House**
16264   **Paperback**